BOLLINGEN SERIES LXXX

The Divine Comedy

❖

Inferno

1: Italian Text and Translation

DANTE ALIGHIERI

The Divine Comedy

TRANSLATED, WITH A COMMENTARY, BY

CHARLES S. SINGLETON

Inferno

1: Italian Text and Translation

BOLLINGEN SERIES LXXX

PRINCETON UNIVERSITY PRESS

THIS IS VOLUME I OF

THE DIVINE COMEDY OF DANTE ALIGHIERI

CONSTITUTING NUMBER LXXX IN BOLLINGEN SERIES

SPONSORED BY BOLLINGEN FOUNDATION.

THIS VOLUME, INFERNO,

IS IN TWO PARTS: ITALIAN TEXT AND TRANSLATION,

AND COMMENTARY

Library of Congress Catalogue card number 68-57090

ISBN 0-691-09855-7

Printed in the United States of America

by Princeton University Press, Princeton, New Jersey

CONTENTS

Inferno

2

Note on the Italian Text
and the Translation

Index

Inferno

Italian Text and Translation

INFERNO

Nᴇʟ ᴍᴇᴢᴢᴏ del cammin di nostra vita
mi ritrovai per una selva oscura,
che la diritta via era smarrita. 3
Ahi quanto a dir qual era è cosa dura
esta selva selvaggia e aspra e forte
che nel pensier rinova la paura! 6
Tant' è amara che poco è più morte;
ma per trattar del ben ch'i' vi trovai,
dirò de l'altre cose ch'i' v'ho scorte. 9
Io non so ben ridir com' i' v'intrai,
tant' era pien di sonno a quel punto
che la verace via abbandonai. 12
Ma poi ch'i' fui al piè d'un colle giunto,
là dove terminava quella valle
che m'avea di paura il cor compunto, 15
guardai in alto e vidi le sue spalle
vestite già de' raggi del pianeta
che mena dritto altrui per ogne calle. 18

CANTO I

MIDWAY in the journey of our life I found myself in a dark wood, for the straight way was lost. Ah, how hard it is to tell what that wood was, wild, rugged, harsh; the very thought of it renews the fear! It is so bitter that death is hardly more so. But, to treat of the good that I found in it, I will tell of the other things I saw there.

I cannot rightly say how I entered it, I was so full of sleep at the moment I left the true way; but when I had reached the foot of a hill, there at the end of the valley that had pierced my heart with fear, I looked up and saw its shoulders already clad in the rays of the planet that leads men aright by every path.

Allor fu la paura un poco queta,
   che nel lago del cor m'era durata
   la notte ch'i' passai con tanta pieta.   *21*
E come quei che con lena affannata,
   uscito fuor del pelago a la riva,
   si volge a l'acqua perigliosa e guata,   *24*
così l'animo mio, ch'ancor fuggiva,
   si volse a retro a rimirar lo passo
   che non lasciò già mai persona viva.   *27*
Poi ch'èi posato un poco il corpo lasso,
   ripresi via per la piaggia diserta,
   sì che 'l piè fermo sempre era 'l più basso.   *30*
Ed ecco, quasi al cominciar de l'erta,
   una lonza leggiera e presta molto,
   che di pel macolato era coverta;   *33*
e non mi si partia dinanzi al volto,
   anzi 'mpediva tanto il mio cammino,
   ch'i' fui per ritornar più volte vòlto.   *36*
Temp' era dal principio del mattino,
   e 'l sol montava 'n sù con quelle stelle
   ch'eran con lui quando l'amor divino   *39*
mosse di prima quelle cose belle;
   sì ch'a bene sperar m'era cagione
   di quella fiera a la gaetta pelle   *42*
l'ora del tempo e la dolce stagione;
   ma non sì che paura non mi desse
   la vista che m'apparve d'un leone.   *45*
Questi parea che contra me venisse
   con la test' alta e con rabbiosa fame,
   sì che parea che l'aere ne tremesse.   *48*

Then the fear was somewhat quieted that had continued in the lake of my heart through the night I had passed so piteously. And as he who with laboring breath has escaped from the deep to the shore turns to look back on the dangerous waters, so my mind which was still fleeing turned back to gaze upon the pass that never left anyone alive.

After I had rested my tired body a little, I again took up my way across the desert strand, so that the firm foot was always the lower. And behold, near the beginning of the steep, a leopard light-footed and very fleet, covered with a spotted hide! And it did not depart from before my eyes, but did so impede my way that more than once I turned round to go back.

It was the beginning of the morning, and the sun was mounting with the stars that were with it when Divine Love first set those beautiful things in motion, so that the hour of the day and the sweet season gave me cause for good hope of that beast with the gay skin; yet not so much that I did not feel afraid at the sight of a lion that appeared to me and seemed to be coming at me, head high and raging with hunger, so that the air seemed to tremble at it;

Ed una lupa, che di tutte brame
  sembiava carca ne la sua magrezza,
  e molte genti fé già viver grame,   51
questa mi porse tanto di gravezza
  con la paura ch'uscia di sua vista,
  ch'io perdei la speranza de l'altezza.   54
E qual è quei che volontieri acquista,
  e giugne 'l tempo che perder lo face,
  che 'n tutti suoi pensier piange e s'attrista;   57
tal mi fece la bestia sanza pace,
  che, venendomi 'ncontro, a poco a poco
  mi ripigneva là dove 'l sol tace.   60
Mentre ch'i' rovinava in basso loco,
  dinanzi a li occhi mi si fu offerto
  chi per lungo silenzio parea fioco.   63
Quando vidi costui nel gran diserto,
  "*Miserere* di me," gridai a lui,
  "qual che tu sii, od ombra od omo certo!"   66
Rispuosemi: "Non omo, omo già fui,
  e li parenti miei furon lombardi,
  mantoani per patrïa ambedui.   69
Nacqui *sub Iulio*, ancor che fosse tardi,
  e vissi a Roma sotto 'l buono Augusto
  nel tempo de li dèi falsi e bugiardi.   72
Poeta fui, e cantai di quel giusto
  figliuol d'Anchise che venne di Troia,
  poi che 'l superbo Ilïón fu combusto.   75
Ma tu perché ritorni a tanta noia?
  perché non sali il dilettoso monte
  ch'è principio e cagion di tutta gioia?"   78

6

and a she-wolf, that in her leanness seemed laden with every craving and had already caused many to live in sorrow: she put such heaviness upon me with the fear that came from sight of her that I lost hope of the height. And like one who is eager in winning, but, when the time comes that makes him lose, weeps and is saddened in all his thoughts, such did that peaceless beast make me, as, coming on against me, she pushed me back, little by little, to where the sun is silent.

While I was ruining down to the depth there appeared before me one who seemed faint through long silence. When I saw him in that vast desert, I cried to him, "Have pity on me whatever you are, shade or living man!"

"No, not a living man, though once I was," he answered me, "and my parents were Lombards, both Mantuans by birth. I was born *sub Julio*, although late, and I lived at Rome under the good Augustus, in the time of the false and lying gods. I was a poet, and I sang of that just son of Anchises who came from Troy after proud Ilium was burned. But you, why do you return to so much woe? Why do you not climb the delectable mountain, the source and cause of every happiness?"

"Or se' tu quel Virgilio e quella fonte
 che spandi di parlar sì largo fiume?"
 rispuos' io lui con vergognosa fronte.   *81*
"O de li altri poeti onore e lume,
 vagliami 'l lungo studio e 'l grande amore
 che m'ha fatto cercar lo tuo volume.   *84*
Tu se' lo mio maestro e 'l mio autore,
 tu se' solo colui da cu' io tolsi
 lo bello stilo che m'ha fatto onore.   *87*
Vedi la bestia per cu' io mi volsi;
 aiutami da lei, famoso saggio,
 ch'ella mi fa tremar le vene e i polsi."   *90*
"A te convien tenere altro vïaggio,"
 rispuose, poi che lagrimar mi vide,
 "se vuo' campar d'esto loco selvaggio;   *93*
ché questa bestia, per la qual tu gride,
 non lascia altrui passar per la sua via,
 ma tanto lo 'mpedisce che l'uccide;   *96*
e ha natura sì malvagia e ria,
 che mai non empie la bramosa voglia,
 e dopo 'l pasto ha più fame che pria.   *99*
Molti son li animali a cui s'ammoglia,
 e più saranno ancora, infin che 'l Veltro
 verrà, che la farà morir con doglia.   *102*
Questi non ciberà terra né peltro,
 ma sapïenza, amore e virtute,
 e sua nazion sarà tra feltro e feltro.   *105*
Di quella umile Italia fia salute
 per cui morì la vergine Cammilla,
 Eurialo e Turno e Niso di ferute.   *108*

"Are you, then, that Virgil, that fount which pours forth so broad a stream of speech?" I answered him, my brow covered with shame. "O glory and light of other poets, may the long study and the great love that have made me search your volume avail me! You are my master and my author. You alone are he from whom I took the fair style that has done me honor. See the beast that has turned me back. Help me against her, famous sage, for she makes my veins and pulses tremble."

"It behooves you to go by another way if you would escape from this wild place," he answered when he saw me weep, "for this beast, the cause of your complaint, lets no man pass her way, but so besets him that she slays him; and she has a nature so vicious and malign that she never sates her greedy appetite and after feeding is hungrier than before. Many are the beasts with which she mates, and there will yet be more, until the Hound shall come who will deal her a painful death. He will not feed on earth or pelf, but on wisdom, love, and virtue, and his birth shall be between felt and felt. He shall be the salvation of that low-lying Italy for which the virgin Camilla and Euryalus, Turnus, and Nisus died of their wounds.

Questi la caccerà per ogne villa,
   fin che l'avrà rimessa ne lo 'nferno,
   là onde 'nvidia prima dipartilla.   *111*
Ond' io per lo tuo me' penso e discerno
   che tu mi segui, e io sarò tua guida,
   e trarrotti di qui per loco etterno;   *114*
ove udirai le disperate strida,
   vedrai li antichi spiriti dolenti,
   ch'a la seconda morte ciascun grida;   *117*
e vederai color che son contenti
   nel foco, perché speran di venire
   quando che sia a le beate genti.   *120*
A le quai poi se tu vorrai salire,
   anima fia a ciò più di me degna:
   con lei ti lascerò nel mio partire;   *123*
ché quello imperador che là sù regna,
   perch' i' fu' ribellante a la sua legge,
   non vuol che 'n sua città per me si vegna.   *126*
In tutte parti impera e quivi regge;
   quivi è la sua città e l'alto seggio:
   oh felice colui cu' ivi elegge!"   *129*
E io a lui: "Poeta, io ti richeggio
   per quello Dio che tu non conoscesti,
   a ciò ch'io fugga questo male e peggio,   *132*
che tu mi meni là dov' or dicesti,
   sì ch'io veggia la porta di san Pietro
   e color cui tu fai cotanto mesti."   *135*
Allor si mosse, e io li tenni dietro.   *136*

He shall hunt her through every town till he
has thrust her back into Hell, whence envy
first sent her forth. Therefore I think and
deem it best that you should follow me, and
I will be your guide and lead you hence
through an eternal place, where you shall
hear the despairing shrieks and see the an-
cient tormented spirits who all bewail the
second death. Then you shall see those who
are content in the fire because they hope
to come among the blessed, whensoever that
may be; and to these if you would then as-
cend, there shall be a soul worthier than I
to guide you; with her I shall leave you at my
departing. For the Emperor who reigns there-
above wills not that I come into His city,
because I was rebellious to His law. In all
parts is His empire, in that part is His king-
dom, there is His city and His lofty seat. Oh,
happy he whom He elects thereto!"

And I to him, "Poet, I beseech you, by that
God whom you did not know, so that I may
escape this ill and worse, lead me whither
you said just now, that I may see St. Peter's
gate and those whom you term so woeful."

Then he set out, and I followed after him.

INFERNO

Lo GIORNO se n'andava, e l'aere bruno
  toglieva li animai che sono in terra
  da le fatiche loro; e io sol uno   3
m'apparecchiava a sostener la guerra
  sì del cammino e sì de la pietate,
  che ritrarrà la mente che non erra.   6
O Muse, o alto ingegno, or m'aiutate;
  o mente che scrivesti ciò ch'io vidi,
  qui si parrà la tua nobilitate.   9
Io cominciai: "Poeta che mi guidi,
  guarda la mia virtù s'ell' è possente,
  prima ch'a l'alto passo tu mi fidi.   12
Tu dici che di Silvïo il parente,
  corruttibile ancora, ad immortale
  secolo andò, e fu sensibilmente.   15
Però, se l'avversario d'ogne male
  cortese i fu, pensando l'alto effetto
  ch'uscir dovea di lui, e 'l chi e 'l quale   18

CANTO II

Day was departing, and the dark air was taking the creatures on earth from their labors; and I alone was making ready to sustain the strife, both of the journey and of the pity, which unerring memory shall retrace. O Muses, O high genius, help me now! O memory that wrote down what I saw, here shall your worthiness appear!

I began, "Poet, you who guide me, consider if my strength is sufficient, before you trust me to the deep way. You tell how the father of Silvius went, while still mortal, to the immortal world and was there in his bodily senses. But that the Adversary of all evil should show him such favor seems not unfitting to an understanding mind, considering the high effect that was to spring from him, and who and what he was;

non pare indegno ad omo d'intelletto;
   ch'e' fu de l'alma Roma e di suo impero
   ne l'empireo ciel per padre eletto: *21*
la quale e 'l quale, a voler dir lo vero,
   fu stabilita per lo loco santo
   u' siede il successor del maggior Piero.   *24*
Per quest' andata onde li dai tu vanto,
   intese cose che furon cagione
   di sua vittoria e del papale ammanto.   *27*
Andovvi poi lo Vas d'elezïone,
   per recarne conforto a quella fede
   ch'è principio a la via di salvazione.   *30*
Ma io, perché venirvi? o chi 'l concede?
   Io non Enëa, io non Paulo sono;
   me degno a ciò né io né altri 'l crede.   *33*
Per che, se del venire io m'abbandono,
   temo che la venuta non sia folle.
   Se' savio; intendi me' ch'i' non ragiono."   *36*
E qual è quei che disvuol ciò che volle
   e per novi pensier cangia proposta,
   sì che dal cominciar tutto si tolle,   *39*
tal mi fec' ïo 'n quella oscura costa,
   perché, pensando, consumai la 'mpresa
   che fu nel cominciar cotanto tosta.   *42*
"S'i' ho ben la parola tua intesa,"
   rispuose del magnanimo quell' ombra,
   "l'anima tua è da viltade offesa;   *45*
la qual molte fïate l'omo ingombra
   sì che d'onrata impresa lo rivolve,
   come falso veder bestia quand' ombra.   *48*

for in the Empyrean heaven he was chosen as father of glorious Rome and of her empire, and both, to say the truth, were established as the holy place where the successor of great Peter has his seat. In this journey, which you affirm he made, he learned things that were the cause of his victory and of the papal mantle. Later, the Chosen Vessel went there, that he might bring thence confirmation of that faith which is the beginning of the way of salvation. But I, why do I come there? And who allows it? I am not Aeneas, I am not Paul; of this neither I nor others think me worthy. Wherefore, if I yield and come, I fear that the coming may be folly. You are wise; you understand better than I explain it." And like one who unwills what he has willed and with new thoughts changes his resolve, so that he quite gives up the thing he had begun, such did I become on that dark slope, for by thinking on it I rendered null the undertaking that had been so suddenly embarked upon.

"If I have well understood what you say," the shade of that magnanimous one replied, "your spirit is beset by cowardice, which oftentimes encumbers a man, turning him from honorable endeavor, as false seeing turns a beast that shies.

Da questa tema a ciò che tu ti solve,
   dirotti perch' io venni e quel ch'io 'ntesi
   nel primo punto che di te mi dolve.   *1*
Io era tra color che son sospesi,
   e donna mi chiamò beata e bella,
   tal che di comandare io la richiesi.   *54*
Lucevan li occhi suoi più che la stella;
   e cominciommi a dir soave e piana,
   con angelica voce, in sua favella: *57*
'O anima cortese mantoana,
   di cui la fama ancor nel mondo dura,
   e durerà quanto 'l mondo lontana,   *60*
l'amico mio, e non de la ventura,
   ne la diserta piaggia è impedito
   sì nel cammin, che vòlt' è per paura;   *63*
e temo che non sia già sì smarrito,
   ch'io mi sia tardi al soccorso levata,
   per quel ch'i' ho di lui nel cielo udito.   *66*
Or movi, e con la tua parola ornata
   e con ciò c'ha mestieri al suo campare,
   l'aiuta sì ch'i' ne sia consolata.   *69*
I' son Beatrice che ti faccio andare;
   vegno del loco ove tornar disio;
   amor mi mosse, che mi fa parlare.   *72*
Quando sarò dinanzi al segnor mio,
   di te mi loderò sovente a lui.'
   Tacette allora, e poi comincia' io: *75*
'O donna di virtù, sola per cui
   l'umana spezie eccede ogne contento
   di quel ciel c'ha minor li cerchi sui,   *78*

To free you from this fear I will tell you why
I came and what it was I heard when I first
felt pity for you. I was among those who are
suspended, and a lady called me, so blessed
and so fair that I prayed her to command
me. Her eyes were more resplendent than the
stars, and she began to say to me, sweetly and
softly, in an angelic voice, 'O courteous Man-
tuan spirit, whose fame still lasts in the world,
and shall last as long as the world, my friend
—and not the friend of Fortune—finds his
way so impeded on the desert slope that he
has turned back in fright; and, from what I
have heard of him in Heaven, I fear he may
already have gone so astray that I am late in
arising to help him. Go now, and with your
fair speech and with whatever is needful for
his deliverance, assist him so that it may con-
sole me. I am Beatrice who send you. I come
from a place to which I long to return. Love
moved me and makes me speak. When I am
before my Lord I will often praise you to
Him.'

"Then she was silent; and I began, 'O Lady
of virtue, through whom alone mankind rises
beyond all that is contained by the heaven
that circles least,

tanto m'aggrada il tuo comandamento,
  che l'ubidir, se già fosse, m'è tardi;
  più non t'è uo' ch'aprirmi il tuo talento.   *81*
Ma dimmi la cagion che non ti guardi
  de lo scender qua giuso in questo centro
  de l'ampio loco ove tornar tu ardi.'   *84*
'Da che tu vuo' saver cotanto a dentro,
  dirotti brievemente,' mi rispuose,
  'perch' i' non temo di venir qua entro.   *87*
Temer si dee di sole quelle cose
  c'hanno potenza di fare altrui male;
  de l'altre no, ché non son paurose.   *90*
I' son fatta da Dio, sua mercé, tale,
  che la vostra miseria non mi tange,
  né fiamma d'esto 'ncendio non m'assale.   *93*
Donna è gentil nel ciel che si compiange
  di questo 'mpedimento ov' io ti mando,
  sì che duro giudicio là sù frange.   *96*
Questa chiese Lucia in suo dimando
  e disse: – Or ha bisogno il tuo fedele
  di te, e io a te lo raccomando–.   *99*
Lucia, nimica di ciascun crudele,
  si mosse, e venne al loco dov' i' era,
  che mi sedea con l'antica Rachele.   *102*
Disse: – Beatrice, loda di Dio vera,
  ché non soccorri quei che t'amò tanto,
  ch'uscì per te de la volgare schiera?   *105*
Non odi tu la pieta del suo pianto,
  non vedi tu la morte che 'l combatte
  su la fiumana ove 'l mar non ha vanto–?   *108*

your command so pleases me, that had I
obeyed already it would be late. You have
only to declare your will to me. But tell me
the reason why you are not wary of descend-
ing to this center from that spacious region
to which you long to return.'

"'Since you wish to know so deeply,' she
answered me, 'I will tell you briefly why I
am not afraid to come within this place.
Those things alone should be feared that have
power to do one harm—not other things, for
they are not fearful. I am made such by God,
of His grace, that your suffering does not
touch me, and no flame of this burning assails
me. In Heaven there is a gracious lady who
has such pity of this impediment to which I
send you that stern judgment is broken there-
above. She called Lucy, in her request, and
said, "Your faithful one has need of you now,
and I commend him to you." Lucy, foe of
every cruelty, arose and, coming to where I
sat with ancient Rachel, said, "Beatrice, true
praise of God, why do you not succor him
who bore you such love that for you he left
the vulgar throng? Do you not hear his pitiful
lament? Do you not see the death that assails
him on that flood over which the sea has no
vaunt?"

Al mondo non fur mai persone ratte
   a far lor pro o a fuggir lor danno,
   com' io, dopo cotai parole fatte,   *111*
venni qua giù del mio beato scanno,
   fidandomi del tuo parlare onesto,
   ch'onora te e quei ch'udito l'hanno.'   *114*
Poscia che m'ebbe ragionato questo,
   li occhi lucenti lagrimando volse,
   per che mi fece del venir più presto.   *117*
E venni a te così com' ella volse:
   d'inanzi a quella fiera ti levai
   che del bel monte il corto andar ti tolse.   *120*
Dunque: che è? perché, perché restai,
   perché tanta viltà nel core allette,
   perché ardire e franchezza non hai,   *123*
poscia che tai tre donne benedette
   curan di te ne la corte del cielo,
   e 'l mio parlar tanto ben ti promette?"   *126*
Quali fioretti dal notturno gelo
   chinati e chiusi, poi che 'l sol li 'mbianca,
   si drizzan tutti aperti in loro stelo,   *129*
tal mi fec' io di mia virtude stanca,
   e tanto buono ardire al cor mi corse,
   ch'i' cominciai come persona franca: *132*
"Oh pietosa colei che mi soccorse!
   e te cortese ch'ubidisti tosto
   a le vere parole che ti porse!   *135*
Tu m'hai con disiderio il cor disposto
   sì al venir con le parole tue,
   ch'i' son tornato nel primo proposto.   *138*

" 'On earth no one was ever so swift to seize advantage or to flee from harm as I was when these words were uttered, to come down here from my blessed seat—trusting in your noble speech, which honors you and all who have heard it.'

"When she had said this to me, she turned her eyes, which shone with tears, making me the more eager to come; and so, even as she wished, I came to you, and rescued you from the beast that was preventing your going the short way up the fair mountain. What, then, is this? Why, why do you hold back? Why do you harbor such cowardice in your heart? Why are you not bold and free, when in Heaven's court three such blessed ladies are mindful of you, and my words pledge you so great a good?"

As little flowers, bent down and closed by chill of night, straighten and all unfold upon their stems when the sun brightens them, such in my faint strength did I become; and so much good courage rushed to my heart that I began, as one set free, "Oh, how compassionate was she who helped me, and how courteous were you, so quick to obey the true words she spoke to you! By your words you have made me so eager to come with you that I have returned to my first resolve.

Or va, ch'un sol volere è d'ambedue:
   tu duca, tu segnore e tu maestro."
   Così li dissi; e poi che mosso fue,
intrai per lo cammino alto e silvestro.   *142*

Now on, for a single will is in us both;
you are my leader, you my master and my
teacher."

So I said to him, and when he moved on,
I entered along the deep and savage way.

INFERNO

PER ME SI VA NE LA CITTÀ DOLENTE,
  PER ME SI VA NE L'ETTERNO DOLORE,
  PER ME SI VA TRA LA PERDUTA GENTE.   *3*
GIUSTIZIA MOSSE IL MIO ALTO FATTORE;
  FECEMI LA DIVINA PODESTATE,
  LA SOMMA SAPÏENZA E 'L PRIMO AMORE.   *6*
DINANZI A ME NON FUOR COSE CREATE
  SE NON ETTERNE, E IO ETTERNO DURO.
  LASCIATE OGNE SPERANZA, VOI CH'INTRATE.   *9*

Queste parole di colore oscuro
  vid' ïo scritte al sommo d'una porta;
  per ch'io: "Maestro, il senso lor m'è duro."   *12*
Ed elli a me, come persona accorta:
  "Qui si convien lasciare ogne sospetto;
  ogne viltà convien che qui sia morta.   *15*
Noi siam venuti al loco ov' i' t'ho detto
  che tu vedrai le genti dolorose
  c'hanno perduto il ben de l'intelletto."   *18*
E poi che la sua mano a la mia puose
  con lieto volto, ond' io mi confortai,
  mi mise dentro a le segrete cose.   *21*

CANTO III

THROUGH ME YOU ENTER THE WOEFUL CITY,
   THROUGH ME YOU ENTER ETERNAL GRIEF,
   THROUGH ME YOU ENTER AMONG THE LOST.
JUSTICE MOVED MY HIGH MAKER:
   THE DIVINE POWER MADE ME,
   THE SUPREME WISDOM, AND THE PRIMAL LOVE.
BEFORE ME NOTHING WAS CREATED
   IF NOT ETERNAL, AND ETERNAL I ENDURE.
   ABANDON EVERY HOPE, YOU WHO ENTER.

These words of obscure color I saw inscribed over a portal; whereupon I said, "Master, their meaning is hard for me." And he to me, as one who understands, "Here must all fear be left behind; here let all cowardice be dead. We have come to the place where I have told you you will see the wretched people who have lost the good of intellect." And when he had placed his hand on mine, with a cheerful look from which I took comfort, he led me among the secret things.

Quivi sospiri, pianti e alti guai
  risonavan per l'aere sanza stelle,
  per ch'io al cominciar ne lagrimai.   *24*
Diverse lingue, orribili favelle,
  parole di dolore, accenti d'ira,
  voci alte e fioche, e suon di man con elle   *27*
facevano un tumulto, il qual s'aggira
  sempre in quell' aura sanza tempo tinta,
  come la rena quando turbo spira.   *30*
E io ch'avea d'error la testa cinta,
  dissi: "Maestro, che è quel ch'i' odo?
  e che gent' è che par nel duol sì vinta?"   *33*
Ed elli a me: "Questo misero modo
  tegnon l'anime triste di coloro
  che visser sanza 'nfamia e sanza lodo.   *36*
Mischiate sono a quel cattivo coro
  de li angeli che non furon ribelli
  né fur fedeli a Dio, ma per sé fuoro.   *39*
Caccianli i ciel per non esser men belli,
  né lo profondo inferno li riceve,
  ch'alcuna gloria i rei avrebber d'elli."   *42*
E io: "Maestro, che è tanto greve
  a lor che lamentar li fa sì forte?"
  Rispuose: "Dicerolti molto breve.   *45*
Questi non hanno speranza di morte,
  e la lor cieca vita è tanto bassa,
  che 'nvidïosi son d'ogne altra sorte.   *48*
Fama di loro il mondo esser non lassa;
  misericordia e giustizia li sdegna:
  non ragioniam di lor, ma guarda e passa." *51*

Here sighs, laments, and loud wailings were resounding through the starless air, so that at first they made me weep. Strange tongues, horrible outcries, utterances of woe, accents of anger, voices shrill and faint, and the beating of hands among them, were making a tumult that swirls unceasingly in that dark and timeless air, like sand when a whirlwind blows. And I, my head circled with error, said, "Master, what is this I hear? And what people are these who seem so overcome by pain?"

And he to me, "Such is the miserable condition of the sorry souls of those who lived without infamy and without praise. They are mingled with that base band of angels who were neither rebellious nor faithful to God, but stood apart. The heavens drive them out, so as not to be less beautiful; and deep Hell does not receive them, lest the wicked have some glory over them."

And I, "Master, what is so grievous to them that it makes them lament so bitterly?"

He answered, "Very briefly I will tell you. These have no hope of death, and their blind life is so abject that they are envious of every other lot. The world does not suffer that report of them shall live. Mercy and justice disdain them. Let us not speak of them, but look, and pass on."

E io, che riguardai, vidi una 'nsegna
  che girando correva tanto ratta,
  che d'ogne posa mi parea indegna;   *54*
e dietro le venìa sì lunga tratta
  di gente, ch'i' non averei creduto
  che morte tanta n'avesse disfatta.   *57*
Poscia ch'io v'ebbi alcun riconosciuto,
  vidi e conobbi l'ombra di colui
  che fece per viltade il gran rifiuto.   *60*
Incontanente intesi e certo fui
  che questa era la setta d'i cattivi,
  a Dio spiacenti e a' nemici sui.   *63*
Questi sciaurati, che mai non fur vivi,
  erano ignudi e stimolati molto
  da mosconi e da vespe ch'eran ivi.   *66*
Elle rigavan lor di sangue il volto,
  che, mischiato di lagrime, a' lor piedi
  da fastidiosi vermi era ricolto.   *69*
E poi ch'a riguardar oltre mi diedi,
  vidi genti a la riva d'un gran fiume;
  per ch'io dissi: "Maestro, or mi concedi   *72*
ch'i' sappia quali sono, e qual costume
  le fa di trapassar parer sì pronte,
  com' i' discerno per lo fioco lume."   *75*
Ed elli a me: "Le cose ti fier conte
  quando noi fermerem li nostri passi
  su la trista riviera d'Acheronte."   *78*
Allor con li occhi vergognosi e bassi,
  temendo no 'l mio dir li fosse grave,
  infino al fiume del parlar mi trassi.   *81*

Looking again, I saw a banner that ran so fast, whirling about, that it seemed it might never have rest, and behind it came so long a train of people that I should never have believed death had undone so many. After I had recognized some among them, I saw and knew the shade of him who from cowardice made the great refusal. Straightway I understood and knew for certain that this was the sorry sect of those who are displeasing to God and to his enemies. These wretches, who never were alive, were naked and were much stung by gadflies and wasps there, which were streaking their faces with blood that mingled with their tears and was gathered by loathsome worms at their feet.

Then, directing my gaze farther on, I saw people at the shore of a great river; wherefore I said, "Master, now grant that I may know who these are, and what law makes them seem so ready to cross over, as I discern through the dim light."

And he to me, "These things will be made known to you when we stay our steps at the dismal stream of Acheron."

Then, with eyes downcast and ashamed, fearing that my words had displeased him, I refrained from speaking till we reached the river.

Ed ecco verso noi venir per nave
    un vecchio, bianco per antico pelo,
    gridando: "Guai a voi, anime prave!   *84*
Non isperate mai veder lo cielo:
    i' vegno per menarvi a l'altra riva
    ne le tenebre etterne, in caldo e 'n gelo.   *87*
E tu che se' costì, anima viva,
    pàrtiti da cotesti che son morti."
    Ma poi che vide ch'io non mi partiva,   *90*
disse: "Per altra via, per altri porti
    verrai a piaggia, non qui, per passare:
    più lieve legno convien che ti porti."   *93*
E 'l duca lui: "Caron, non ti crucciare:
    vuolsi così colà dove si puote
    ciò che si vuole, e più non dimandare."   *96*
Quinci fuor quete le lanose gote
    al nocchier de la livida palude,
    che 'ntorno a li occhi avea di fiamme rote.   *99*
Ma quell' anime, ch'eran lasse e nude,
    cangiar colore e dibattero i denti,
    ratto che 'nteser le parole crude.   *102*
Bestemmiavano Dio e lor parenti,
    l'umana spezie e 'l loco e 'l tempo e 'l seme
    di lor semenza e di lor nascimenti.   *105*
Poi si ritrasser tutte quante insieme,
    forte piangendo, a la riva malvagia
    ch'attende ciascun uom che Dio non teme.   *108*
Caron dimonio, con occhi di bragia
    loro accennando, tutte le raccoglie;
    batte col remo qualunque s'adagia.   *111*

And behold, an old man, his hair white with age, coming towards us in a boat and shouting, "Woe to you, wicked souls! Do not hope to see Heaven ever! I come to carry you to the other shore, into eternal darkness, into fire and cold. And you there, living soul, stand aside from these that are dead." But when he saw that I did not do so, he said, "By another way, by other ports, not here, you shall cross to shore. A lighter bark must carry you."

And my leader to him, "Charon, do not rage. Thus is it willed there where that can be done which is willed; and ask no more."

Thereon the grizzled cheeks of the ferryman of the livid marsh, who had wheels of flame about his eyes, were quiet. But those forlorn and naked souls changed color, their teeth chattering, as soon as they heard the cruel words. They cursed God, their parents, the human race, the place, the time, the seed of their begetting and of their birth. Then, weeping loudly, all drew to the evil shore that awaits every man who fears not God. The demon Charon, his eyes like glowing coals, beckons to them and collects them all, beating with his oar whoever lingers.

Come d'autunno si levan le foglie
   l'una appresso de l'altra, fin che 'l ramo
   vede a la terra tutte le sue spoglie,   *114*
similemente il mal seme d'Adamo
   gittansi di quel lito ad una ad una,
   per cenni come augel per suo richiamo.   *117*
Così sen vanno su per l'onda bruna,
   e avanti che sien di là discese,
   anche di qua nuova schiera s'auna.   *120*
"Figliuol mio," disse 'l maestro cortese,
   "quelli che muoion ne l'ira di Dio
   tutti convegnon qui d'ogne paese;   *123*
e pronti sono a trapassar lo rio,
   ché la divina giustizia li sprona,
   sì che la tema si volve in disio.   *126*
Quinci non passa mai anima buona;
   e però, se Caron di te si lagna,
   ben puoi sapere omai che 'l suo dir suona." *129*
Finito questo, la buia campagna
   tremò sì forte, che de lo spavento
   la mente di sudore ancor mi bagna.   *132*
La terra lagrimosa diede vento,
   che balenò una luce vermiglia
   la qual mi vinse ciascun sentimento;
e caddi come l'uom cui sonno piglia.   *136*

As the leaves fall away in autumn, one after another, till the bough sees all its spoils upon the ground, so there the evil seed of Adam: one by one they cast themselves from that shore at signals, like a bird at its call. Thus they go over the dark water, and before they have landed on the other shore, on this side a new throng gathers.

"My son," said the courteous master, "those who die in the wrath of God all come together here from every land; and they are eager to cross the stream, for Divine Justice so spurs them that their fear is changed to desire. No good soul ever passes this way; therefore, if Charon complains of you, you can now well understand the meaning of his words."

When he had ended, the gloomy plain shook so violently that even now the memory of my terror bathes me in sweat. The tear-soaked ground gave forth a wind that flashed a crimson light which overcame all my senses, and I fell like one who is seized by sleep.

INFERNO

Ruppemi l'alto sonno ne la testa
    un greve truono, sì ch'io mi riscossi
    come persona ch'è per forza desta;   *3*
e l'occhio riposato intorno mossi,
    dritto levato, e fiso riguardai
    per conoscer lo loco dov' io fossi.   *6*
Vero è che 'n su la proda mi trovai
    de la valle d'abisso dolorosa
    che 'ntrono accoglie d'infiniti guai.   *9*
Oscura e profonda era e nebulosa
    tanto che, per ficcar lo viso a fondo,
    io non vi discernea alcuna cosa.   *12*
"Or discendiam qua giù nel cieco mondo,"
    cominciò il poeta tutto smorto.
    "Io sarò primo, e tu sarai secondo."   *15*
E io, che del color mi fui accorto,
    dissi: "Come verrò, se tu paventi
    che suoli al mio dubbiare esser conforto?"   *18*

CANTO IV

A HEAVY thunderclap broke the deep sleep in my head, so that I started like one who is awakened by force; and, standing up, I moved my rested eyes around, gazing intently to make out the place where I was. True it is that I found myself on the brink of the chasm of pain, which holds the clamor of endless wailings. It was so dark and deep and misty that, though I peered intently down into the depth, I could make out nothing there.

"Let us descend now into the blind world here below," the poet began, all pale. "I will be first, and you second."

And I, noting his pallor, said, "How shall I come, if you are afraid, who are wont to encourage me when I hesitate?"

Ed elli a me: "L'angoscia de le genti
   che son qua giù, nel viso mi dipigne
   quella pietà che tu per tema senti.   21
Andiam, ché la via lunga ne sospigne."
   Così si mise e così mi fé intrare
   nel primo cerchio che l'abisso cigne.   24
Quivi, secondo che per ascoltare,
   non avea pianto mai che di sospiri
   che l'aura etterna facevan tremare;   27
ciò avvenia di duol sanza martìri,
   ch'avean le turbe, ch'eran molte e grandi,
   d'infanti e di femmine e di viri.   30
Lo buon maestro a me: "Tu non dimandi
   che spiriti son questi che tu vedi?
   Or vo' che sappi, innanzi che più andi,   33
ch'ei non peccaro; e s'elli hanno mercedi,
   non basta, perché non ebber battesmo,
   ch'è porta de la fede che tu credi;   36
e s' e' furon dinanzi al cristianesmo,
   non adorar debitamente a Dio:
   e di questi cotai son io medesmo.   39
Per tai difetti, non per altro rio,
   semo perduti, e sol di tanto offesi
   che sanza speme vivemo in disio."   42
Gran duol mi prese al cor quando lo 'ntesi,
   però che gente di molto valore
   conobbi che 'n quel limbo eran sospesi.   45
"Dimmi, maestro mio, dimmi, segnore,"
   comincia' io per volere esser certo
   di quella fede che vince ogne errore: 48

And he to me, "The anguish of the people here below paints my face with the pity that you take for fear. Let us go, for the long way urges us." So he entered, and had me enter, the first circle that girds the abyss.

Here there was no plaint, that could be heard, except of sighs, which caused the eternal air to tremble; and this arose from the sadness, without torments, of the crowds that were many and great, both of children and of women and men.

The good master said to me, "Do you not ask what spirits are these that you see? Now, before you go farther, I will have you know that they did not sin; but if they have merit, that does not suffice, for they did not have baptism, which is the portal of the faith you hold; and if they were before Christianity, they did not worship God aright, and I myself am one of these. Because of these shortcomings, and for no other fault, we are lost, and only so far afflicted that without hope we live in longing."

Great sadness seized my heart when I heard him, for I recognized that people of great worth were suspended in that Limbo.

"Tell me, master, tell me, sir," I began, wishing to be assured of the faith that conquers every error,

"uscicci mai alcuno, o per suo merto
 o per altrui, che poi fosse beato?"
   E quei che 'ntese il mio parlar coverto,   *51*
rispuose: "Io era nuovo in questo stato,
   quando ci vidi venire un possente,
   con segno di vittoria coronato.   *54*
Trasseci l'ombra del primo parente,
   d'Abèl suo figlio e quella di Noè,
   di Moïsè legista e ubidente;   *57*
Abraàm patrïarca e Davìd re,
   Israèl con lo padre e co' suoi nati
   e con Rachele, per cui tanto fé,   *60*
e altri molti, e feceli beati.
   E vo' che sappi che, dinanzi ad essi,
   spiriti umani non eran salvati."   *63*
Non lasciavam l'andar perch' ei dicessi,
   ma passavam la selva tuttavia,
   la selva, dico, di spiriti spessi.   *66*
Non era lunga ancor la nostra via
   di qua dal sonno, quand' io vidi un foco
   ch'emisperio di tenebre vincia.   *69*
Di lungi n'eravamo ancora un poco,
   ma non sì ch'io non discernessi in parte
   ch'orrevol gente possedea quel loco.   *72*
"O tu ch'onori scïenzïa e arte,
   questi chi son c'hanno cotanta onranza,
   che dal modo de li altri li diparte?"   *75*
E quelli a me: "L'onrata nominanza
   che di lor suona sù ne la tua vita,
   grazïa acquista in ciel che sì li avanza."   *78*

"did ever anyone go forth from here, either by his own or by another's merit, who afterwards was blessed?"

And he, who understood my covert speech, replied, "I was new in this condition when I saw a Mighty One come here, crowned with sign of victory. He took hence the shade of our first parent, Abel his son, and Noah, and Moses, obedient giver of laws, Abraham the patriarch and David the king, Israel with his father and his children and with Rachel, for whom he did so much, and many others; and He made them blessed. And I would have you know that before these no human souls were saved."

We did not cease going on because he spoke, but all the while were passing through the wood, I mean the wood of thronging spirits; nor had we yet gone far from the place of my slumber when I saw a fire, which overcame a hemisphere of darkness. We were still a little distant from it, yet not so far but that I might in part discern that honorable folk possessed this place.

"O you who honor science and art, who are these that have such honor that it sets them apart from the condition of the rest?"

And he to me, "Their honored fame, which resounds in your life above, wins grace in Heaven, which thus advances them."

Intanto voce fu per me udita:
　　"Onorate l'altissimo poeta;
　　l'ombra sua torna, ch'era dipartita."　　　*81*
Poi che la voce fu restata e queta,
　　vidi quattro grand' ombre a noi venire:
　　sembianz' avevan né trista né lieta.　　　*84*
Lo buon maestro cominciò a dire:
　　"Mira colui con quella spada in mano,
　　che vien dinanzi ai tre sì come sire:　　　*87*
quelli è Omero poeta sovrano;
　　l'altro è Orazio satiro che vene;
　　Ovidio è 'l terzo, e l'ultimo Lucano.　　　*90*
Però che ciascun meco si convene
　　nel nome che sonò la voce sola,
　　fannomi onore, e di ciò fanno bene."　　　*93*
Così vid' i' adunar la bella scola
　　di quel segnor de l'altissimo canto
　　che sovra li altri com' aquila vola.　　　*96*
Da ch'ebber ragionato insieme alquanto,
　　volsersi a me con salutevol cenno,
　　e 'l mio maestro sorrise di tanto;　　　*99*
e più d'onore ancora assai mi fenno,
　　ch'e' sì mi fecer de la loro schiera,
　　sì ch'io fui sesto tra cotanto senno.　　　*102*
Così andammo infino a la lumera,
　　parlando cose che 'l tacere è bello,
　　sì com' era 'l parlar colà dov' era.　　　*105*
Venimmo al piè d'un nobile castello,
　　sette volte cerchiato d'alte mura,
　　difeso intorno d'un bel fiumicello.　　　*108*

Meanwhile I heard a voice which said, "Honor the great Poet! His shade, which had departed, now returns."

After the voice had ceased and was still, I saw four great shades coming to us, in semblance neither sad nor joyful. The good master began, "Note him there with sword in hand who comes before the other three as their lord. He is Homer, sovereign poet; next is Horace, satirist; Ovid comes third, and Lucan last. Since each shares with me the name the single voice has uttered, they do me honor, and in that they do well."

Thus I saw assembled the fair school of that lord of highest song who, like an eagle, soars above the rest. After they had talked awhile together, they turned to me with sign of salutation, at which my master smiled; and far more honor still they showed me, for they made me one of their company, so that I was sixth amid so much wisdom. Thus we went onward to the light, talking of things it is well to pass in silence, even as it was well to speak of them there.

We came to the foot of a noble castle, seven times encircled by lofty walls and defended round about by a fair stream.

Questo passammo come terra dura;
  per sette porte intrai con questi savi:
  giugnemmo in prato di fresca verdura.   *111*
Genti v'eran con occhi tardi e gravi,
  di grande autorità ne' lor sembianti:
  parlavan rado, con voci soavi.   *114*
Traemmoci così da l'un de' canti,
  in loco aperto, luminoso e alto,
  sì che veder si potien tutti quanti.   *117*
Colà diritto, sovra 'l verde smalto,
  mi fuor mostrati li spiriti magni,
  che del vedere in me stesso m'essalto.   *120*
I' vidi Eletra con molti compagni,
  tra ' quai conobbi Ettòr ed Enea,
  Cesare armato con li occhi grifagni.   *123*
Vidi Cammilla e la Pantasilea;
  da l'altra parte vidi 'l re Latino
  che con Lavina sua figlia sedea.   *126*
Vidi quel Bruto che cacciò Tarquino,
  Lucrezia, Iulia, Marzïa e Corniglia;
  e solo, in parte, vidi 'l Saladino.   *129*
Poi ch'innalzai un poco più le ciglia,
  vidi 'l maestro di color che sanno
  seder tra filosofica famiglia.   *132*
Tutti lo miran, tutti onor li fanno:
  quivi vid' ïo Socrate e Platone,
  che 'nnanzi a li altri più presso li stanno;   *135*
Democrito che 'l mondo a caso pone,
  Dïogenès, Anassagora e Tale,
  Empedoclès, Eraclito e Zenone;   *138*

This we crossed, as on solid ground, and through seven gates I entered with these sages. We came to a meadow of fresh verdure, where there were people with grave and slow-moving eyes and looks of great authority; they spoke seldom and with gentle voices.

Then we drew to one side, into an open place which was luminous and high, so that we could see all of them. There before me, on the enameled green, the great spirits were shown to me, so that I glory within me for having seen them. I saw Electra with many companions, among whom I knew Hector, and Aeneas, and falcon-eyed Caesar armed. I saw Camilla and Penthesilea; and on the other side I saw King Latinus, who sat with his daughter Lavinia. I saw that Brutus who drove out the Tarquin, I saw Lucretia, Julia, Marcia, and Cornelia; and by himself apart I saw Saladin.

When I raised my eyes a little higher, I saw the Master of those who know, seated in a philosophic family. All look to him, all do him honor. There, nearest to him and in front of the rest, I saw Socrates and Plato; I saw Democritus, who ascribes the world to chance, Diogenes, Anaxagoras, and Thales, Empedocles, Heraclitus, and Zeno.

e vidi il buono accoglitor del quale,
  Dïascoride dico; e vidi Orfeo,
  Tulïo e Lino e Seneca morale;   *141*
Euclide geomètra e Tolomeo,
  Ipocràte, Avicenna e Galïeno,
  Averoìs che 'l gran comento feo.   *144*
Io non posso ritrar di tutti a pieno,
  però che sì mi caccia il lungo tema,
  che molte volte al fatto il dir vien meno.   *147*
La sesta compagnia in due si scema:
  per altra via mi mena il savio duca,
  fuor de la queta, ne l'aura che trema.
E vegno in parte ove non è che luca.   *151*

I saw the good collector of the qualities of
things—I mean Dioscorides—and I saw Or-
pheus, Tully, Linus, and Seneca the moralist,
Euclid the geometer, and Ptolemy, Hippo-
crates, Avicenna, Galen, and Averroës, who
made the great commentary. I cannot give
full account of them all, for my long theme
so drives me on, that many times the telling
comes short of the fact.

The company of six diminishes to two; by
another way my wise guide leads me, out of
the quiet, into the trembling air; and I come
to a part where there is naught that shines.

INFERNO

Così discesi del cerchio primaio
giù nel secondo, che men loco cinghia
e tanto più dolor, che punge a guaio.   *3*
Stavvi Minòs orribilmente, e ringhia:
essamina le colpe ne l'intrata;
giudica e manda secondo ch'avvinghia.   *6*
Dico che quando l'anima mal nata
li vien dinanzi, tutta si confessa;
e quel conoscitor de le peccata   *9*
vede qual loco d'inferno è da essa;
cignesi con la coda tante volte
quantunque gradi vuol che giù sia messa.   *12*
Sempre dinanzi a lui ne stanno molte:
vanno a vicenda ciascuna al giudizio,
dicono e odono e poi son giù volte.   *15*
"O tu che vieni al doloroso ospizio,"
disse Minòs a me quando mi vide,
lasciando l'atto di cotanto offizio,   *18*

CANTO V

Thus I descended from the first circle into the second, which girds less space, and so much greater woe that it goads to wailing. There stands Minos, horrible and snarling: upon the entrance he examines their offenses, and judges and dispatches them according as he entwines. I mean that when the ill-begotten soul comes before him, it confesses all; and that discerner of sins sees which shall be its place in Hell, then girds himself with his tail as many times as the grades he wills that it be sent down. Always before him stands a crowd of them; they go, each in his turn, to the judgment; they tell, and hear, and then are hurled below.

"O you who come to the abode of pain," said Minos to me, when he saw me, pausing in the act of that great office,

"guarda com' entri e di cui tu ti fide;
   non t'inganni l'ampiezza de l'intrare!"
   E 'l duca mio a lui: "Perché pur gride?   *21*
Non impedir lo suo fatale andare:
   vuolsi così colà dove si puote
   ciò che si vuole, e più non dimandare."   *24*
Or incomincian le dolenti note
   a farmisi sentire; or son venuto
   là dove molto pianto mi percuote.   *27*
Io venni in loco d'ogne luce muto,
   che mugghia come fa mar per tempesta,
   se da contrari venti è combattuto.   *30*
La bufera infernal, che mai non resta,
   mena li spirti con la sua rapina;
   voltando e percotendo li molesta.   *33*
Quando giungon davanti a la ruina,
   quivi le strida, il compianto, il lamento;
   bestemmian quivi la virtù divina.   *36*
Intesi ch'a così fatto tormento
   enno dannati i peccator carnali,
   che la ragion sommettono al talento.   *39*
E come li stornei ne portan l'ali
   nel freddo tempo, a schiera larga e piena,
   così quel fiato li spiriti mali   *42*
di qua, di là, di giù, di sù li mena;
   nulla speranza li conforta mai,
   non che di posa, ma di minor pena.   *45*
E come i gru van cantando lor lai,
   faccendo in aere di sé lunga riga,
   così vid' io venir, traendo guai,   *48*

"beware how you enter and in whom you trust; let not the breadth of the entrance deceive you!" And my leader to him, "Why do you too cry out? Do not hinder his fated going: thus is it willed there where that can be done which is willed; and ask no more."

Now the doleful notes begin to reach me; now I am come where much wailing smites me. I came into a place mute of all light, which bellows like the sea in tempest when it is assailed by warring winds. The hellish hurricane, never resting, sweeps along the spirits with its rapine; whirling and smiting, it torments them. When they arrive before the ruin, there the shrieks, the moans, the lamentations; there they curse the divine power. I learned that to such torment are condemned the carnal sinners, who subject reason to desire.

And as their wings bear the starlings along in the cold season, in wide, dense flocks, so does that blast the sinful spirits; hither, thither, downward, upward, it drives them. No hope of less pain, not to say of rest, ever comforts them. And as the cranes go chanting their lays, making a long line of themselves in the air, so I saw shades come, uttering wails,

ombre portate da la detta briga;
   per ch'i' dissi: "Maestro, chi son quelle
   genti che l'aura nera sì gastiga?"   *51*
"La prima di color di cui novelle
   tu vuo' saper," mi disse quelli allotta,
   "fu imperadrice di molte favelle.   *54*
A vizio di lussuria fu sì rotta,
   che libito fé licito in sua legge,
   per tòrre il biasmo in che era condotta.   *57*
Ell' è Semiramìs, di cui si legge
   che succedette a Nino e fu sua sposa:
   tenne la terra che 'l Soldan corregge.   *60*
L'altra è colei che s'ancise amorosa,
   e ruppe fede al cener di Sicheo;
   poi è Cleopatràs lussurïosa.   *63*
Elena vedi, per cui tanto reo
   tempo si volse, e vedi 'l grande Achille,
   che con amore al fine combatteo.   *66*
Vedi Parìs, Tristano"; e più di mille
   ombre mostrommi e nominommi a dito,
   ch'amor di nostra vita dipartille.   *69*
Poscia ch'io ebbi 'l mio dottore udito
   nomar le donne antiche e ' cavalieri,
   pietà mi giunse, e fui quasi smarrito.   *72*
I' cominciai: "Poeta, volontieri
   parlerei a que' due che 'nsieme vanno,
   e paion sì al vento esser leggieri."   *75*
Ed elli a me: "Vedrai quando saranno
   più presso a noi; e tu allor li priega
   per quello amor che i mena, ed ei verranno."   *78*

borne by that strife; wherefore I said, "Master, who are these people that are so lashed by the black air?"

"The first of these of whom you wish to know," he said to me then, "was empress of many tongues. She was so given to lechery that she made lust licit in her law, to take away the blame she had incurred. She is Semiramis, of whom we read that she succeeded Ninus and had been his wife: she held the land the Sultan rules. The next is she who slew herself for love and broke faith to the ashes of Sichaeus; next is wanton Cleopatra. See Helen, for whom so many years of ill revolved; and see the great Achilles, who fought at the last with love. See Paris, Tristan," and more than a thousand shades whom love had parted from our life he showed me, pointing them out and naming them.

When I heard my teacher name the ladies and the knights of old, pity overcame me and I was as one bewildered. "Poet," I began, "willingly would I speak with those two that go together and seem to be so light upon the wind."

And he to me, "You shall see when they are nearer to us; and do you entreat them then by that love which leads them, and they will come."

Sì tosto come il vento a noi li piega,
  mossi la voce: "O anime affannate,
  venite a noi parlar, s'altri nol niega!"   *81*
Quali colombe dal disio chiamate
  con l'ali alzate e ferme al dolce nido
  vegnon per l'aere, dal voler portate;   *84*
cotali uscir de la schiera ov' è Dido,
  a noi venendo per l'aere maligno,
  sì forte fu l'affettüoso grido.   *87*
"O animal grazïoso e benigno
  che visitando vai per l'aere perso
  noi che tignemmo il mondo di sanguigno,   *90*
se fosse amico il re de l'universo,
  noi pregheremmo lui de la tua pace,
  poi c'hai pietà del nostro mal perverso.   *93*
Di quel che udire e che parlar vi piace,
  noi udiremo e parleremo a voi,
  mentre che 'l vento, come fa, ci tace.   *96*
Siede la terra dove nata fui
  su la marina dove 'l Po discende
  per aver pace co' seguaci sui.   *99*
Amor, ch'al cor gentil ratto s'apprende,
  prese costui de la bella persona
  che mi fu tolta; e 'l modo ancor m'offende.   *102*
Amor, ch'a nullo amato amar perdona,
  mi prese del costui piacer sì forte,
  che, come vedi, ancor non m'abbandona.   *105*
Amor condusse noi ad una morte.
  Caina attende chi a vita ci spense."
  Queste parole da lor ci fuor porte.   *108*

As soon as the wind bends them to us, I raised my voice, "O wearied souls! come speak with us, if Another forbid it not."

As doves called by desire, with wings raised and steady, come through the air, borne by their will to their sweet nest, so did these issue from the troop where Dido is, coming to us through the malignant air, such force had my compassionate cry.

"O living creature, gracious and benign, that go through the black air visiting us who stained the world with blood, if the King of the universe were friendly to us, we would pray Him for your peace, since you have pity on our perverse ill. Of that which it pleases you to hear and to speak, we will hear and speak with you, while the wind, as now, is silent for us.

"The city where I was born lies on that shore where the Po descends to be at peace with its followers. Love, which is quickly kindled in a gentle heart, seized this one for the fair form that was taken from me—and the way of it afflicts me still. Love, which absolves no loved one from loving, seized me so strongly with delight in him, that, as you see, it does not leave me even now. Love brought us to one death. Caina awaits him who quenched our life."

These words were borne to us from them.

53

Quand' io intesi quell' anime offense,
   china' il viso, e tanto il tenni basso,
   fin che 'l poeta mi disse: "Che pense?"   *111*
Quando rispuosi, cominciai: "Oh lasso,
   quanti dolci pensier, quanto disio
   menò costoro al doloroso passo!"   *114*
Poi mi rivolsi a loro e parla' io,
   e cominciai: "Francesca, i tuoi martìri
   a lagrimar mi fanno tristo e pio.   *117*
Ma dimmi: al tempo d'i dolci sospiri,
   a che e come concedette amore
   che conosceste i dubbiosi disiri?"   *120*
E quella a me: "Nessun maggior dolore
   che ricordarsi del tempo felice
   ne la miseria; e ciò sa 'l tuo dottore.   *123*
Ma s'a conoscer la prima radice
   del nostro amor tu hai cotanto affetto,
   dirò come colui che piange e dice.   *126*
Noi leggiavamo un giorno per diletto
   di Lancialotto come amor lo strinse;
   soli eravamo e sanza alcun sospetto.   *129*
Per più fïate li occhi ci sospinse
   quella lettura, e scolorocci il viso;
   ma solo un punto fu quel che ci vinse.   *132*
Quando leggemmo il disïato riso
   esser basciato da cotanto amante,
   questi, che mai da me non fia diviso,   *135*
la bocca mi basciò tutto tremante.
   Galeotto fu 'l libro e chi lo scrisse:
   quel giorno più non vi leggemmo avante."   *138*

And when I heard those afflicted souls I bowed my head and held it bowed until the poet said to me, "What are you thinking of?"

When I answered, I began, "Alas! How many sweet thoughts, what great desire, brought them to the woeful pass!"

Then I turned again to them, and I began, "Francesca, your torments make me weep for grief and pity; but tell me, in the time of the sweet sighs, by what and how did Love grant you to know the dubious desires?"

And she to me, "There is no greater sorrow than to recall, in wretchedness, the happy time; and this your teacher knows. But if you have such great desire to know the first root of our love, I will tell as one who weeps and tells. One day, for pastime, we read of Lance-lot, how love constrained him; we were alone, suspecting nothing. Several times that reading urged our eyes to meet and took the color from our faces, but one moment alone it was that overcame us. When we read how the longed-for smile was kissed by so great a lover, this one, who never shall be parted from me, kissed my mouth all trembling. A Galle-hault was the book and he who wrote it; that day we read no farther in it."

Mentre che l'uno spirto questo disse,
 l'altro piangëa; sì che di pietade
 io venni men così com' io morisse.
E caddi come corpo morto cade.   *142*

While the one spirit said this, the other wept,
so that for pity I swooned, as if in death, and
fell as a dead body falls.

INFERNO

Al tornar de la mente, che si chiuse
  dinanzi a la pietà d'i due cognati,
  che di trestizia tutto mi confuse,   3
novi tormenti e novi tormentati
  mi veggio intorno, come ch'io mi mova
  e ch'io mi volga, e come che io guati.   6
Io sono al terzo cerchio, de la piova
  etterna, maladetta, fredda e greve;
  regola e qualità mai non l' è nova.   9
Grandine grossa, acqua tinta e neve
  per l'aere tenebroso si riversa;
  pute la terra che questo riceve.   12
Cerbero, fiera crudele e diversa,
  con tre gole caninamente latra
  sovra la gente che quivi è sommersa.   15
Li occhi ha vermigli, la barba unta e atra,
  e 'l ventre largo, e unghiate le mani;
  graffia li spirti ed iscoia ed isquatra.   18

CANTO VI

At the return of my mind which had closed itself before the piteousness of the two kinsfolk that had quite overwhelmed me with sadness, I see about me new torments and new tormented souls, whichever way I move and turn about to gaze. I am in the third circle of the eternal, accursed, cold and heavy rain: its measure and its quality are never new; huge hail, foul water, and snow pour down through the murky air; the ground that receives it stinks. Cerberus, monstrous beast and cruel, with three throats barks dog-like over the people who are here submerged. His eyes are red, his beard greasy and black, his belly wide and his hands taloned; he claws the spirits, flays and quarters them.

Urlar li fa la pioggia come cani;
   de l'un de' lati fanno a l'altro schermo;
   volgonsi spesso i miseri profani.   *21*
Quando ci scorse Cerbero, il gran vermo,
   le bocche aperse e mostrocci le sanne;
   non avea membro che tenesse fermo.   *24*
E 'l duca mio distese le sue spanne,
   prese la terra, e con piene le pugna
   la gittò dentro a le bramose canne.   *27*
Qual è quel cane ch'abbaiando agogna,
   e si racqueta poi che 'l pasto morde,
   ché solo a divorarlo intende e pugna,   *30*
cotai si fecer quelle facce lorde
   de lo demonio Cerbero, che 'ntrona
   l'anime sì, ch'esser vorrebber sorde.   *33*
Noi passavam su per l'ombre che adona
   la greve pioggia, e ponavam le piante
   sovra lor vanità che par persona.   *36*
Elle giacean per terra tutte quante,
   fuor d'una ch'a seder si levò, ratto
   ch'ella ci vide passarsi davante.   *39*
"O tu che se' per questo 'nferno tratto,"
   mi disse, "riconoscimi, se sai:
   tu fosti, prima ch'io disfatto, fatto."   *42*
E io a lui: "L'angoscia che tu hai
   forse ti tira fuor de la mia mente,
   sì che non par ch'i' ti vedessi mai.   *45*
Ma dimmi chi tu se' che 'n sì dolente
   loco se' messo, e hai sì fatta pena,
   che, s'altra è maggio, nulla è sì spiacente."   *48*

The rain makes them howl like dogs; the profane wretches often turn themselves, making of one side a screen for the other.

When Cerberus the great worm perceived us, he opened his mouths and showed his fangs; he was aquiver in every limb. And my leader, reaching out his open hands, took up earth, and with full fists threw it into the ravenous gullets. As the dog that barking craves, and then grows quiet when he snaps up his food, straining and struggling only to devour it, such became the foul faces of the demon Cerberus, who so thunders on the souls that they would fain be deaf.

We were passing over the shades whom the heavy rain subdues, and we were setting our feet upon their emptiness, which seems real bodies. All were lying on the ground, save one, who sat up as soon as he saw us pass before him.

"O you that are led through this Hell," he said to me, "recognize me if you can: you were made before I was unmade."

And I to him, "The anguish you endure perhaps takes you from my memory, so that I do not seem ever to have seen you; but tell me who you are, who are set in a place so grievous and who suffer such punishment that, if any is greater, none is so loathsome."

Ed elli a me: "La tua città, ch'è piena
    d'invidia sì che già trabocca il sacco,
    seco mi tenne in la vita serena.   *51*
Voi cittadini mi chiamaste Ciacco:
    per la dannosa colpa de la gola,
    come tu vedi, a la pioggia mi fiacco.   *54*
E io anima trista non son sola,
    ché tutte queste a simil pena stanno
    per simil colpa." E più non fé parola.   *57*
Io li rispuosi: "Ciacco, il tuo affanno
    mi pesa sì, ch'a lagrimar mi 'nvita;
    ma dimmi, se tu sai, a che verranno   *60*
li cittadin de la città partita;
    s'alcun v'è giusto; e dimmi la cagione
    per che l'ha tanta discordia assalita."   *63*
E quelli a me: "Dopo lunga tencione
    verranno al sangue, e la parte selvaggia
    caccerà l'altra con molta offensione.   *66*
Poi appresso convien che questa caggia
    infra tre soli, e che l'altra sormonti
    con la forza di tal che testé piaggia.   *69*
Alte terrà lungo tempo le fronti,
    tenendo l'altra sotto gravi pesi,
    come che di ciò pianga o che n'aonti.   *72*
Giusti son due, e non vi sono intesi;
    superbia, invidia e avarizia sono
    le tre faville c'hanno i cuori accesi."   *75*
Qui puose fine al lagrimabil suono.
    E io a lui: "Ancor vo' che mi 'nsegni
    e che di più parlar mi facci dono.   *78*

And he to me, "Your city, which is so full of envy that already the sack runs over, held me in it, in the bright life. You citizens called me Ciacco: for the ruinous fault of gluttony, as you see, I am broken by the rain; and I, in my misery, am not alone, for all these endure the same penalty for the same fault." And he said no more.

I answered him, "Ciacco, your misery so weighs upon me that it bids me weep. But tell me, if you can, what the citizens of the divided city will come to; and if any one in it is just; and tell me why such discord has assailed it."

And he to me, "After long contention they will come to blood, and the rustic party will drive out the other with much offense. Then, through the power of one who presently is temporizing, that party is destined to fall within three years, and the other to prevail, long holding its head high and keeping the other under heavy burdens, however it may lament and feel the shame. Two men are just, and are not heeded there. Pride, envy, and avarice are the three sparks that have inflamed their hearts." Here he ended his grievous words.

And I to him, "I would have you instruct me further, and make me a gift of further speech:

Farinata e 'l Tegghiaio, che fuor sì degni,
   Iacopo Rusticucci, Arrigo e 'l Mosca
   e li altri ch'a ben far puoser li 'ngegni,   *81*
dimmi ove sono e fa ch'io li conosca;
   ché gran disio mi stringe di savere
   se 'l ciel li addolcia o lo 'nferno li attosca."   *84*
E quelli: "Ei son tra l'anime più nere;
   diverse colpe giù li grava al fondo:
   se tanto scendi, là i potrai vedere.   *87*
Ma quando tu sarai nel dolce mondo,
   priegoti ch'a la mente altrui mi rechi:
   più non ti dico e più non ti rispondo."   *90*
Li diritti occhi torse allora in biechi;
   guardommi un poco e poi chinò la testa:
   cadde con essa a par de li altri ciechi.   *93*
E 'l duca disse a me: "Più non si desta
   di qua dal suon de l'angelica tromba,
   quando verrà la nimica podesta: *96*
ciascun rivederà la trista tomba,
   ripiglierà sua carne e sua figura,
   udirà quel ch'in etterno rimbomba."   *99*
Sì trapassammo per sozza mistura
   de l'ombre e de la pioggia, a passi lenti,
   toccando un poco la vita futura;   *102*
per ch'io dissi: "Maestro, esti tormenti
   creserann' ei dopo la gran sentenza,
   o fier minori, o saran sì cocenti?"   *105*

Farinata and Tegghiaio, who were so worthy, Jacopo Rusticucci, Arrigo, and Mosca, and the others who set their minds on doing good, tell me where they are and give me to know them, for great desire urges me to learn whether Heaven soothes or Hell envenoms them."

And he, "They are among the blackest souls, and different faults weigh them down toward the bottom; if you descend that far, there you can see them. But when you shall be in the sweet world I pray you recall me to men's memory. More I do not tell you, nor do I answer you more." Thereon he twisted his straight eyes asquint, looked at me for a moment, then bent his head and fell down with the other blind ones.

And my leader said to me, "He wakes no more until the angel's trumpet sounds and the hostile Power comes, when each shall find again his dismal tomb and take again his flesh and form, and hear that which resounds to all eternity."

Thus with slow steps we passed along through the foul mixture of the shades and of the rain, touching a little on the future life; wherefore I said, "Master, these torments, will they increase after the great Judgment, or will they grow less, or will they be just as burning as now?"

Ed elli a me: "Ritorna a tua scïenza,
  che vuol, quanto la cosa è più perfetta,
  più senta il bene, e così la doglienza.   *108*
Tutto che questa gente maladetta
  in vera perfezion già mai non vada,
  di là più che di qua essere aspetta."   *111*
Noi aggirammo a tondo quella strada,
  parlando più assai ch'i' non ridico;
  venimmo al punto dove si digrada:
quivi trovammo Pluto, il gran nemico.   *115*

And he to me, "Return to your science, which has it that the more a thing is perfect, the more it feels the good, and so the pain. Although this accursed folk can never come to true perfection, yet they look to be nearer it then than now."

We went round along that road, speaking much more than I repeat, and we came to the place where the descent is; there we found Plutus, the great enemy.

INFERNO

"Pape Satàn, pape Satàn aleppe!"
   cominciò Pluto con la voce chioccia;
   e quel savio gentil, che tutto seppe,   *3*
disse per confortarmi: "Non ti noccia
   la tua paura; ché, poder ch'elli abbia,
   non ci torrà lo scender questa roccia."   *6*
Poi si rivolse a quella 'nfiata labbia,
   e disse: "Taci, maladetto lupo!
   consuma dentro te con la tua rabbia.   *9*
Non è sanza cagion l'andare al cupo:
   vuolsi ne l'alto, là dove Michele
   fé la vendetta del superbo strupo."   *12*
Quali dal vento le gonfiate vele
   caggiono avvolte, poi che l'alber fiacca,
   tal cadde a terra la fiera crudele.   *15*
Così scendemmo ne la quarta lacca,
   pigliando più de la dolente ripa
   che 'l mal de l'universo tutto insacca.   *18*

CANTO VII

"*P*ape *Satàn, pape Satàn aleppe!*" Plutus began with a clucking voice; and that gentle sage who knew all, said, to reassure me, "Do not let your fear harm you; for, whatever power he have, he shall not keep us from descending this rock." Then he turned back to that bloated visage and said, "Silence, accursed wolf! Consume yourself inwardly with your own rage. Not without cause is this journey to the depth; so is it willed on high, there where Michael avenged the proud rebellion." As sails swollen by the wind fall in a heap when the mainmast snaps, so fell that cruel beast to the ground.

Thus we descended into the fourth hollow, taking in more of the dismal bank which insacks all the evil of the universe.

Ahi giustizia di Dio! tante chi stipa
　　nove travaglie e pene quant' io viddi?
　　e perché nostra colpa sì ne scipa?　　　　　*21*
Come fa l'onda là sovra Cariddi,
　　che si frange con quella in cui s'intoppa,
　　così convien che qui la gente riddi.　　　　*24*
Qui vid' i' gente più ch'altrove troppa,
　　e d'una parte e d'altra, con grand' urli,
　　voltando pesi per forza di poppa.　　　　　*27*
Percotëansi 'ncontro; e poscia pur lì
　　si rivolgea ciascun, voltando a retro,
　　gridando: "Perché tieni?" e "Perché burli?"　*30*
Così tornavan per lo cerchio tetro
　　da ogne mano a l'opposito punto,
　　gridandosi anche loro ontoso metro;　　　　*33*
poi si volgea ciascun, quand' era giunto,
　　per lo suo mezzo cerchio a l'altra giostra.
　　E io, ch'avea lo cor quasi compunto,　　　　*36*
dissi: "Maestro mio, or mi dimostra
　　che gente è questa, e se tutti fuor cherci
　　questi chercuti a la sinistra nostra."　　　*39*
Ed elli a me: "Tutti quanti fuor guerci
　　sì de la mente in la vita primaia,
　　che con misura nullo spendio ferci.　　　　*42*
Assai la voce lor chiaro l'abbaia,
　　quando vegnono a' due punti del cerchio
　　dove colpa contraria li dispaia.　　　　　*45*
Questi fuor cherci, che non han coperchio
　　piloso al capo, e papi e cardinali,
　　in cui usa avarizia il suo soperchio."　　　*48*

70

Ah, justice of God! who crams together so
many new travails and penalties as I saw?
And why does our guilt so waste us? As does
the wave, there over Charybdis, breaking it-
self against the wave it meets, so must the folk
here dance their round. Here I saw far more
people than elsewhere, both on the one side
and on the other, howling loudly, rolling
weights, which they pushed with their chests;
they clashed together, and then right there
each wheeled round, rolling back his weight,
shouting, "Why do you hoard?" and "Why
do you squander?" Thus they returned along
the gloomy circle on either hand to the op-
posite point, shouting at each other again
their reproachful refrain; then, having reached
that point, each turned back through his
half-circle to the next joust.

And I, heart-wrung at this, said, "Master,
now declare to me who are these people, and
if all these tonsured ones on our left were
clerics."

And he to me, "Each and all of these were
so asquint of mind in the first life that they
followed there no right measure in their
spending; most clearly do they bark this out
when they come to the two points of the circle
where opposite fault divides them. These who
have no covering of hair on their head were
clerics, and popes and cardinals, in whom
avarice wreaks its excess."

E io: "Maestro, tra questi cotali
　　dovre' io ben riconoscere alcuni
　　che furo immondi di cotesti mali."　　　　*51*
Ed elli a me: "Vano pensiero aduni:
　　la sconoscente vita che i fé sozzi,
　　ad ogne conoscenza or li fa bruni.　　　　*54*
In etterno verranno a li due cozzi:
　　questi resurgeranno del sepulcro
　　col pugno chiuso, e questi coi crin mozzi.　*57*
Mal dare e mal tener lo mondo pulcro
　　ha tolto loro, e posti a questa zuffa:
　　qual ella sia, parole non ci appulcro.　　*60*
Or puoi, figliuol, veder la corta buffa
　　d'i ben che son commessi a la fortuna,
　　per che l'umana gente si rabuffa;　　　　*63*
ché tutto l'oro ch'è sotto la luna
　　e che già fu, di quest' anime stanche
　　non poterebbe farne posare una."　　　　*66*
"Maestro mio," diss' io, "or mi dì anche:
　　questa fortuna di che tu mi tocche,
　　che è, che i ben del mondo ha sì tra branche?"*69*
E quelli a me: "Oh creature sciocche,
　　quanta ignoranza è quella che v'offende!
　　Or vo' che tu mia sentenza ne 'mbocche.　*72*
Colui lo cui saver tutto trascende,
　　fece li cieli e diè lor chi conduce
　　sì, ch'ogne parte ad ogne parte splende,　*75*
distribuendo igualmente la luce.
　　Similemente a li splendor mondani
　　ordinò general ministra e duce　　　　　*78*

And I said, "Master, among such as these
I ought surely to recognize some who were
polluted with these evils." And he to me,
"You harbor a vain thought: the undiscern-
ing life that made them foul now makes them
dim to all discernment. They will come for-
ever to the two buttings; these will rise from
the grave with closed fist, and these with
cropped hair. Ill-giving and ill-keeping have
robbed them of the fair world and set them
to this scuffle—what that is, I spend no fair
words to say. Now can you see, my son, the
brief mockery of the goods that are com-
mitted to Fortune, for which humankind
contend with one another; because all the
gold that is beneath the moon, or ever was,
would not give rest to a single one of these
weary souls."

"Master," I said, "now tell me further: this
Fortune which you touch on here, what is it,
which has the goods of the world so in its
clutches?"

And he to me, "O foolish creatures, how
great is the ignorance that besets you! I
would have you receive my judgment on this
now. He whose wisdom transcends all, made
the heavens and gave them guides, so that
every part shines to every part, equally dis-
tributing the light. In like manner, for world-
ly splendors He ordained a general minister
and guide

73

che permutasse a tempo li ben vani
   di gente in gente e d'uno in altro sangue,
   oltre la difension d'i senni umani;   *81*
per ch'una gente impera e l'altra langue,
   seguendo lo giudicio di costei,
   che è occulto come in erba l'angue.   *84*
Vostro saver non ha contasto a lei:
   questa provede, giudica, e persegue
   suo regno come il loro li altri dèi.   *87*
Le sue permutazion non hanno triegue:
   necessità la fa esser veloce;
   sì spesso vien chi vicenda consegue.   *90*
Quest' è colei ch'è tanto posta in croce
   pur da color che le dovrien dar lode,
   dandole biasmo a torto e mala voce;   *93*
ma ella s'è beata e ciò non ode:
   con l'altre prime creature lieta
   volve sua spera e beata si gode.   *96*
Or discendiamo omai a maggior pieta;
   già ogne stella cade che saliva
   quand' io mi mossi, e 'l troppo star si vieta." *99*
Noi ricidemmo il cerchio a l'altra riva
   sovr' una fonte che bolle e riversa
   per un fossato che da lei deriva.   *102*
L'acqua era buia assai più che persa;
   e noi, in compagnia de l'onde bige,
   intrammo giù per una via diversa.   *105*
In la palude va c'ha nome Stige
   questo tristo ruscel, quand' è disceso
   al piè de le maligne piagge grige.   *108*

who should in due time transfer the vain goods from race to race, and from one to another blood, beyond the prevention of human wit, so that one race rules and another languishes, pursuant to her judgment, which is hidden like the snake in the grass. Your wisdom cannot withstand her: she foresees, judges, and pursues her reign, as theirs the other gods. Her changes know no truce. Necessity compels her to be swift, so fast do men come to their turns. This is she who is much reviled even by those who ought to praise her, but do wrongfully blame her and defame her. But she is blest and does not hear it. Happy with the other primal creatures she turns her sphere and rejoices in her bliss.

"Now let us descend to greater wretchedness: already every star sinks that was rising when I set out, and to stay overlong is forbidden."

We crossed the circle to the other edge, above a fount that boils and pours over by a trench leading from it. The water was far darker than perse; and we, in company with the murky waves, entered down through a strange way. This dismal little stream, when it has descended to the foot of the malign gray slopes, flows into the marsh that is named Styx;

E io, che di mirare stava inteso,
    vidi genti fangose in quel pantano,
    ignude tutte, con sembiante offeso.   *111*
Queste si percotean non pur con mano,
    ma con la testa e col petto e coi piedi,
    troncandosi co' denti a brano a brano.   *114*
Lo buon maestro disse: "Figlio, or vedi
    l'anime di color cui vinse l'ira;
    e anche vo' che tu per certo credi   *117*
che sotto l'acqua è gente che sospira,
    e fanno pullular quest' acqua al summo,
    come l'occhio ti dice, u' che s'aggira.   *120*
Fitti nel limo dicon: 'Tristi fummo
    ne l'aere dolce che dal sol s'allegra,
    portando dentro accidïoso fummo: *123*
or ci attristiam ne la belletta negra.'
    Quest' inno si gorgoglian ne la strozza,
    ché dir nol posson con parola integra."   *126*
Così girammo de la lorda pozza
    grand' arco, tra la ripa secca e 'l mézzo,
    con li occhi vòlti a chi del fango ingozza.
Venimmo al piè d'una torre al da sezzo.   *130*

and I, who was standing intent to gaze, saw a muddy people in that bog, all naked and with looks of rage. They were smiting each other not with hand only, but with head and chest and feet, and tearing each other piecemeal with their teeth.

The good master said, "Son, you see now the souls of those whom anger overcame; and I would also have you know for certain that down under the water are people who sigh and make it bubble at the surface, as your eye tells you wherever it turns. Fixed in the slime they say, 'We were sullen in the sweet air that is gladdened by the sun, bearing within us the sluggish fumes; now we are sullen in the black mire.' This hymn they gurgle in their throats, for they cannot speak it in full words."

Thus we compassed a great arc of that foul pond between the dry bank and the slough, with eyes turned on those that swallow the mire; and we came at length to the foot of a tower.

INFERNO

Io DICO, seguitando, ch'assai prima
 che noi fossimo al piè de l'alta torre,
 li occhi nostri n'andar suso a la cima   *3*
per due fiammette che i vedemmo porre,
 e un'altra da lungi render cenno,
 tanto ch'a pena il potea l'occhio tòrre.   *6*
E io mi volsi al mar di tutto 'l senno;
 dissi: "Questo che dice? e che risponde
 quell' altro foco? e chi son quei che 'l fenno?" *9*
Ed elli a me: "Su per le sucide onde
 già scorgere puoi quello che s'aspetta,
 se 'l fummo del pantan nol ti nasconde." *12*
Corda non pinse mai da sé saetta
 che sì corresse via per l'aere snella,
 com' io vidi una nave piccioletta   *15*
venir per l'acqua verso noi in quella,
 sotto 'l governo d'un sol galeoto,
 che gridava: "Or se' giunta, anima fella!" *18*

CANTO VIII

I SAY, continuing, that long before we had come to the foot of the high tower, our eyes went upward to its summit because of two little flames we saw set there, while yet another returned the signal from so far off that the eye could hardly catch it. And I turned to the sea of all wisdom and said, "This one, what does it mean? And that other fire, what does it answer? And who are they that have made it?" And he to me, "Over the foul waves you can already make out what is expected, if the fumes of the marsh do not hide it from you."

Bowstring never drove arrow from itself that coursed so swiftly through the air as a little bark I saw come towards us then through the water, piloted by a single boatman, who cried, "Now you are caught, fell spirit!"

"Flegïàs, Flegïàs, tu gridi a vòto,"
 disse lo mio segnore, "a questa volta:
 più non ci avrai che sol passando il loto." *21*
Qual è colui che grande inganno ascolta
 che li sia fatto, e poi se ne rammarca,
 fecesi Flegïàs ne l'ira accolta. *24*
Lo duca mio discese ne la barca,
 e poi mi fece intrare appresso lui;
 e sol quand' io fui dentro parve carca. *27*
Tosto che 'l duca e io nel legno fui,
 segando se ne va l'antica prora
 de l'acqua più che non suol con altrui. *30*
Mentre noi corravam la morta gora,
 dinanzi mi si fece un pien di fango,
 e disse: "Chi se' tu che vieni anzi ora?" *33*
E io a lui: "S'i' vegno, non rimango;
 ma tu chi se', che sì se' fatto brutto?"
 Rispuose: "Vedi che son un che piango.' *36*
E io a lui: "Con piangere e con lutto,
 spirito maladetto, ti rimani;
 ch'i' ti conosco, ancor sie lordo tutto." *39*
Allor distese al legno ambo le mani;
 per che 'l maestro accorto lo sospinse,
 dicendo: "Via costà con li altri cani!" *42*
Lo collo poi con le braccia mi cinse;
 basciommi 'l volto e disse: "Alma sdegnosa,
 benedetta colei che 'n te s'incinse! *45*
Quei fu al mondo persona orgogliosa;
 bontà non è che sua memoria fregi:
 così s'è l'ombra sua qui furïosa. *48*

"Phlegyas, Phlegyas, this time you shout in vain," said my lord. "You shall not have us longer than while crossing the mire." As one who listens to some great deception that has been practiced on him, and then repines at it, such Phlegyas became in his gathered wrath.

My leader got into the bark, then had me enter after him—and only when I was in it did it seem laden.

As soon as he and I had embarked, the ancient prow moves off, cutting more of the water than it is wont with others. While we were running through the dead channel, there rose before me one covered with mud, and said, "Who are you that come before your time?"

And I to him, "If I come, I do not remain. But you, who are you that have become so foul?"

He answered, "You see that I am one who weeps."

And I to him, "In weeping and in sorrow do you remain, accursed spirit, for I know you, even if you are all filthy."

Then he stretched both his hands to the boat, whereat the wary master thrust him off, saying, "Away there with the other dogs!" Then he put his arms about my neck, kissed my face, and said, "Indignant soul, blessed is she who bore you! He was an arrogant one in the world. No goodness whatever adorns his memory; so is his shade furious here.

Quanti si tegnon or là sù gran regi
  che qui staranno come porci in brago,
  di sé lasciando orribili dispregi!"   *51*
E io: "Maestro, molto sarei vago
  di vederlo attuffare in questa broda
  prima che noi uscissimo del lago."   *54*
Ed elli a me: "Avante che la proda
  ti si lasci veder, tu sarai sazio:
  di tal disïo convien che tu goda."   *57*
Dopo ciò poco vid' io quello strazio
  far di costui a le fangose genti,
  che Dio ancor ne lodo e ne ringrazio.   *60*
Tutti gridavano: "A Filippo Argenti!"
  e 'l fiorentino spirito bizzarro
  in sé medesmo si volvea co' denti.   *63*
Quivi il lasciammo, che più non ne narro;
  ma ne l'orecchie mi percosse un duolo,
  per ch'io avante l'occhio intento sbarro.   *66*
Lo buon maestro disse: "Omai, figliuolo,
  s'appressa la città c'ha nome Dite,
  coi gravi cittadin, col grande stuolo."   *69*
E io: "Maestro, già le sue meschite
  là entro certe ne la valle cerno,
  vermiglie come se di foco uscite   *72*
fossero." Ed ei mi disse: "Il foco etterno
  ch'entro l'affoca le dimostra rosse,
  come tu vedi in questo basso inferno."   *75*
Noi pur giugnemmo dentro a l'alte fosse
  che vallan quella terra sconsolata:
  le mura mi parean che ferro fosse.   *78*

How many up there now account themselves great kings, that here shall lie like swine in mire, leaving behind them horrible dispraises."

And I, "Master, I should like well to see him soused in this soup, before we quit the lake."

And he to me, "Before the shore comes into view you shall be satisfied. It is fitting that in such a wish you should be gratified."

A little after this I saw such rending of him by the muddy folk that I still praise and thank God for it. All cried, "At Filippo Argenti!"—and the irascible Florentine spirit turned on himself with his teeth.

Here we left him, and I tell no more of him; but on my ears smote a sound of wailing, at which I bend my eyes intently forward. The good master said, "Now, my son, the city that is named Dis draws near, with its grave citizens, with its great garrison."

And I, "Master, already I distinctly discern its mosques there within the valley, red as if they had come out of the fire."

And he to me, "The eternal fire that blazes there within makes them show red, as you see, in this nether Hell."

We came at last into the deep moats entrenching that doleful city. The walls seemed to me to be of iron,

Non sanza prima far grande aggirata,
  venimmo in parte dove il nocchier forte
  "Usciteci," gridò: "qui è l'intrata."   *81*
Io vidi più di mille in su le porte
  da ciel piovuti, che stizzosamente
  dicean: "Chi è costui che sanza morte   *84*
va per lo regno de la morta gente?"
  E 'l savio mio maestro fece segno
  di voler lor parlar segretamente.   *87*
Allor chiusero un poco il gran disdegno
  e disser: "Vien tu solo, e quei sen vada
  che sì ardito intrò per questo regno.   *90*
Sol si ritorni per la folle strada:
  pruovi, se sa; ché tu qui rimarrai,
  che li ha' iscorta sì buia contrada."   *93*
Pensa, lettor, se io mi sconfortai
  nel suon de le parole maladette,
  ché non credetti ritornarci mai.   *96*
"O caro duca mio, che più di sette
  volte m'hai sicurtà renduta e tratto
  d'alto periglio che 'ncontra mi stette,   *99*
non mi lasciar," diss' io, "così disfatto;
  e se 'l passar più oltre ci è negato,
  ritroviam l'orme nostre insieme ratto."   *102*
E quel segnor che lì m'avea menato,
  mi disse: "Non temer; ché 'l nostro passo
  non ci può tòrre alcun: da tal n'è dato.   *105*
Ma qui m'attendi, e lo spirito lasso
  conforta e ciba di speranza buona,
  ch'i' non ti lascernò nel mondo basso."   *108*

and not until we had made a great circuit
did we come to a place where the boatman
loudly cried, "Out with you here! This is
the entrance."

Above the gates I saw more than a thou-
sand of those rained down from Heaven,
who cried angrily, "Who is this that without
death goes through the kingdom of the
dead?" And my wise master made a sign
that he wished to speak with them apart.
Then they restrained somewhat their great
disdain, and said, "You come alone, and let
that one depart, who has entered so daringly
into this kingdom. Let him retrace alone his
foolish way; try, if he can!—for you shall
stay here, who have escorted him through so
dark a country."

Judge, reader, if I did not lose heart at the
sound of the accursed words, for I did not
think I should ever return here.

"O my dear leader, who seven times and
more have restored my confidence and drawn
me from great peril confronting me, do not
leave me thus undone," I said. "And if going
farther is denied us, let us quickly retrace our
steps together."

And that lord who had led me thither
said to me, "Do not fear, for no one can take
from us our passage, by such a One is it
granted us; but wait for me here, and com-
fort your weary spirit and feed it with good
hope, for I will not forsake you in the nether
world."

Così sen va, e quivi m'abbandona
  lo dolce padre, e io rimagno in forse,
  che sì e no nel capo mi tenciona.   *111*

Udir non potti quello ch'a lor porse;
  ma ei non stette là con essi guari,
  che ciascun dentro a pruova si ricorse.   *114*

Chiuser le porte que' nostri avversari
  nel petto al mio segnor, che fuor rimase
  e rivolsesi a me con passi rari.   *117*

Li occhi a la terra e le ciglia avea rase
  d'ogne baldanza, e dicea ne' sospiri:
  "Chi m'ha negate le dolenti case!"   *120*

E a me disse: "Tu, perch' io m'adiri,
  non sbigottir, ch'io vincerò la prova,
  qual ch'a la difension dentro s'aggiri.   *123*

Questa lor tracotanza non è nova;
  ché già l'usaro a men segreta porta,
  la qual sanza serrame ancor si trova.   *126*

Sovr' essa vedestù la scritta morta:
  e già di qua da lei discende l'erta,
  passando per li cerchi sanza scorta,
tal che per lui ne fia la terra aperta."   *130*

So he goes away and leaves me there, the
gentle father, and I remain in doubt, as yes
and no contend within my head.

I could not hear what he proposed to them;
but he was not long there with them when
they all scrambled to get back in. These our
adversaries shut the gates in the face of
my lord, who remained without and turned
back to me with slow steps. He had his eyes
upon the ground, and his brows were shorn
of all boldness, and he was saying with sighs,
"Who has denied me the abodes of pain?"
And to me he said, "Be not dismayed be-
cause of my vexation, for I shall prevail in
this, whatever be contrived within to hinder
us. This insolence of theirs is nothing new,
for they showed it once at a less secret gate,
which still stands without a bolt. Over it you
saw the dead inscription; and already, on this
side of it, there comes down the steep, passing
the circles without escort, one by whom the
city shall be opened to us."

INFERNO

Quel color che viltà di fuor mi pinse
  veggendo il duca mio tornare in volta,
  più tosto dentro il suo novo ristrinse.   *3*
Attento si fermò com' uom ch'ascolta;
  ché l'occhio nol potea menare a lunga
  per l'aere nero e per la nebbia folta.   *6*
"Pur a noi converrà vincer la punga,"
  cominciò el, "se non . . . Tal ne s'offerse.
  Oh quanto tarda a me ch'altri qui giunga!"   *9*
I' vidi ben sì com' ei ricoperse
  lo cominciar con l'altro che poi venne,
  che fur parole a le prime diverse;   *12*
ma nondimen paura il suo dir dienne,
  perch' io traeva la parola tronca
  forse a peggior sentenzia che non tenne.   *15*
"In questo fondo de la trista conca
  discende mai alcun del primo grado,
  che sol per pena ha la speranza cionca?"   *18*

CANTO IX

That color which cowardice painted out-
wardly on me when I saw my leader turn
back, repressed more speedily his own new
color. He stopped attentive, like a man that
listens, for his eye could not lead him far
through the dark air and the dense fog.

"Yet we must win this fight," he began,
"or else . . . such did she offer herself to us!
Oh, how long to me it seems till someone
come!" I saw well how he covered up the
beginning with the rest that came after,
which were words different from the first;
but none the less his speech gave me fear,
because I drew his broken phrase perhaps to
a worse meaning than it held.

"Into this depth of the dismal hollow does
any ever descend from the first circle where
the sole punishment is hope cut off?" I asked;

Questa question fec' io; e quei "Di rado
   incontra," mi rispuose, "che di noi
   faccia il cammino alcun per qual io vado.   *21*
Ver è ch'altra fïata qua giù fui,
   congiurato da quella Eritón cruda
   che richiamava l'ombre a' corpi sui.   *24*
Di poco era di me la carne nuda,
   ch'ella mi fece intrar dentr' a quel muro,
   per trarne un spirto del cerchio di Giuda.   *27*
Quell' è 'l più basso loco e 'l più oscuro,
   e 'l più lontan dal ciel che tutto gira:
   ben so 'l cammin; però ti fa sicuro.   *30*
Questa palude che 'l gran puzzo spira
   cigne dintorno la città dolente,
   u' non potemo intrare omai sanz' ira."   *33*
E altro disse, ma non l'ho a mente;
   però che l'occhio m'avea tutto tratto
   ver' l'alta torre a la cima rovente,   *36*
dove in un punto furon dritte ratto
   tre furïe infernal di sangue tinte,
   che membra feminine avieno e atto,   *39*
e con idre verdissime eran cinte;
   serpentelli e ceraste avien per crine,
   onde le fiere tempie erano avvinte.   *42*
E quei, che ben conobbe le meschine
   de la regina de l'etterno pianto,
   "Guarda," mi disse, "le feroci Erine.   *45*
Quest' è Megera dal sinistro canto;
   quella che piange dal destro è Aletto;
   Tesifón è nel mezzo"; e tacque a tanto.   *48*

and he answered, "It seldom happens that any of us makes the journey on which I go. It is true that once before I was down here, conjured by that cruel Erichtho who was wont to call back shades into their bodies. My flesh had been but short while divested of me, when she made me enter within that wall to draw forth a spirit from the circle of Judas. That is the lowest place, and the darkest, and farthest from the heaven that encircles all. Well do I know the way, so reassure yourself. This marsh, which exhales the mighty stench, girds round the sorrowful city, wherein now we cannot enter without anger."

And more he said, but I have it not in memory, for my eye had wholly drawn me to the high tower with the glowing summit, where all at once three hellish blood-stained Furies had instantly risen up. They had the limbs and bearing of women, and they were girt with greenest hydras. For hair they had little serpents and cerastes bound about their savage temples. And he, who well recognized the handmaids of the queen of eternal lamentation, said to me, "See the fierce Erinyes! That is Megaera on the left; she that wails on the right is Alecto; Tisiphone is in the middle"; and with that he was silent.

Con l'unghie si fendea ciascuna il petto;
　　battiensi a palme e gridavan sì alto,
　　ch'i' mi strinsi al poeta per sospetto.　　　　*51*
"Vegna Medusa: sì 'l farem di smalto,"
　　dicevan tutte riguardando in giuso;
　　"mal non vengiammo in Tesëo l'assalto."　　*54*
"Volgiti 'n dietro e tien lo viso chiuso;
　　ché se 'l Gorgón si mostra e tu 'l vedessi,
　　nulla sarebbe di tornar mai suso."　　　　*57*
Così disse 'l maestro; ed elli stessi
　　mi volse, e non si tenne a le mie mani,
　　che con le sue ancor non mi chiudessi.　　*60*
O voi ch'avete li 'ntelletti sani,
　　mirate la dottrina che s'asconde
　　sotto 'l velame de li versi strani.　　　　*63*
E già venìa su per le torbide onde
　　un fracasso d'un suon, pien di spavento,
　　per cui tremavano amendue le sponde,　　*66*
non altrimenti fatto che d'un vento
　　impetüoso per li avversi ardori,
　　che fier la selva e sanz' alcun rattento　　*69*
li rami schianta, abbatte e porta fori;
　　dinanzi polveroso va superbo,
　　e fa fuggir le fiere e li pastori.　　　　*72*
Li occhi mi sciolse e disse: "Or drizza il nerbo
　　del viso su per quella schiuma antica
　　per indi ove quel fummo è più acerbo."　　*75*
Come le rane innanzi a la nimica
　　biscia per l'acqua si dileguan tutte,
　　fin ch'a la terra ciascuna s'abbica,　　　　*78*

Each was tearing her breast with her nails;
and they were beating themselves with their
hands, and crying out so loudly that in fear
I pressed close to the poet.

"Let Medusa come and we'll turn him to
stone," they all cried, looking downward.
"Poorly did we avenge the assault of The-
seus."

"Turn your back, and keep your eyes shut;
for should the Gorgon show herself and you
see her, there would be no returning above."
Thus said the master, and he himself turned
me round and, not trusting to my hands,
covered my face with his own hands as well.

O you who have sound understanding,
mark the doctrine that is hidden under the
veil of the strange verses!

And now there came over the turbid waves
a crash of fearful sound, at which both shores
trembled: a sound as of a wind, violent from
conflicting heats, which strikes the forest and
with unchecked course shatters the branches,
beats them down and sweeps them away,
haughtily driving onward in its cloud of dust
and putting wild beasts and shepherds to
flight.

He loosed my eyes, and said, "Now direct
your sight across that ancient scum, there
where that fume is harshest."

As the frogs before their enemy the snake
all vanish through the water, till each cocks
itself on the bottom,

vid' io più di mille anime distrutte
    fuggir così dinanzi ad un ch'al passo
    passava Stige con le piante asciutte.   *81*
Dal volto rimovea quell' aere grasso,
    menando la sinistra innanzi spesso;
    e sol di quell' angoscia parea lasso.   *84*
Ben m'accorsi ch'elli era da ciel messo,
    e volsimi al maestro; e quei fé segno
    ch'i' stessi queto ed inchinassi ad esso.   *87*
Ahi quanto mi parea pien di disdegno!
    Venne a la porta e con una verghetta
    l'aperse, che non v'ebbe alcun ritegno.   *90*
"O cacciati del ciel, gente dispetta,"
    cominciò elli in su l'orribil soglia,
    "ond' esta oltracotanza in voi s'alletta?   *93*
Perché recalcitrate a quella voglia
    a cui non puote il fin mai esser mozzo,
    e che più volte v'ha cresciuta doglia?   *96*
Che giova ne le fata dar di cozzo?
    Cerbero vostro, se ben vi ricorda,
    ne porta ancor pelato il mento e 'l gozzo."   *99*
Poi si rivolse per la strada lorda,
    e non fé motto a noi, ma fé sembiante
    d'omo cui altra cura stringa e morda   *102*
che quella di colui che li è davante;
    e noi movemmo i piedi inver' la terra,
    sicuri appresso le parole sante.   *105*
Dentro li 'ntrammo sanz' alcuna guerra;
    e io, ch'avea di riguardar disio
    la condizion che tal fortezza serra,   *108*

I saw more than a thousand ruined souls
flee before one that strode dry-shod over
Styx. He was clearing that gross air from
before his face, often moving his left hand
before him, and only with that annoyance
did he seem weary. Well did I perceive that
he was a messenger from Heaven; and I
turned to the master, who signed to me that
I should stand quiet and bow down to him.
Ah, how full of disdain he seemed to me! He
came to the gate, and with a little wand he
opened it, and there was no resistance.

"O outcasts from Heaven, race despised,"
he began upon the horrible threshold, "why
is this insolence harbored in you? Why
do you kick against that Will which can
never be thwarted of its end, and which
many times has increased your pain? What
does it avail to butt against the fates? Your
Cerberus, if you well remember, still bears
his chin and his throat peeled for doing so."
Then he turned back on the filthy way, and
spoke not a word to us, but looked like one
whom other care urges and incites than that
of those who stand before him.

Then we moved our steps toward the city,
secure after the holy words. We entered it
without any strife; and I, who was eager
to behold the condition which such a fortress
encloses,

com' io fui dentro, l'occhio intorno invio:
 e veggio ad ogne man grande campagna,
 piena di duolo e di tormento rio. *111*
Sì come ad Arli, ove Rodano stagna,
 sì com' a Pola, presso del Carnaro
 ch'Italia chiude e suoi termini bagna, *114*
fanno i sepulcri tutt' il loco varo,
 così facevan quivi d'ogne parte,
 salvo che 'l modo v'era più amaro; *117*
ché tra li avelli fiamme erano sparte,
 per le quali eran sì del tutto accesi,
 che ferro più non chiede verun' arte. *120*
Tutti li lor coperchi eran sospesi,
 e fuor n'uscivan sì duri lamenti,
 che ben parean di miseri e d'offesi. *123*
E io: "Maestro, quai son quelle genti
 che, seppellite dentro da quell' arche,
 si fan sentir coi sospiri dolenti?" *126*
E quelli a me: "Qui son li eresïarche
 con lor seguaci, d'ogne setta, e molto
 più che non credi son le tombe carche. *129*
Simile qui con simile è sepolto,
 e i monimenti son più e men caldi."
 E poi ch'a la man destra si fu vòlto,
passammo tra i martìri e li alti spaldi. *133*

cast my eye round about, as soon as I was in; and on every hand I see a great plain full of woe and of cruel torment. As at Arles, where the Rhone slackens its course, and as at Pola, near the Quarnero, which shuts Italy in and bathes her borders, the sepulchers make all the place uneven, so they did here on every side, save that the manner here was more bitter; for among the tombs flames were scattered, whereby they were made to glow all over, hotter than iron need be for any craft. Their covers were all raised up, and such dire laments were issuing forth from them as truly seemed to come from people wretched and suffering.

And I, "Master, what are these people who, buried within these chests, make themselves heard by their woeful sighs?"

And he to me, "Here are the heresiarchs with their followers of every sect, and the tombs are laden far more than you think. Like with like is buried here, and the monuments are more and less hot."

Then, after he had turned to the right hand, we passed between the tortures and the high battlements.

INFERNO

Ora sen va per un secreto calle,
  tra 'l muro de la terra e li martìri,
  lo mio maestro, e io dopo le spalle.   3
"O virtù somma, che per li empi giri
  mi volvi," cominciai, "com' a te piace,
  parlami, e sodisfammi a' miei disiri.   6
La gente che per li sepolcri giace
  potrebbesi veder? già son levati
  tutt' i coperchi, e nessun guardia face."   9
E quelli a me: "Tutti saran serrati
  quando di Iosafàt qui torneranno
  coi corpi che là sù hanno lasciati.   12
Suo cimitero da questa parte hanno
  con Epicuro tutti suoi seguaci,
  che l'anima col corpo morta fanno.   15
Però a la dimanda che mi faci
  quinc' entro satisfatto sarà tosto,
  e al disio ancor che tu mi taci."   18

CANTO X

Now, along a solitary path between the wall of the city and the torments my master goes on, and I follow after him.

"O supreme virtue," I began, "who lead me round as you will through the impious circles, speak to me and satisfy my desires. Might these people who lie within the sepulchers be seen? Indeed, the covers are all raised, and no one keeps guard."

And he to me, "All shall be closed when from Jehoshaphat they return here with the bodies which they have left above. In this part Epicurus with all his followers, who make the soul die with the body, have their burial-place. Therefore, to the question which you ask me you shall soon have satisfaction here within, and also to the wish which you hold from me."

E io: "Buon duca, non tegno riposto
   a te mio cuor se non per dicer poco,
   e tu m'hai non pur mo a ciò disposto."   *21*
"O Tosco che per la città del foco
   vivo ten vai così parlando onesto,
   piacciati di restare in questo loco.   *24*
La tua loquela ti fa manifesto
   di quella nobil patrïa natio,
   a la qual forse fui troppo molesto."   *27*
Subitamente questo suono uscìo
   d'una de l'arche; però m'accostai,
   temendo, un poco più al duca mio.   *30*
Ed el mi disse: "Volgiti! Che fai?
   Vedi là Farinata che s'è dritto:
   da la cintola in sù tutto 'l vedrai."   *33*
Io avea già il mio viso nel suo fitto;
   ed el s'ergea col petto e con la fronte
   com' avesse l'inferno a gran dispitto.   *36*
E l'animose man del duca e pronte
   mi pinser tra le sepulture a lui,
   dicendo: "Le parole tue sien conte."   *39*
Com' io al piè de la sua tomba fui,
   guardommi un poco, e poi, quasi sdegnoso,
   mi dimandò: "Chi fuor li maggior tui?"   *42*
Io ch'era d'ubidir disideroso,
   non gliel celai, ma tutto gliel' apersi;
   ond' ei levò le ciglia un poco in suso;   *45*
poi disse: "Fieramente furo avversi
   a me e a miei primi e a mia parte,
   sì che per due fiate li dispersi."   *48*

And I, "Good leader, I do not keep my heart hidden from you except in order to speak little, and to this you have before now disposed me."

"O Tuscan, who go alive through the city of fire speaking thus modestly, may it please you to stop in this place. Your speech clearly shows you a native of that noble fatherland to which I perhaps did too much harm." Suddenly this sound issued from one of the coffers, whereat in fear I drew a little nearer to my leader. And he to me, "Turn round! what are you doing? See there Farinata who has risen erect: from the waist upwards you will see him all."

Already I had fixed my eyes on his, and he rose upright with chest and brow thrown back as if he had great scorn of Hell; and the bold and ready hands of my leader pushed me between the tombs to him, and he said, "Let your words be fitting."

When I was at the foot of his tomb, he looked at me for a moment, then, as if in disdain, asked me, "Who were your ancestors?"

And I, who was eager to obey, concealed nothing, but made all plain to him; whereupon he raised his brows a little; then he said, "They were fiercely adverse to me and to my forebears and to my party, so that twice over I scattered them."

"S'ei fur cacciati, ei tornar d'ogne parte,"
   rispuos' io lui, "l'una e l'altra fiata;
   ma i vostri non appreser ben quell' arte."   *51*
Allor surse a la vista scoperchiata
   un'ombra, lungo questa, infino al mento:
   credo che s'era in ginocchie levata.   *54*
Dintorno mi guardò, come talento
   avesse di veder s'altri era meco;
   e poi che 'l sospecciar fu tutto spento,   *57*
piangendo disse: "Se per questo cieco
   carcere vai per altezza d'ingegno,
   mio figlio ov' è? e perché non è teco?"   *60*
E io a lui: "Da me stesso non vegno:
   colui ch'attende là per qui mi mena,
   forse cui Guido vostro ebbe a disdegno."   *63*
Le sue parole e 'l modo de la pena
   m'avean di costui già letto il nome;
   però fu la risposta così piena.   *66*
Di sùbito drizzato gridò: "Come?
   dicesti 'elli ebbe'? non viv' elli ancora?
   non fiere li occhi suoi lo dolce lume?"   *69*
Quando s'accorse d'alcuna dimora
   ch'io facëa dinanzi a la risposta,
   supin ricadde e più non parve fora.   *72*
Ma quell' altro magnanimo, a cui posta
   restato m'era, non mutò aspetto,
   né mosse collo, né piegò sua costa;   *75*
e sé continüando al primo detto,
   "S'elli han quell' arte," disse, "male appresa,
   ciò mi tormenta più che questo letto.   *78*

"If they were driven forth, they returned from every quarter, both times," I answered him, "but yours have not learned that art well."

Then there arose to sight alongside of him a shade, visible to the chin: I think he had raised himself on his knees. He looked round about me as though he wished to see whether someone was with me, but when his expectation was quite spent, he said, weeping, "If you go through this blind prison by reason of high genius, where is my son, and why is he not with you?"

And I to him, "I come not of myself. He who waits yonder, whom perhaps your Guido had in disdain, is leading me through here."

Already his words and the manner of his punishment had read his name to me: hence was my answer so full.

Suddenly straightening up, he cried, "How? Did you say 'he had'? Does he not still live? Does the sweet light not strike his eyes?" And when he perceived that I made some delay in answering, he fell supine again and showed himself no more.

But the other, that great soul at whose instance I had stopped, changed not his aspect, nor moved his neck, nor bent his side. "And if," he said, continuing his first discourse, "they have ill learned that art, that fact torments me more than this bed.

Ma non cinquanta volte fia raccesa
  la faccia de la donna che qui regge,
  che tu saprai quanto quell' arte pesa.   *81*
E se tu mai nel dolce mondo regge,
  dimmi: perché quel popolo è sì empio
  incontr' a' miei in ciascuna sua legge?"   *84*
Ond' io a lui: "Lo strazio e 'l grande scempio
  che fece l'Arbia colorata in rosso,
  tal orazion fa far nel nostro tempio."   *87*
Poi ch'ebbe sospirando il capo mosso,
  "A ciò non fu' io sol," disse, "né certo
  sanza cagion con li altri sarei mosso.   *90*
Ma fu' io solo, là dove sofferto
  fu per ciascun di tòrre via Fiorenza,
  colui che la difesi a viso aperto."   *93*
"Deh, se riposi mai vostra semenza,"
  prega' io lui, "solvetemi quel nodo
  che qui ha 'nviluppata mia sentenza.   *96*
El par che voi veggiate, se ben odo,
  dinanzi quel che 'l tempo seco adduce,
  e nel presente tenete altro modo."   *99*
"Noi veggiam, come quei c'ha mala luce,
  le cose," disse, "che ne son lontano;
  cotanto ancor ne splende il sommo duce.   *102*
Quando s'appressano o son, tutto è vano
  nostro intelletto; e s'altri non ci apporta,
  nulla sapem di vostro stato umano.   *105*
Però comprender puoi che tutta morta
  fia nostra conoscenza da quel punto
  che del futuro fia chiusa la porta."   *108*

But the face of the Lady who rules here will not be kindled fifty times before you shall know how much that art weighs. And, so may you return some time to the sweet world, tell me, why is that people so fierce against my kindred in all its laws?" Whereon I to him, "The havoc and the great slaughter, which dyed the Arbia red, cause such prayers to be made in our temple."

He sighed, and shook his head, then said, "I was not alone in that, nor surely without cause would I have moved with the others; but I was alone there where all agreed to make an end of Florence, the one who defended her before them all."

"Ah, so may your seed sometime find peace," I prayed him, "solve the knot which has here entangled my judgment. It seems, if I hear aright, that you see beforehand what time brings with it, but have a different manner with the present."

"Like one who has bad light, we see the things," he said, "which are remote from us: so much does the Supreme Ruler still shine on us; but when they draw near, or are, our intelligence is wholly vain, and unless others bring us word, we know nothing of your human state; wherefore you can comprehend that all our knowledge will be dead from that moment when the door of the future shall be closed."

Allor, come di mia colpa compunto,
   dissi: "Or direte dunque a quel caduto
   che 'l suo nato è co' vivi ancor congiunto;   *111*
e s'i' fui, dianzi, a la risposta muto,
   fate i saper che 'l fei perché pensava
   già ne l'error che m'avete soluto."   *114*
E già 'l maestro mio mi richiamava;
   per ch'i' pregai lo spirto più avaccio
   che mi dicesse chi con lu' istava.   *117*
Dissemi: "Qui con più di mille giaccio:
   qua dentro è 'l secondo Federico
   e 'l Cardinale; e de li altri mi taccio."   *120*
Indi s'ascose; e io inver' l'antico
   poeta volsi i passi, ripensando
   a quel parlar che mi parea nemico.   *123*
Elli si mosse; e poi, così andando,
   mi disse: "Perché se' tu sì smarrito?"
   E io li sodisfeci al suo dimando.   *126*
"La mente tua conservi quel ch'udito
   hai contra te," mi comandò quel saggio;
   "e ora attendi qui," e drizzò 'l dito: *129*
"quando sarai dinanzi al dolce raggio
   di quella il cui bell' occhio tutto vede,
   da lei saprai di tua vita il vïaggio."   *132*
Appresso mosse a man sinistra il piede:
   lasciammo il muro e gimmo inver' lo mezzo
   per un sentier ch'a una valle fiede,
che 'nfin là sù facea spiacer suo lezzo.   *136*

Then, compunctious for my fault, I said, "Will you, now, tell him who fell back that his son is still among the living? And let him know that, if I was silent in response to him before, it was because my thoughts were already in that error which you have resolved for me."

And now my master was recalling me; wherefore with more haste I begged the spirit to tell me who were there with him; and he said to me, "Here I lie with more than a thousand. Here within is the second Frederick, and the Cardinal; and of the rest I do not speak."

With that he hid himself; and I turned my steps to the ancient poet, thinking on the words that seemed hostile to me. He set out, and then, as we went, he said to me, "Why are you so disturbed?" And I satisfied him in his question.

"Let your memory preserve what you have heard against yourself," that sage bade me, "and now give heed here—" and he raised his finger; "when you are before her sweet radiance whose fair eyes see all, from her you shall know of your life's journey."

Then he turned his steps to the left and, leaving the wall, we made our way toward the middle by a path that strikes into a valley which even up there annoyed us with its stench.

INFERNO

In su l'estremità d'un'alta ripa
    che facevan gran pietre rotte in cerchio,
    venimmo sopra più crudele stipa;   *3*
e quivi, per l'orribile soperchio
    del puzzo che 'l profondo abisso gitta,
    ci raccostammo, in dietro, ad un coperchio   *6*
d'un grand' avello, ov' io vidi una scritta
    che dicea: "Anastasio papa guardo,
    lo qual trasse Fotin de la via dritta."   *9*
"Lo nostro scender conviene esser tardo,
    sì che s'ausi un poco in prima il senso
    al tristo fiato; e poi no i fia riguardo."   *12*
Così 'l maestro; e io "Alcun compenso,"
    dissi lui, "trova che 'l tempo non passi
    perduto." Ed elli: "Vedi ch'a ciò penso."   *15*
"Figliuol mio, dentro da cotesti sassi,"
    cominciò poi a dir, "son tre cerchietti
    di grado in grado, come que' che lassi.   *18*

CANTO XI

On the edge of a high bank, formed by huge broken rocks in a circle, we came above a more cruel pen; and here, because of the horrible excess of the stench which the deep abyss throws out, we drew back to the cover of a great tomb, on which I saw an inscription that said, "I hold Pope Anastasius, whom Photinus drew from the right path."

"We must delay our descent, that the sense may first accustom itself a little to the vile breath, and then we shall not heed it." Thus my master; and I said to him, "Pray find some compensation, that the time may not be lost." And he, "Know that I am so minded."

"My son, within these rocks," he then began, "are three lesser circles, one below another, like those you are leaving.

Tutti son pien di spirti maladetti;
  ma perché poi ti basti pur la vista,
  intendi come e perché son costretti.   21
D'ogne malizia, ch'odio in cielo acquista,
  ingiuria è 'l fine, ed ogne fin cotale
  o con forza o con frode altrui contrista.   24
Ma perché frode è de l'uom proprio male,
  più spiace a Dio; e però stan di sotto
  li frodolenti, e più dolor li assale.   27
Di vïolenti il primo cerchio è tutto;
  ma perché si fa forza a tre persone,
  in tre gironi è distinto e costrutto.   30
A Dio, a sé, al prossimo si pòne
  far forza, dico in loro e in lor cose,
  come udirai con aperta ragione.   33
Morte per forza e ferute dogliose
  nel prossimo si danno, e nel suo avere
  ruine, incendi e tollette dannose;   36
onde omicide e ciascun che mal fiere,
  guastatori e predon, tutti tormenta
  lo giron primo per diverse schiere.   39
Puote omo avere in sé man vïolenta
  e ne' suoi beni; e però nel secondo
  giron convien che sanza pro si penta   42
qualunque priva sé del vostro mondo,
  biscazza e fonde la sua facultade,
  e piange là dov' esser de' giocondo.   45

All are full of accursed spirits; but in order that hereafter the sight alone may suffice you, hear how and why they are impounded.

"Of every malice that gains hatred in Heaven the end is injustice; and every such end, either by force or by fraud, afflicts another. But because fraud is an evil peculiar to man, it more displeases God, and therefore the fraudulent are the lower, and more pain assails them.

"All the first circle is for the violent: but because violence is done to three persons, it is divided and constructed in three rings. To God, to one's self, and to one's neighbor may violence be done: I say to them and to their things, as I shall make plain to you.

"By violence death and grievous wounds may be inflicted upon one's neighbor; and on his substance, ruins, burnings, and injurious extortions; wherefore the first ring torments all homicides and every one who smites wrongfully, despoilers and plunderers, in various troops.

"A man may lay violent hand upon himself, and upon his own property; and therefore in the second ring must every one repent in vain who deprives himself of your world, gambles away and dissipates his substance, and weeps there where he should be joyous.

Puossi far forza ne la deïtade,
    col cor negando e bestemmiando quella,
    e spregiando natura e sua bontade;   *48*
e però lo minor giron suggella
    del segno suo e Soddoma e Caorsa
    e chi, spregiando Dio col cor, favella.   *51*
La frode, ond' ogne coscïenza è morsa,
    può l'omo usare in colui che 'n lui fida
    e in quel che fidanza non imborsa.   *54*
Questo modo di retro par ch'incida
    pur lo vinco d'amor che fa natura;
    onde nel cerchio secondo s'annida   *57*
ipocresia, lusinghe e chi affattura,
    falsità, ladroneccio e simonia,
    ruffian, baratti e simile lordura.   *60*
Per l'altro modo quell' amor s'oblia
    che fa natura, e quel ch'è poi aggiunto,
    di che la fede spezïal si cria;   *63*
onde nel cerchio minore, ov' è 'l punto
    de l'universo in su che Dite siede,
    qualunque trade in etterno è consunto."   *66*
E io: "Maestro, assai chiara procede
    la tua ragione, e assai ben distingue
    questo baràtro e 'l popol ch'e' possiede.   *69*
Ma dimmi: quei de la palude pingue,
    che mena il vento, e che batte la pioggia,
    e che s'incontran con sì aspre lingue,   *72*
perché non dentro da la città roggia
    sono ei puniti, se Dio li ha in ira?
    e se non li ha, perché sono a tal foggia?"   *75*

"Violence may be done against the Deity, by denying and blaspheming Him in the heart, and despising Nature and her goodness; and therefore the smallest ring seals with its mark both Sodom and Cahors, and all who speak contemning God in their heart.

"Fraud, which gnaws every conscience, a man may practice upon one who trusts in him, or upon one who reposes no confidence. This latter way seems to sever only the bond of love which nature makes; wherefore in the second circle hypocrisy, flatteries, sorcerers, falsity, theft, simony, panders, barratry, and like filth have their nest.

"By the other way both that love which Nature makes is forgotten, and that also which is added to it and which creates a special trust; therefore, in the smallest circle, at the center of the universe and the seat of Dis, every traitor is consumed eternally."

And I, "Master, your discourse proceeds most clearly, and full well distinguishes this chasm and the people that it holds; but tell me: they of the fat marsh, and they whom the wind drives, and they whom the rain beats, and they who clash with such rough tongues, why are they not punished within the ruddy city, if God's anger is upon them? And if it is not, why are they in such plight?"

Ed elli a me "Perché tanto delira,"
  disse, "lo 'ngegno tuo da quel che sòle?
  o ver la mente dove altrove mira?   78
Non ti rimembra di quelle parole
  con le quai la tua Etica pertratta
  le tre disposizion che 'l ciel non vole,   81
incontenenza, malizia e la matta
  bestialitade? e come incontenenza
  men Dio offende e men biasimo accatta?   84
Se tu riguardi ben questa sentenza,
  e rechiti a la mente chi son quelli
  che sù di fuor sostegnon penitenza,   87
tu vedrai ben perché da questi felli
  sien dipartiti, e perché men crucciata
  la divina vendetta li martelli."   90
"O sol che sani ogne vista turbata,
  tu mi contenti sì quando tu solvi,
  che, non men che saver, dubbiar m'aggrata.   93
Ancora in dietro un poco ti rivolvi,"
  diss' io, "là dove di' ch'usura offende
  la divina bontade, e 'l groppo solvi."   96
"Filosofia," mi disse, "a chi la 'ntende,
  nota, non pure in una sola parte,
  come natura lo suo corso prende   99
dal divino 'ntelletto e da sua arte;
  e se tu ben la tua Fisica note,
  tu troverai, non dopo molte carte,   102
che l'arte vostra quella, quanto pote,
  segue, come 'l maestro fa 'l discente;
  sì che vostr' arte a Dio quasi è nepote.   105

And he said to me, "Why does your wit so wander beyond its wont? Or your mind, whither does it gaze? Do you not remember the words with which your *Ethics* treats the three dispositions which Heaven wills not: incontinence, malice, and mad bestiality? and how incontinence less offends God and incurs less blame? If you consider well this doctrine, and bring to mind who they are that suffer punishment above, outside, you will see clearly why they are divided from these wicked spirits, and why the divine vengeance smites them with less wrath."

"O sun that heal every troubled vision, you do content me so, when you solve, that questioning, no less than knowing, pleases me; but turn back a little," I said, "to where you say that usury offends the divine Goodness, and loose the knot."

"Philosophy, for one who understands it," he said to me, "points out, not in one place alone, how Nature takes her course from divine Intellect and from Its art; and if you note well your *Physics*, you will find, after not many pages, that your art, as far as it can, follows her, as the pupil does his master; so that your art is as it were grandchild of God.

Da queste due, se tu ti rechi a mente
   lo Genesì dal principio, convene
   prender sua vita e avanzar la gente;   *108*
e perché l'usuriere altra via tene,
   per sé natura e per la sua seguace
   dispregia, poi ch'in altro pon la spene.   *111*
Ma seguimi oramai che 'l gir mi piace;
   ché i Pesci guizzan su per l'orizzonta,
   e 'l Carro tutto sovra 'l Coro giace,
e 'l blazo via là oltra si dismonta."   *115*

By these two, if you remember Genesis at the beginning, it behooves man to gain his bread and to prosper. But because the usurer takes another way, he contemns Nature in herself and in her follower, for he puts his hope elsewhere.

"But follow me now, for it pleases me to go: the Fishes are quivering on the horizon, and all the Wain lies over Caurus, and there, farther on, is the descent of the cliff."

Era lo loco ov' a scender la riva
   venimmo, alpestro e, per quel che v'er' anco,
   tal, ch'ogne vista ne sarebbe schiva.   *3*
Qual è quella ruina che nel fianco
   di qua da Trento l'Adice percosse,
   o per tremoto o per sostegno manco,   *6*
che da cima del monte, onde si mosse,
   al piano è sì la roccia discoscesa,
   ch'alcuna via darebbe a chi sù fosse: *9*
cotal di quel burrato era la scesa;
   e 'n su la punta de la rotta lacca
   l'infamïa di Creti era distesa   *12*
che fu concetta ne la falsa vacca;
   e quando vide noi, sé stesso morse,
   sì come quei cui l'ira dentro fiacca.   *15*
Lo savio mio inver' lui gridò: "Forse
   tu credi che qui sia 'l duca d'Atene,
   che sù nel mondo la morte ti porse?   *18*
Pàrtiti, bestia, ché questi non vene
   ammaestrato da la tua sorella,
   ma vassi per veder le vostre pene."   *21*

CANTO XII

The place where we came for the descent
of the bank was alpine, and such, because of
what was there, that every eye would shun it.

Like the ruin which struck the Adige in
its flank, on this side of Trent, either by
earthquake or through failure of support,
where, from the top of the mountain whence
it started, to the plain, the rock is so tum-
bled down as to give some passage to anyone
above—such was the descent of that ravine;
and on the edge of the broken chasm was
outstretched the infamy of Crete that was
conceived in the false cow. And when he
saw us he bit himself, like one whom wrath
rends inwardly.

My sage cried out toward him, "Perhaps
you believe that here is the Duke of Athens,
who dealt you your death up in the world.
Get you gone, beast, for this man does not
come tutored by your sister, but journeys
here to see your punishments."

Qual è quel toro che si slaccia in quella
  c'ha ricevuto già 'l colpo mortale,
  che gir non sa, ma qua e là saltella,   *24*
vid' io lo Minotauro far cotale;
  e quello accorto gridò: "Corri al varco;
  mentre ch'e' 'nfuria, è buon che tu ti cale."   *27*
Così prendemmo via giù per lo scarco
  di quelle pietre, che spesso moviensi
  sotto i miei piedi per lo novo carco.   *30*
Io gia pensando; e quei disse: "Tu pensi
  forse a questa ruina, ch'è guardata
  da quell' ira bestial ch'i' ora spensi.   *33*
Or vo' che sappi che l'altra fïata
  ch'i' discesi qua giù nel basso inferno,
  questa roccia non era ancor cascata.   *36*
Ma certo poco pria, se ben discerno,
  che venisse colui che la gran preda
  levò a Dite del cerchio superno,   *39*
da tutte parti l'alta valle feda
  tremò sì, ch'i' pensai che l'universo
  sentisse amor, per lo qual è chi creda   *42*
più volte il mondo in caòsso converso;
  e in quel punto questa vecchia roccia,
  qui e altrove, tal fece riverso.   *45*
Ma ficca li occhi a valle, ché s'approccia
  la riviera del sangue in la qual bolle
  qual che per vïolenza in altrui noccia."   *48*
Oh cieca cupidigia e ira folle,
  che sì ci sproni ne la vita corta,
  e ne l'etterna poi sì mal c'immolle!   *51*

As a bull that breaks loose in the moment
when it has received the mortal blow, and
cannot go, but plunges this way and that, so
I saw the Minotaur do. And my wary guide
cried, "Run to the passage: while he is in fury
it is well that you descend."

So we took our way down over that rocky
debris, which often moved under my feet with
the new weight. I was going along thinking,
and he said, "Perhaps you are thinking on this
ruin, guarded by that bestial wrath which I
quelled just now. Know then that the other
time I came down here into the nether Hell
this rock had not yet fallen. But certainly, if
I reckon rightly, it was a little before He
came who took from Dis the great spoil of
the uppermost circle, that the deep foul val-
ley trembled so on all sides that I thought
the universe felt love, whereby, as some
believe, the world has many times been
turned to chaos; and at that moment this
ancient rock, here and elsewhere, made such
downfall. But fix your eyes below, for the
river of blood draws near, in which boils
everyone who by violence injures others."

O blind cupidity and mad rage, which in
the brief life so goad us on, and then, in the
eternal, steep us so bitterly!

Io vidi un'ampia fossa in arco torta,
   come quella che tutto 'l piano abbraccia,
   secondo ch'avea detto la mia scorta;   *54*
e tra 'l piè de la ripa ed essa, in traccia
   corrien centauri, armati di saette,
   come solien nel mondo andare a caccia.   *57*
Veggendoci calar, ciascun ristette,
   e de la schiera tre si dipartiro
   con archi e asticciuole prima elette;   *60*
e l'un gridò da lungi: "A qual martiro
   venite voi che scendete la costa?
   Ditel costinci; se non, l'arco tiro."   *63*
Lo mio maestro disse: "La risposta
   farem noi a Chirón costà di presso:
   mal fu la voglia tua sempre sì tosta."   *66*
Poi mi tentò, e disse: "Quelli è Nesso,
   che morì per la bella Deianira,
   e fé di sé la vendetta elli stesso.   *69*
E quel di mezzo, ch'al petto si mira,
   è il gran Chirón, il qual nodrì Achille;
   quell' altro è Folo, che fu sì pien d'ira.   *72*
Dintorno al fosso vanno a mille a mille,
   saettando qual anima si svelle
   del sangue più che sua colpa sortille."   *75*
Noi ci appressammo a quelle fiere isnelle:
   Chirón prese uno strale, e con la cocca
   fece la barba in dietro a le mascelle.   *78*
Quando s'ebbe scoperta la gran bocca,
   disse a' compagni: "Siete voi accorti
   che quel di retro move ciò ch'el tocca?   *81*

I saw a wide ditch bent in an arc, as one embracing all the plain, according as my guide had said, and between it and the foot of the bank were centaurs running in a file, armed with arrows, as in the world they were wont to go to the chase. Seeing us coming down they all stopped and from the band three came forward, with bows and shafts which they first selected; and one cried from a distance, "To what torment do you come, you who descend the slope? Tell us from there; if not, I draw my bow!"

My master said, "Our answer we will make to Chiron there beside you; to your own hurt was your will ever thus hasty." Then he nudged me and said, "That is Nessus, who died for the beautiful Dejanira and himself wrought vengeance for himself; and the one in the middle, who gazes on his own breast, is the great Chiron, he who brought up Achilles; the other is Pholus, who was so full of rage. Around the ditch they go by thousands, piercing with their arrows whatever spirit lifts itself out of the blood more than its guilt has allotted to it."

We drew near to those fleet beasts; and Chiron took an arrow and, with the notch of it, brushed back his beard upon his jaws; and when he had uncovered his great mouth, he said to his companions, "Have you observed that the one behind moves what he touches?

Così non soglion far li piè d'i morti."
   E 'l mio buon duca, che già li er' al petto,
   dove le due nature son consorti,   *84*
rispuose: "Ben è vivo, e sì soletto
   mostrar li mi convien la valle buia;
   necessità 'l ci 'nduce, e non diletto.   *87*
Tal si partì da cantare alleluia
   che mi commise quest' officio novo:
   non è ladron, né io anima fuia.   *90*
Ma per quella virtù per cu' io movo
   li passi miei per sì selvaggia strada,
   danne un de' tuoi, a cui noi siamo a provo,   *93*
e che ne mostri là dove si guada,
   e che porti costui in su la groppa,
   ché non è spirto che per l'aere vada."   *96*
Chirón si volse in su la destra poppa,
   e disse a Nesso: "Torna, e sì li guida,
   e fa cansar s'altra schiera v'intoppa."   *99*
Or ci movemmo con la scorta fida
   lungo la proda del bollor vermiglio,
   dove i bolliti facieno alte strida.   *102*
Io vidi gente sotto infino al ciglio;
   e 'l gran centauro disse: "E' son tiranni
   che dier nel sangue e ne l'aver di piglio.   *105*
Quivi si piangon li spietati danni;
   quivi è Alessandro, e Dïonisio fero
   che fé Cicilia aver dolorosi anni.   *108*
E quella fronte c'ha 'l pel così nero,
   è Azzolino; e quell' altro ch'è biondo,
   è Opizzo da Esti, il qual per vero   *111*

The feet of the dead are not wont to do so."

And my good leader, who was now at his breast, where the two natures are consorted, replied, "Indeed he is alive, and thus alone have I to show him the dark valley: necessity brings him to it, and not sport. From singing halleluiah, came one who gave me this new office. He is no robber, nor I a thievish spirit; but by that Power by which I move my steps on so wild a road, give us one of your band whom we may keep beside, that he may show us where the ford is, and carry this one on his back, who is not a spirit that can go through the air."

Chiron bent round on his right breast and said to Nessus: "Go back and guide them, then; and if another troop encounters you, make it give way."

We moved on then with the trusty escort, along the edge of the crimson boiling, in which the boiled were uttering piercing shrieks. I saw people in it, down even to the eyebrows, and the great centaur said, "These are tyrants who took to blood and plunder. Here they lament their merciless crimes: here is Alexander, and cruel Dionysius who made Sicily have woeful years; and that brow with the hair so black is Azzolino, and that other blond one is Opizzo of Este who up

fu spento dal figliastro sù nel mondo."
    Allor mi volsi al poeta, e quei disse:
    "Questi ti sia or primo, e io secondo."   *114*
Poco più oltre il centauro s'affisse
    sovr' una gente che 'nfino a la gola
    parea che di quel bulicame uscisse.   *117*
Mostrocci un'ombra da l'un canto sola,
    dicendo: "Colui fesse in grembo a Dio
    lo cor che 'n su Tamisi ancor si cola."   *120*
Poi vidi gente che di fuor del rio
    tenean la testa e ancor tutto 'l casso;
    e di costoro assai riconobb' io.   *123*
Così a più a più si facea basso
    quel sangue, sì che cocea pur li piedi;
    e quindi fu del fosso il nostro passo.   *126*
"Sì come tu da questa parte vedi
    lo bulicame che sempre si scema,"
    disse 'l centauro, "voglio che tu credi   *129*
che da quest' altra a più a più giù prema
    lo fondo suo, infin ch'el si raggiunge
    ove la tirannia convien che gema.   *132*
La divina giustizia di qua punge
    quell' Attila che fu flagello in terra,
    e Pirro e Sesto; e in etterno munge   *135*
le lagrime, che col bollor diserra,
    a Rinier da Corneto, a Rinier Pazzo,
    che fecero a le strade tanta guerra."
Poi si rivolse e ripassossi 'l guazzo.   *139*

in the world was indeed slain by his step-
son." Then I turned to the poet, and he
said, "Let him be first guide to you now,
and me second."

A little farther on the centaur stopped be-
side a people who seemed to issue from
that boiling stream as far as the throat. He
showed us a spirit on one side alone and said,
"That one clove, in God's bosom, the heart
which on the Thames still drips with blood."

Then some I saw who had their heads, and
even all their chests, out of the stream; and
of these I recognized many. Thus more and
more that blood sank down till it cooked
only the feet; and here was our passage of
the ditch.

"As on this hand you see that the boiling
stream continually diminishes," said the cen-
taur, "so I would have you believe that on
this other it lowers its bed more and more,
until it comes round again to the place where
tyranny must groan. Divine justice there
goads that Attila who was a scourge on earth,
and Pyrrhus and Sextus; and forever milks
the tears, unlocked by the boiling, from
Rinier of Corneto and Rinier Pazzo, who
made such warfare upon the highways."

Then he turned back and crossed the ford
again.

INFERNO

Non era ancor di là Nesso arrivato,
   quando noi ci mettemmo per un bosco
   che da neun sentiero era segnato.   *3*
Non fronda verde, ma di color fosco;
   non rami schietti, ma nodosi e 'nvolti;
   non pomi v'eran, ma stecchi con tòsco.   *6*
Non han sì aspri sterpi né sì folti
   quelle fiere selvagge che 'n odio hanno
   tra Cecina e Corneto i luoghi cólti.   *9*
Quivi le brutte Arpie lor nidi fanno,
   che cacciar de le Strofade i Troiani
   con tristo annunzio di futuro danno.   *12*
Ali hanno late, e colli e visi umani,
   piè con artigli, e pennuto 'l gran ventre;
   fanno lamenti in su li alberi strani.   *15*
E 'l buon maestro "Prima che più entre,
   sappi che se' nel secondo girone,"
   mi cominciò a dire, "e sarai mentre   *18*

CANTO XIII

Nᴇssᴜs had not yet reached the other side when we moved forward through a wood which was not marked by any path. No green leaves, but of dusky hue; no smooth boughs, but gnarled and warped; no fruits were there, but thorns with poison. Those wild beasts that hate tilled lands between Cecina and Corneto do not have thickets so rough or dense. Here the foul Harpies make their nests, who drove the Trojans from the Strophades with dismal announcement of future ill; they have broad wings, and human necks and faces, feet with claws, and their great bellies are feathered; they make lament on the strange trees.

And the good master began to say to me, "Before you enter farther, know that you are in the second ring, and shall be, until

che tu verrai ne l'orribil sabbione.
 Però riguarda ben; sì vederai
 cose che torrien fede al mio sermone."   *21*
Io sentia d'ogne parte trarre guai
 e non vedea persona che 'l facesse;
 per ch'io tutto smarrito m'arrestai.   *24*
Cred' ïo ch'ei credette ch'io credesse
 che tante voci uscisser, tra quei bronchi,
 da gente che per noi si nascondesse.   *27*
Però disse 'l maestro: "Se tu tronchi
 qualche fraschetta d'una d'este piante,
 li pensier c'hai si faran tutti monchi."   *30*
Allor porsi la mano un poco avante
 e colsi un ramicel da un gran pruno;
 e 'l tronco suo gridò: "Perché mi schiante?" *33*
Da che fatto fu poi di sangue bruno,
 ricominciò a dir: "Perché mi scerpi?
 non hai tu spirto di pietade alcuno?   *36*
Uomini fummo, e or siam fatti sterpi:
 ben dovrebb' esser la tua man più pia,
 se state fossimo anime di serpi."   *39*
Come d'un stizzo verde ch'arso sia
 da l'un de' capi, che da l'altro geme
 e cigola per vento che va via,   *42*
sì de la scheggia rotta usciva insieme
 parole e sangue; ond' io lasciai la cima
 cadere, e stetti come l'uom che teme.   *45*
"S'elli avesse potuto creder prima,"
 rispuose 'l savio mio, "anima lesa,
 ciò c'ha veduto pur con la mia rima,   *48*

you come to the horrible sand. Look well,
therefore, and you shall see things that would
make my words incredible."

I heard wailings uttered on every side, and
saw no one who made them; wherefore, all
bewildered, I stopped. I believe that he be-
lieved that I believed that all those voices
from amid the trunks came from people
who were hidden from us. Therefore the
master said, "If you break off a little branch
from one of these plants, the thoughts you
have will all be cut short." Then I stretched
my hand a little forward and plucked a twig
from a great thornbush, and its stub cried,
"Why do you break me?" And when it had
become dark with blood, it began again to
cry, "Why do you tear me? Have you no
spirit of pity? We were men, and now are
turned to stocks. Truly your hand ought to
be more merciful had we been souls of ser-
pents."

As from a green brand that is burning at
one end, and drips from the other, hissing
with the escaping air, so from that broken
twig came out words and blood together;
whereon I let fall the tip, and stood like
one who is afraid.

"If he, O wounded spirit, had been able to
believe before," replied my sage, "what he
had never seen save in my verses,

131

non averebbe in te la man distesa;
　　ma la cosa incredibile mi fece
　　indurlo ad ovra ch'a me stesso pesa.　　　　*51*
Ma dilli chi tu fosti, sì che 'n vece
　　d'alcun' ammenda tua fama rinfreschi
　　nel mondo sù, dove tornar li lece."　　　　*54*
E 'l tronco: "Sì col dolce dir m'adeschi,
　　ch'i' non posso tacere; e voi non gravi
　　perch' ïo un poco a ragionar m'inveschi.　　*57*
Io son colui che tenni ambo le chiavi
　　del cor di Federigo, e che le volsi,
　　serrando e diserrando, sì soavi,　　　　　　*60*
che dal secreto suo quasi ogn' uom tolsi;
　　fede portai al glorïoso offizio,
　　tanto ch'i' ne perde' li sonni e ' polsi.　　*63*
La meretrice che mai da l'ospizio
　　di Cesare non torse li occhi putti,
　　morte comune e de le corti vizio,　　　　　*66*
infiammò contra me li animi tutti;
　　e li 'nfiammati infiammar sì Augusto,
　　che ' lieti onor tornaro in tristi lutti.　　*69*
L'animo mio, per disdegnoso gusto,
　　credendo col morir fuggir disdegno,
　　ingiusto fece me contra me giusto.　　　　　*72*
Per le nove radici d'esto legno
　　vi giuro che già mai non ruppi fede
　　al mio segnor, che fu d'onor sì degno.　　　*75*
E se di voi alcun nel mondo riede,
　　conforti la memoria mia, che giace
　　ancor del colpo che 'nvidia le diede."　　　*78*

he would not have stretched forth his hand against you; but the incredible thing made me prompt him to a deed that grieves me. But tell him who you were, so that by way of some amends he may refresh your fame in the world above, whither it is allowed him to return."

And the stub said, "You so allure me with your sweet words that I cannot keep silent; and may it not burden you that I am enticed to talk a little. I am he who held both the keys of Frederick's heart, and turned them, locking and unlocking, so softly that from his secrets I kept almost every one. So faithful was I to the glorious office that for it I lost both sleep and life. The harlot that never turned her whorish eyes from Caesar's household—the common death and vice of courts— inflamed all minds against me; and they, inflamed, did so inflame Augustus that my glad honors were changed to dismal woes. My mind, in scornful temper, thinking by dying to escape from scorn, made me unjust against my just self. By the new roots of this tree I swear to you that I never broke faith with my lord, who was so worthy of honor. And if one of you returns to the world, let him comfort my memory which still lies prostrate from the blow that envy gave it."

Un poco attese, e poi "Da ch'el si tace,"
  disse 'l poeta a me, "non perder l'ora;
  ma parla, e chiedi a lui, se più ti piace."   *81*
Ond' ïo a lui: "Domandal tu ancora
  di quel che credi ch'a me satisfaccia;
  ch'i' non potrei, tanta pietà m'accora."   *84*
Perciò ricominciò: "Se l'om ti faccia
  liberamente ciò che 'l tuo dir priega,
  spirito incarcerato, ancor ti piaccia   *87*
di dirne come l'anima si lega
  in questi nocchi; e dinne, se tu puoi,
  s'alcuna mai di tai membra si spiega."   *90*
Allor soffiò il tronco forte, e poi
  si convertì quel vento in cotal voce:
  "Brievemente sarà risposto a voi.   *93*
Quando si parte l'anima feroce
  dal corpo ond' ella stessa s'è disvelta,
  Minòs la manda a la settima foce.   *96*
Cade in la selva, e non l'è parte scelta;
  ma là dove fortuna la balestra,
  quivi germoglia come gran di spelta.   *99*
Surge in vermena e in pianta silvestra:
  l'Arpie, pascendo poi de le sue foglie,
  fanno dolore, e al dolor fenestra.   *102*
Come l'altre verrem per nostre spoglie,
  ma non però ch'alcuna sen rivesta,
  ché non è giusto aver ciò ch'om si toglie.   *105*
Qui le strascineremo, e per la mesta
  selva saranno i nostri corpi appesi,
  ciascuno al prun de l'ombra sua molesta."   *108*

The poet waited a little, then said to me, "Since he is silent, do not lose time, but speak and ask of him, if you would know more."

To which I answered, "Do you ask him further of what you think may satisfy me, for I cannot, such pity fills my heart."

Therefore he began again, "So may this man do freely what you ask of him, imprisoned spirit, may it please you to tell us further how the soul is bound in these knots; and tell us, if you can, whether from such members any soul is ever loosed."

Then the stub puffed hard, and soon that breath was changed into this voice, "You shall be answered briefly. When the fierce soul quits the body from which it has uprooted itself, Minos sends it to the seventh gullet. It falls into the woods, and no part is chosen for it, but wherever fortune flings it, there it sprouts like a grain of spelt; it shoots up to a sapling, and to a wild growth; the Harpies, feeding then upon its leaves, give pain and to the pain an outlet. Like the rest we shall come, each for his cast-off body, but not, however, that any may inhabit it again; for it is not just that a man have what he robs himself of. Hither shall we drag them, and through the mournful wood our bodies will be hung, each on the thornbush of its nocuous shade."

Noi eravamo ancora al tronco attesi,
   credendo ch'altro ne volesse dire,
   quando noi fummo d'un romor sorpresi,   *111*
similemente a colui che venire
   sente 'l porco e la caccia a la sua posta,
   ch'ode le bestie, e le frasche stormire.   *114*
Ed ecco due da la sinistra costa,
   nudi e graffiati, fuggendo sì forte,
   che de la selva rompieno ogne rosta.   *117*
Quel dinanzi: "Or accorri, accorri, morte!"
   E l'altro, cui pareva tardar troppo,
   gridava: "Lano, sì non furo accorte   *120*
le gambe tue a le giostre dal Toppo!"
   E poi che forse li fallia la lena,
   di sé e d'un cespuglio fece un groppo.   *123*
Di rietro a loro era la selva piena
   di nere cagne, bramose e correnti
   come veltri ch'uscisser di catena.   *126*
In quel che s'appiattò miser li denti,
   e quel dilaceraro a brano a brano;
   poi sen portar quelle membra dolenti.   *129*
Presemi allor la mia scorta per mano,
   e menommi al cespuglio che piangea
   per le rotture sanguinenti in vano.   *132*
"O Iacopo," dicea, "da Santo Andrea,
   che t'è giovato di me fare schermo?
   che colpa ho io de la tua vita rea?"   *135*
Quando 'l maestro fu sovr' esso fermo,
   disse: "Chi fosti, che per tante punte
   soffi con sangue doloroso sermo?"   *138*

We were still attentive to the stub, believing it might wish to say more to us, when like one aware of the wild boar and the chase approaching his post, who hears the beasts and the branches crashing, we were surprised by an uproar. And behold, two on the left hand, naked and torn, fleeing so hard that they were breaking every tangle of the wood. The one in front was shouting, "Now come, come quickly, death!" and the other, thinking himself too slow, "Lano, your legs were not so nimble at the jousts of the Toppo!" and perhaps because breath was failing him, he made one knot of himself and of a bush. Behind them the wood was full of black bitches, eager and fleet, like greyhounds loosed from the leash. On him who had squatted they set their teeth and tore him piecemeal, then carried off those woeful limbs.

My escort then took me by the hand and led me to the bush, which was lamenting in vain through its bleeding fractures. "O Jacopo da Santo Andrea," it cried, "what have you gained by making a screen of me? What blame have I for your sinful life?"

When my master had stopped beside it, he said, "Who were you, that through so many wounds blow forth with blood your doleful speech?"

137

Ed elli a noi: "O anime che giunte
   siete a veder lo strazio disonesto
   c'ha le mie fronde sì da me disgiunte,   *141*
raccoglietele al piè del tristo cesto.
   I' fui de la città che nel Batista
   mutò 'l primo padrone; ond' ei per questo   *144*
sempre con l'arte sua la farà trista;
   e se non fosse che 'n sul passo d'Arno
   rimane ancor di lui alcuna vista,   *147*
que' cittadin che poi la rifondarno
   sovra 'l cener che d'Attila rimase,
   avrebber fatto lavorare indarno.
Io fei gibetto a me de le mie case."   *151*

And it to us, "O souls, who have arrived to see the shameful havoc that has thus torn my leaves from me, collect them at the foot of the wretched bush. I was of the city that changed her first patron for the Baptist, on which account he with his art will ever make her sorrowful; and were it not that at the passage of the Arno some semblance of him still remains, those citizens who afterwards rebuilt it on the ashes left by Attila would have labored in vain. I made me a gibbet of my own house."

INFERNO

Poi che la carità del natio loco
    mi strinse, raunai le fronde sparte
    e rende'le a colui, ch'era già fioco.   *3*
Indi venimmo al fine ove si parte
    lo secondo giron dal terzo, e dove
    si vede di giustizia orribil arte.   *6*
A ben manifestar le cose nove,
    dico che arrivammo ad una landa
    che dal suo letto ogne pianta rimove.   *9*
La dolorosa selva l'è ghirlanda
    intorno, come 'l fosso tristo ad essa;
    quivi fermammo i passi a randa a randa.   *12*
Lo spazzo era una rena arida e spessa,
    non d'altra foggia fatta che colei
    che fu da' piè di Caton già soppressa.   *15*
O vendetta di Dio, quanto tu dei
    esser temuta da ciascun che legge
    ciò che fu manifesto a li occhi mei!   *18*

CANTO XIV

Because the love of my native place con-
strained me, I gathered up the scattered twigs
and gave them back to him who was already
faint of voice. Thence we came to the con-
fine, where the second ring is divided from
the third and where a horrible mode of jus-
tice is seen.

To make these new things clear, I say we
reached a plain which rejects all plants from
its bed. The woeful wood is a garland round
about it, as round the wood the dismal ditch.
Here we stayed our steps at the very edge.
The ground was a dry deep sand, not differ-
ent in its fashion from that which once was
trodden by the feet of Cato.

O vengeance of God, how much should
you be feared by all who read what was re-
vealed to my eyes!

D'anime nude vidi molte gregge
   che piangean tutte assai miseramente,
   e parea posta lor diversa legge.   *21*
Supin giacea in terra alcuna gente,
   alcuna si sedea tutta raccolta,
   e altra andava continüamente.   *24*
Quella che giva 'ntorno era più molta,
   e quella men che giacëa al tormento,
   ma più al duolo avea la lingua sciolta.   *27*
Sovra tutto 'l sabbion, d'un cader lento,
   piovean di foco dilatate falde,
   come di neve in alpe sanza vento.   *30*
Quali Alessandro in quelle parti calde
   d'Indïa vide sopra 'l süo stuolo
   fiamme cadere infino a terra salde,   *33*
per ch'ei provide a scalpitar lo suolo
   con le sue schiere, acciò che lo vapore
   mei si stingueva mentre ch'era solo: *36*
tale scendeva l'etternale ardore;
   onde la rena s'accendea, com' esca
   sotto focile, a doppiar lo dolore.   *39*
Sanza riposo mai era la tresca
   de le misere mani, or quindi or quinci
   escotendo da sé l'arsura fresca.   *42*
I' cominciai: "Maestro, tu che vinci
   tutte le cose, fuor che ' demon duri
   ch'a l'intrar de la porta incontra uscinci,   *45*
chi è quel grande che non par che curi
   lo 'ncendio e giace dispettoso e torto,
   sì che la pioggia non par che 'l maturi?"   *48*

I saw many herds of naked souls, who were all lamenting very miserably; and different laws seemed to be imposed upon them. Some were lying supine upon the ground, some sitting all crouched up, and others were going about incessantly. Those who moved about were far more numerous, and those who were lying in the torment were fewer, but they gave more tongue to their pain.

Over all the sand huge flakes of fire were falling slowly, like snow in the mountains without a wind. As the flames which Alexander, in those hot regions of India, saw fall upon his army, entire to the ground, whereat he had his legions tramp the soil, because the flakes were better extinguished before they spread, so did the eternal burning descend there, and the sand was kindled by it like tinder under the flint, to redouble the pain. The dance of the wretched hands was ever without repose, now here, now there, as they beat off the fresh burning.

I began, "Master, you who overcome all things except the obdurate demons that came out against us at the entrance of the gate, who is that great one who seems not to heed the fire, and lies disdainful and scowling, so that the rain seems not to ripen him?"

143

E quel medesmo, che si fu accorto
   ch'io domandava il mio duca di lui,
   gridò: "Qual io fui vivo, tal son morto.   *51*
Se Giove stanchi 'l suo fabbro da cui
   crucciato prese la folgore aguta
   onde l'ultimo dì percosso fui;   *54*
o s'elli stanchi li altri a muta a muta
   in Mongibello a la focina negra,
   chiamando 'Buon Vulcano, aiuta, aiuta!'   *57*
sì com' el fece a la pugna di Flegra,
   e me saetti con tutta sua forza:
   non ne potrebbe aver vendetta allegra."   *60*
Allora il duca mio parlò di forza
   tanto, ch'i' non l'avea sì forte udito:
   "O Capaneo, in ciò che non s'ammorza   *63*
la tua superbia, se' tu più punito;
   nullo martiro, fuor che la tua rabbia,
   sarebbe al tuo furor dolor compito."   *66*
Poi si rivolse a me con miglior labbia,
   dicendo: "Quei fu l'un d'i sette regi
   ch'assiser Tebe; ed ebbe e par ch'elli abbia   *69*
Dio in disdegno, e poco par che 'l pregi;
   ma, com' io dissi lui, li suoi dispetti
   sono al suo petto assai debiti fregi.   *72*
Or mi vien dietro, e guarda che non metti,
   ancor, li piedi ne la rena arsiccia;
   ma sempre al bosco tien li piedi stretti."   *75*
Tacendo divenimmo là 've spiccia
   fuor de la selva un picciol fiumicello,
   lo cui rossore ancor mi raccapriccia.   *78*

And that same one, who had perceived that I was asking my leader about him, cried out, "What I was living, that am I dead. Though Jove weary out his smith, from whom in anger he took the sharp bolt by which on my last day I was smitten; and though he weary out the others, turn by turn, in Mongibello at the black forge, crying, 'Good Vulcan, help, help!' even as he did at the fight of Phlegra, and hurl at me with all his might, he would not have thereby glad vengeance."

Then my leader spoke with such force as I had not heard him use before, "O Capaneus! in that your pride remains unquenched you are punished the more: no torment save your own raging would be pain to match your fury." Then he turned round to me with gentler look, saying, "That was one of the seven kings who besieged Thebes, and held, and seems to hold, God in disdain and prize Him little; but as I said to him, his revilings are quite fitting adornments to his breast. Now come along behind me, and see that you do not set your feet upon the burning sand, but keep them back ever close to the woods."

In silence we came to where there spurts forth from the forest a little stream whose redness makes me shudder yet.

Quale del Bulicame esce ruscello
 che parton poi tra lor le peccatrici,
 tal per la rena giù sen giva quello.   *81*
Lo fondo suo e ambo le pendici
 fatt' era 'n pietra, e ' margini da lato;
 per ch'io m'accorsi che 'l passo era lici.   *84*
"Tra tutto l'altro ch'i' t'ho dimostrato,
 poscia che noi intrammo per la porta
 lo cui sogliare a nessuno è negato,   *87*
cosa non fu da li tuoi occhi scorta
 notabile com' è 'l presente rio,
 che sovra sé tutte fiammelle ammorta."   *90*
Queste parole fuor del duca mio;
 per ch'io 'l pregai che mi largisse 'l pasto
 di cui largito m'avëa il disio.   *93*
"In mezzo mar siede un paese guasto,"
 diss' elli allora, "che s'appella Creta,
 sotto 'l cui rege fu già 'l mondo casto.   *96*
Una montagna v'è che già fu lieta
 d'acqua e di fronde, che si chiamò Ida;
 or è diserta come cosa vieta.   *99*
Rëa la scelse già per cuna fida
 del suo figliuolo, e per celarlo meglio,
 quando piangea, vi facea far le grida.   *102*
Dentro dal monte sta dritto un gran veglio,
 che tien volte le spalle inver' Dammiata
 e Roma guarda come süo speglio.   *105*
La sua testa è di fin oro formata,
 e puro argento son le braccia e 'l petto,
 poi è di rame infino a la forcata;   *108*

As issues from the Bulicame a rivulet which
then the sinful women share among them-
selves, so this ran down across the sand. Its
bottom and both its banks were made of
stone, as were the margins on the side; where-
fore I perceived that our passage was there.

"In all that I have shown to you since we
entered through the gate whose threshold is
denied to no one, nothing has been discerned
by your eyes so notable as the present stream,
which quenches every flame above it." These
were the words of my leader; wherefore I
prayed him to bestow on me the food for
which he had bestowed the appetite.

"In the middle of the sea there lies a wasted
country," he then said, "which is named
Crete, under whose king the world once was
chaste. A mountain is there, called Ida, which
once was glad with waters and with foli-
age; now it is deserted like a thing outworn.
Rhea chose it of old for the faithful cradle
of her son and, the better to conceal him
when he cried, made them raise shouts
there. Within the mountain stands the great
figure of an Old Man, who holds his back
turned toward Damietta, and gazes on
Rome as on his mirror: his head is fashioned
of fine gold, his arms and breast are pure
silver, then down to the fork he is of brass,

da indi in giuso è tutto ferro eletto,
    salvo che 'l destro piede è terra cotta;
    e sta 'n su quel, più che 'n su l'altro, eretto.   *111*
Ciascuna parte, fuor che l'oro, è rotta
    d'una fessura che lagrime goccia,
    le quali, accolte, fóran quella grotta.   *114*
Lor corso in questa valle si diroccia;
    fanno Acheronte, Stige e Flegetonta;
    poi sen van giù per questa stretta doccia,   *117*
infin, là dove più non si dismonta,
    fanno Cocito; e qual sia quello stagno
    tu lo vedrai, però qui non si conta."   *120*
E io a lui: "Se 'l presente rigagno
    si diriva così dal nostro mondo,
    perché ci appar pur a questo vivagno?"   *123*
Ed elli a me: "Tu sai che 'l loco è tondo;
    e tutto che tu sie venuto molto,
    pur a sinistra, giù calando al fondo,   *126*
non se' ancor per tutto 'l cerchio vòlto;
    per che, se cosa n'apparisce nova,
    non de' addur maraviglia al tuo volto."   *129*
E io ancor: "Maestro, ove si trova
    Flegetonta e Letè? ché de l'un taci,
    e l'altro di' che si fa d'esta piova."   *132*
"In tutte tue question certo mi piaci,"
    rispuose, "ma 'l bollor de l'acqua rossa
    dovea ben solver l'una che tu faci.   *135*

and down from there is all of choice iron,
except that the right foot is baked clay, and
he rests more on this than on the other. Every
part except the gold is cleft by a fissure that
drips with tears which, collected, force a pas-
sage through the cavern there. Their course
is from rock to rock into this valley: they
form Acheron, Styx, and Phlegethon; then
their way is down by this narrow channel
until, there where there is no more descend-
ing, they form Cocytus—and what that pool
is, you shall see; here therefore I do not de-
scribe it."

And I to him, "If the present stream flows
down thus from our world, why does it ap-
pear to us only at this border?"

And he to me, "You know that the place
is circular; and though you have come far,
always to the left in descending to the bot-
tom, you have not yet turned through the
whole circle; wherefore if aught new appears
to us, it should not bring wonder to your
face."

And I again, "Master, where are Phlege-
thon and Lethe found? for about the one
you are silent, and the other you say is formed
by this rain."

"Truly you please me in all your ques-
tions," he answered, "but the boiling of the
red water should well solve one that you ask.

Letè vedrai, ma fuor di questa fossa,
  là dove vanno l'anime a lavarsi
  quando la colpa pentuta è rimossa." *138*
Poi disse: "Omai è tempo da scostarsi
  dal bosco; fa che di retro a me vegne:
  li margini fan via, che non son arsi,
e sopra loro ogne vapor si spegne." *142*

Lethe you shall see, but out of this abyss,
there where the souls go to wash themselves,
when the fault repented of has been re-
moved."

Then he said, "Now it is time to quit the
wood; see that you come behind me: the
margins, which are not burning, form a path,
and over them every flame is quenched."

INFERNO

Ora cen porta l'un de' duri margini;
    e 'l fummo del ruscel di sopra aduggia,
    sì che dal foco salva l'acqua e li argini.   *3*
Quali Fiamminghi tra Guizzante e Bruggia,
    temendo 'l fiotto che 'nver' lor s'avventa,
    fanno lo schermo perché 'l mar si fuggia;   *6*
e quali Padoan lungo la Brenta,
    per difender lor ville e lor castelli,
    anzi che Carentana il caldo senta: *9*
a tale imagine eran fatti quelli,
    tutto che né sì alti né sì grossi,
    qual che si fosse, lo maestro félli.   *12*
Già eravam da la selva rimossi
    tanto, ch'i' non avrei visto dov' era,
    perch' io in dietro rivolto mi fossi,   *15*
quando incontrammo d'anime una schiera
    che venian lungo l'argine, e ciascuna
    ci riguardava come suol da sera   *18*

CANTO XV

Now one of the hard margins bears us on, and the vapor from the stream over-shades, so that it shelters the water and the banks from the fire. As the Flemings between Wissant and Bruges, fearing the tide that rushes in on them, make the bulwark to drive back the sea; and as the Paduans do along the Brenta, to protect their towns and castles before Carentana feels the heat; in like fashion were these banks made, except that the builder, whoever he was, made them neither so high nor so thick.

We were already so far removed from the wood that I should not have seen where it was had I turned to look back, when we met a troop of souls that were coming alongside the bank, and each looked at us as men look

guardare uno altro sotto nuova luna;
   e sì ver' noi aguzzavan le ciglia
   come 'l vecchio sartor fa ne la cruna.   *21*
Così adocchiato da cotal famiglia,
   fui conosciuto da un, che mi prese
   per lo lembo e gridò: "Qual maraviglia!"   *24*
E io, quando 'l suo braccio a me distese,
   ficcaï li occhi per lo cotto aspetto,
   sì che 'l viso abbrusciato non difese   *27*
la conoscenza süa al mio 'ntelletto;
   e chinando la mano a la sua faccia,
   rispuosi: "Siete voi qui, ser Brunetto?"   *30*
E quelli: "O figliuol mio, non ti dispiaccia
   se Brunetto Latino un poco teco
   ritorna 'n dietro e lascia andar la traccia."   *33*
I' dissi lui: "Quanto posso, ven preco;
   e se volete che con voi m'asseggia,
   faròl, se piace a costui che vo seco."   *36*
"O figliuol," disse, "qual di questa greggia
   s'arresta punto, giace poi cent' anni
   sanz' arrostarsi quando 'l foco il feggia.   *39*
Però va oltre: i' ti verrò a' panni;
   e poi rigiugnerò la mia masnada,
   che va piangendo i suoi etterni danni."   *42*
Io non osava scender de la strada
   per andar par di lui; ma 'l capo chino
   tenea com' uom che reverente vada.   *45*
El cominciò: "Qual fortuna o destino
   anzi l'ultimo dì qua giù ti mena?
   e chi è questi che mostra 'l cammino?"   *48*

at one another under a new moon at dusk;
and they knit their brows at us as the old
tailor does at the eye of his needle.

Eyed thus by that company, I was recog-
nized by one who took me by the hem, and
cried, "What a marvel!" And I, when he
reached out his arm to me, fixed my eyes on
his scorched face, so that the baked features
did not prevent my knowing him, and reach-
ing down my hand toward his face, I an-
swered, "Are you here, ser Brunetto!"

And he, "O my son, let it not displease
you if Brunetto Latino turns back a little
with you, and lets the train go on."

"I beg it of you with all my heart," I said
to him, "and if you wish me to sit with you,
I will, if it please him there with whom
I go."

"O son," he said, "whoever of this flock
stops even for an instant must then lie a hun-
dred years without brushing off the fire
when it strikes him. Therefore go on: I will
come at your skirts, and then will rejoin my
band who go lamenting their eternal woes."

I dared not descend from the path to go
on a level with him, but I kept my head
bowed like one who walks in reverence. He
began, "What chance or destiny brings you
down here before your last day, and who is
this that shows the way?"

"Là sù di sopra, in la vita serena,"
   rispuos' io lui, "mi smarri' in una valle,
   avanti che l'età mia fosse piena.   *51*
Pur ier mattina le volsi le spalle:
   questi m'apparve, tornand' ïo in quella,
   e reducemi a ca per questo calle."   *54*
Ed elli a me: "Se tu segui tua stella,
   non puoi fallire a glorïoso porto,
   se ben m'accorsi ne la vita bella;   *57*
e s'io non fossi sì per tempo morto,
   veggendo il cielo a te così benigno,
   dato t'avrei a l'opera conforto.   *60*
Ma quello ingrato popolo maligno
   che discese di Fiesole *ab* antico,
   e tiene ancor del monte e del macigno,   *63*
ti si farà, per tuo ben far, nimico;
   ed è ragion, ché tra li lazzi sorbi
   si disconvien fruttare al dolce fico.   *66*
Vecchia fama nel mondo li chiama orbi;
   gent' è avara, invidiosa e superba:
   dai lor costumi fa che tu ti forbi.   *69*
La tua fortuna tanto onor ti serba,
   che l'una parte e l'altra avranno fame
   di te; ma lungi fia dal becco l'erba.   *72*
Faccian le bestie fiesolane strame
   di lor medesme, e non tocchin la pianta,
   s'alcuna surge ancora in lor letame,   *75*
in cui riviva la sementa santa
   di que' Roman che vi rimaser quando
   fu fatto il nido di malizia tanta."   *78*

"There above, in the bright life," I answered him, "I went astray in a valley, before my age was at the full. Only yesterday morning I turned my back on it. He appeared to me, as I was returning into it, and by this path he leads me home."

And he to me, "If you follow your star you cannot fail of a glorious port, if, in the fair life, I discerned aright; and if I had not died so soon, seeing heaven so kind to you, I would have cheered you in your work. But that thankless, malignant people, who of old came down from Fiesole, and still smack of the mountain and the rock, will make themselves an enemy to you because of your good deeds; and there is cause: for among the bitter sorb-trees it is not fitting that the sweet fig should come to fruit. Old report in the world calls them blind; it is a people avaricious, envious and proud: look that you cleanse yourself of their customs. Your fortune holds for you such honor that the one party and the other shall be ravenous against you, but the grass shall be far from the goat. Let the Fiesolan beasts make fodder of themselves, and not touch the plant (if any spring yet upon their dungheap) in which survives the holy seed of those Romans who remained there when it became the nest of so much wickedness."

"Se fosse tutto pieno il mio dimando,"
　　rispuos' io lui, "voi non sareste ancora
　　de l'umana natura posto in bando;　　　　　　*81*
ché 'n la mente m'è fitta, e or m'accora,
　　la cara e buona imagine paterna
　　di voi quando nel mondo ad ora ad ora　　　*84*
m'insegnavate come l'uom s'etterna:
　　e quant' io l'abbia in grado, mentr' io vivo
　　convien che ne la mia lingua si scerna.　　*87*
Ciò che narrate di mio corso scrivo,
　　e serbolo a chiosar con altro testo
　　a donna che saprà, s'a lei arrivo.　　　　　　*90*
Tanto vogl' io che vi sia manifesto,
　　pur che mia coscïenza non mi garra,
　　ch'a la Fortuna, come vuol, son presto.　　*93*
Non è nuova a li orecchi miei tal arra:
　　però giri Fortuna la sua rota
　　come le piace, e 'l villan la sua marra."　　*96*
Lo mio maestro allora in su la gota
　　destra si volse in dietro e riguardommi;
　　poi disse: "Bene ascolta chi la nota."　　　*99*
Né per tanto di men parlando vommi
　　con ser Brunetto, e dimando chi sono
　　li suoi compagni più noti e più sommi.　　*102*
Ed elli a me: "Saper d'alcuno è buono;
　　de li altri fia laudabile tacerci,
　　ché 'l tempo saria corto a tanto suono.　　*105*
In somma sappi che tutti fur cherci
　　e litterati grandi e di gran fama,
　　d'un peccato medesmo al mondo lerci.　　　*108*

"If my prayer were all fulfilled," I an-
swered him, "you would not yet be banished
from human nature, for in my memory is
fixed, and now saddens my heart, the dear,
kind, paternal image of you, when in the
world hour by hour you taught me how man
makes himself eternal; and how much I hold
it in gratitude it behooves me, while I live,
to declare in my speech. That which you tell
me of my course I write, and keep with a
text to be glossed by a lady who will know
how, if I reach her. This much I would have
you know: so conscience chide me not, I am
prepared for Fortune as she wills. Such ear-
nest is not strange to my ears; therefore let
Fortune whirl her wheel as pleases her, and
the yokel his mattock."

Thereon my master turned round on his
right and looked at me, then said, "He who
notes it listens well."

None the less I go on speaking with ser
Brunetto, and ask him who are the most
noted and most eminent of his companions.

And he to me, "It is well to know of
some of them; about the rest it is well
that we be silent, as the time would be too
short for so much talk. In brief, know that
all were clerks, and great men of letters and
of great fame, in the world defiled by one
same sin.

Priscian sen va con quella turba grama,
    e Francesco d'Accorso anche; e vedervi,
    s'avessi avuto di tal tigna brama,   111
colui potei che dal servo de' servi
    fu trasmutato d'Arno in Bacchiglione,
    dove lasciò li mal protesi nervi.   114
Di più direi; ma 'l venire e 'l sermone
    più lungo esser non può, però ch'i' veggio
    là surger nuovo fummo del sabbione.   117
Gente vien con la quale esser non deggio.
    Sieti raccomandato il mio Tesoro,
    nel qual io vivo ancora, e più non cheggio."   120
Poi si rivolse e parve di coloro
    che corrono a Verona il drappo verde
    per la campagna; e parve di costoro
quelli che vince, non colui che perde.   124

Priscian goes on with that wretched crowd, and Francesco d'Accorso too; and you could also have seen there, had you hankered for such scurf, him who was transferred by the Servant of Servants from Arno to Bacchiglione, where he left his sinfully distended muscles. I would say more, but my going and my speech must not be longer, for I see yonder a new smoke rising from the sand: people are coming with whom I must not be. Let my *Treasure*, in which I yet live, be commended to you, and I ask no more."

Then he turned back, and seemed like one of those who run for the green cloth in the field at Verona, and of them seemed he who wins, not he who loses.

INFERNO

Già era in loco onde s'udia 'l rimbombo
de l'acqua che cadea ne l'altro giro,
simile a quel che l'arnie fanno rombo,　　　*3*
quando tre ombre insieme si partiro,
correndo, d'una torma che passava
sotto la pioggia de l'aspro martiro.　　　*6*
Venian ver' noi, e ciascuna gridava:
"Sòstati tu ch'a l'abito ne sembri
essere alcun di nostra terra prava."　　　*9*
Ahimè, che piaghe vidi ne' lor membri,
ricenti e vecchie, da le fiamme incese!
Ancor men duol pur ch'i' me ne rimembri.　　　*12*
A le lor grida il mio dottor s'attese;
volse 'l viso ver' me, e "Or aspetta,"
disse, "a costor si vuole esser cortese.　　　*15*
E se non fosse il foco che saetta
la natura del loco, i' dicerei
che meglio stesse a te che a lor la fretta."　　　*18*

CANTO XVI

Already I was in a place where the re-
sounding of the water which was falling into
the next circle was heard, like the hum which
beehives make, when three shades set out
together running, from a troop that was pass-
ing under the rain of the fierce torment. They
came towards us, each crying, "Stop, you who
by your dress seem to us to be from our
degenerate city!" Ah me, what wounds old
and new I saw in their members, burnt in
by the flames! It pains me yet, only to re-
member it.

My teacher gave heed to their cries, then
turned his face to me and said, "Now wait:
to these one should show courtesy; and were
it not for the fire which the nature of this
place darts, I should say that haste befitted
you more than them."

Ricominciar, come noi restammo, ei
        l'antico verso; e quando a noi fuor giunti,
        fenno una rota di sé tutti e trei.   21
Qual sogliono i campion far nudi e unti,
        avvisando lor presa e lor vantaggio,
        prima che sien tra lor battuti e punti,   24
così rotando, ciascuno il visaggio
        drizzava a me, sì che 'n contraro il collo
        faceva ai piè continüo vïaggio.   27
E "Se miseria d'esto loco sollo
        rende in dispetto noi e nostri prieghi,"
        cominciò l'uno, "e 'l tinto aspetto e brollo,   30
la fama nostra il tuo animo pieghi
        a dirne chi tu se', che i vivi piedi
        così sicuro per lo 'nferno freghi.   33
Questi, l'orme di cui pestar mi vedi,
        tutto che nudo e dipelato vada,
        fu di grado maggior che tu non credi: 36
nepote fu de la buona Gualdrada;
        Guido Guerra ebbe nome, e in sua vita
        fece col senno assai e con la spada.   39
L'altro, ch'appresso me la rena trita,
        è Tegghiaio Aldobrandi, la cui voce
        nel mondo sù dovria esser gradita.   42
E io, che posto son con loro in croce,
        Iacopo Rusticucci fui, e certo
        la fiera moglie più ch'altro mi nuoce."   45
S'i' fossi stato dal foco coperto,
        gittato mi sarei tra lor di sotto,
        e credo che 'l dottor l'avria sofferto;   48

As we stopped, they resumed their ancient
wail, and when they reached us, all three
made of themselves a wheel. As champions,
naked and oiled, are wont to do, eying their
grip and vantage before exchanging thrusts
and blows; thus each, wheeling, directed his
face on me so that his neck kept turning in
a direction contrary to his feet.

And, "If the wretchedness of this sandy
place and our blackened and hairless faces,"
one of them began, "bring us and our prayers
into contempt, let our fame move you to tell
us who you are, that thus securely move liv-
ing feet through Hell. He whose tracks you
see me trample, though he goes naked and
peeled, was of greater degree than you think:
grandson of the good Gualdrada, his name
was Guido Guerra, and in his lifetime he
did much with counsel and with sword.
This other, who treads the sand behind me, is
Tegghiaio Aldobrandi, whose voice should
have been prized up in the world; and I who
am placed with them in torment was Jacopo
Rusticucci, and truly my fierce wife more
than aught else has wrought me ill."

Had I been sheltered from the fire I would
have thrown myself down among them, and
I think my teacher would have permitted it;

ma perch' io mi sarei brusciato e cotto,
   vinse paura la mia buona voglia
   che di loro abbracciar mi facea ghiotto.   *51*
Poi cominciai: "Non dispetto, ma doglia
   la vostra condizion dentro mi fisse,
   tanta che tardi tutta si dispoglia,   *54*
tosto che questo mio segnor mi disse
   parole per le quali i' mi pensai
   che qual voi siete, tal gente venisse.   *57*
Di vostra terra sono, e sempre mai
   l'ovra di voi e li onorati nomi
   con affezion ritrassi e ascoltai.   *60*
Lascio lo fele e vo per dolci pomi
   promessi a me per lo verace duca;
   ma 'nfino al centro pria convien ch'i' tomi."   *63*
"Se lungamente l'anima conduca
   le membra tue," rispuose quelli ancora,
   "e se la fama tua dopo te luca,   *66*
cortesia e valor dì se dimora
   ne la nostra città sì come suole,
   o se del tutto se n'è gita fora;   *69*
ché Guiglielmo Borsiere, il qual si duole
   con noi per poco e va là coi compagni,
   assai ne cruccia con le sue parole."   *72*
"La gente nuova e i sùbiti guadagni
   orgoglio e dismisura han generata,
   Fiorenza, in te, sì che tu già ten piagni."   *75*
Così gridai con la faccia levata;
   e i tre, che ciò inteser per risposta,
   guardar l'un l'altro com' al ver si guata.   *78*

but since I should have been burnt and
baked, fear overcame my good will which
made me greedy to embrace them. Then I
began, "Not contempt, but sorrow, your con-
dition fixed within me, so deeply that it will
not leave me soon, when this my lord said to
me words by which I felt that such men as
you might be coming. I am of your city, and
always have I rehearsed and heard with af-
fection your deeds and honored names. I am
leaving the gall, and I go for sweet fruits
promised me by my truthful leader; but first
I must go down to the center."

"So may your soul long direct your limbs,
and your fame shine after you," he then re-
plied, "tell us if courtesy and valor abide in
our city as once they did, or if they are quite
gone from it, for Guiglielmo Borsiere, who
has been but short while in pain with us and
goes yonder with our company, greatly af-
flicts us with his words."

"The new people and the sudden gains
have engendered pride and excess in you,
O Florence, so that already you weep for it!"
This I cried with uplifted face; and the three,
who understood this to be my answer,
looked at each other as men look on hearing
the truth.

"Se l'altre volte sì poco ti costa,"
   rispuoser tutti, "il satisfare altrui,
   felice te se sì parli a tua posta!   *81*
Però, se campi d'esti luoghi bui
   e torni a riveder le belle stelle,
   quando ti gioverà dicere 'I' fui,'   *84*
fa che di noi a la gente favelle."
   Indi rupper la rota, e a fuggirsi
   ali sembiar le gambe loro isnelle.   *87*
Un amen non saria possuto dirsi
   tosto così com' e' fuoro spariti;
   per ch'al maestro parve di partirsi.   *90*
Io lo seguiva, e poco eravam iti,
   che 'l suon de l'acqua n'era sì vicino,
   che per parlar saremmo a pena uditi.   *93*
Come quel fiume c'ha proprio cammino
   prima dal Monte Viso 'nver' levante,
   da la sinistra costa d'Apennino,   *96*
che si chiama Acquacheta suso, avante
   che si divalli giù nel basso letto,
   e a Forlì di quel nome è vacante,   *99*
rimbomba là sovra San Benedetto
   de l'Alpe per cadere ad una scesa
   ove dovea per mille esser recetto;   *102*
così, giù d'una ripa discoscesa,
   trovammo risonar quell' acqua tinta,
   sì che 'n poc' ora avria l'orecchia offesa.   *105*
Io avea una corda intorno cinta,
   e con essa pensai alcuna volta
   prender la lonza a la pelle dipinta.   *108*

"If at other times it costs you so little to
satisfy others," they all replied, "happy you
if you can speak thus at will. Therefore, if
you escape from these dark regions and re-
turn to see again the beautiful stars, when
you shall rejoice to say, 'I was there,' see that
you speak of us to others." Then they broke
their wheel and in their flight their nimble
legs seemed wings; an "Amen" could not
have been uttered so quickly as they van-
ished; wherefore it seemed well to my master
to depart. I followed him; and we had gone
but a little way when the sound of the water
was so near that we could scarcely have heard
each other speak. As that river which is first
to hold its own course from Mount Viso east-
ward, on the left slope of the Apennine—
called the Acquacheta above, before it de-
scends into its low bed, and at Forlì loses
that name—roars there over San Benedetto
dell'Alpe, falling in one cataract when there
might well have been a thousand; thus, down
from a precipitous bank we found that dark
water resounding, so that in short while it
would have hurt our ears.

I had a cord girt round me, and with
it I once thought to take the gay-skinned
leopard.

Poscia ch'io l'ebbi tutta da me sciolta,
  sì come 'l duca m'avea comandato,
  porsila a lui aggroppata e ravvolta.   *111*
Ond' ei si volse inver' lo destro lato,
  e alquanto di lunge da la sponda
  la gittò giuso in quell' alto burrato.   *114*
"E' pur convien che novità risponda,"
  dicea fra me medesmo, "al novo cenno
  che 'l maestro con l'occhio sì seconda."   *117*
Ahi quanto cauti li uomini esser dienno
  presso a color che non veggion pur l'ovra,
  ma per entro i pensier miran col senno!   *120*
El disse a me: "Tosto verrà di sovra
  ciò ch'io attendo e che il tuo pensier sogna;
  tosto convien ch'al tuo viso si scovra."   *123*
Sempre a quel ver c'ha faccia di menzogna
  de' l'uom chiuder le labbra fin ch'el puote,
  però che sanza colpa fa vergogna;   *126*
ma qui tacer nol posso; e per le note
  di questa comedìa, lettor, ti giuro,
  s'elle non sien di lunga grazia vòte,   *129*
ch'i' vidi per quell' aere grosso e scuro
  venir notando una figura in suso,
  maravigliosa ad ogne cor sicuro,   *132*
sì come torna colui che va giuso
  talora a solver l'àncora ch'aggrappa
  o scoglio o altro che nel mare è chiuso,
che 'n sù si stende e da piè si rattrappa.   *136*

After I had quite loosed it from me, as my leader bade, I passed it to him knotted and coiled. Whereon he, turning to the right, flung it some distance out from the edge, down into the depth of that abyss.

"Surely," I said to myself, "something strange will answer the strange signal which the master so follows with his eye."

Ah, how careful one should be with those who not only see the deed, but have the wit to read one's thoughts! "Soon will come up what I look for and what your mind dreams of," he said to me; "soon must it be discovered to your sight."

To that truth which has the face of a lie a man should always close his lips so far as he can, for through no fault of his it brings reproach; but here I cannot be silent; and, reader, I swear to you by the notes of this Comedy—so may they not fail of lasting favor—that I saw, through that thick and murky air, come swimming upwards a figure amazing to every steadfast heart, even as he returns who sometimes goes down to loose the anchor that is caught on a reef or something else hidden in the sea, who stretches upwards his arms and draws in his feet.

INFERNO

"Ecco la fiera con la coda aguzza,
   che passa i monti e rompe i muri e l'armi!
   Ecco colei che tutto 'l mondo appuzza!"   *3*
Sì cominciò lo mio duca a parlarmi;
   e accennolle che venisse a proda,
   vicino al fin d'i passeggiati marmi.   *6*
E quella sozza imagine di froda
   sen venne, e arrivò la testa e 'l busto,
   ma 'n su la riva non trasse la coda.   *9*
La faccia sua era faccia d'uom giusto,
   tanto benigna avea di fuor la pelle,
   e d'un serpente tutto l'altro fusto;   *12*
due branche avea pilose insin l'ascelle;
   lo dosso e 'l petto e ambedue le coste
   dipinti avea di nodi e di rotelle.   *15*
Con più color, sommesse e sovraposte
   non fer mai drappi Tartari né Turchi,
   né fuor tai tele per Aragne imposte.   *18*

CANTO XVII

"Behold the beast with the pointed tail, that passes mountains and breaks walls and weapons! Behold him that infects all the world!" Thus my leader began to speak to me; and he beckoned him to come to shore near the end of our rocky path. And that foul image of fraud came onward, and landed his head and his bust, but he did not draw his tail onto the bank. His face was the face of a just man, so benign was its outward aspect, and all his trunk was that of a serpent; he had two paws, hairy to the armpits; his back and breast and both his sides were painted with knots and circlets. Tartars or Turks never made cloth with more colors of groundwork and pattern, nor were such webs laid on the loom by Arachne.

Come talvolta stanno a riva i burchi,
   che parte sono in acqua e parte in terra,
   e come là tra li Tedeschi lurchi   21
lo bivero s'assetta a far sua guerra,
   così la fiera pessima si stava
   su l'orlo ch'è di pietra e 'l sabbion serra.   24
Nel vano tutta sua coda guizzava,
   torcendo in sù la venenosa forca
   ch'a guisa di scorpion la punta armava.   27
Lo duca disse: "Or convien che si torca
   la nostra via un poco insino a quella
   bestia malvagia che colà si corca."   30
Però scendemmo a la destra mammella,
   e diece passi femmo in su lo stremo,
   per ben cessar la rena e la fiammella.   33
E quando noi a lei venuti semo,
   poco più oltre veggio in su la rena
   gente seder propinqua al loco scemo.   36
Quivi 'l maestro "Acciò che tutta piena
   esperïenza d'esto giron porti,"
   mi disse, "va, e vedi la lor mena.   39
Li tuoi ragionamenti sian là corti;
   mentre che torni, parlerò con questa,
   che ne conceda i suoi omeri forti."   42
Così ancor su per la strema testa
   di quel settimo cerchio tutto solo
   andai, dove sedea la gente mesta.   45
Per li occhi fora scoppiava lor duolo;
   di qua, di là soccorrien con le mani
   quando a' vapori, e quando al caldo suolo: 48

As sometimes boats lie at the shore, part
in the water and part on land, and as there
among the guzzling Germans the beaver
settles himself to wage his war, so lay that
worst of beasts upon the edge of stone which
bounds the sand. All his tail was quivering
in the void, twisting upward its venom-
ous fork, which had the point armed like a
scorpion's.

My leader said, "Now we must bend our
way a little, as far as that evil beast which is
couching yonder." We descended, therefore,
on the right hand side and took ten steps
upon the verge, so as to keep well away
from the sand and the flames. And when we
had come to him, I see upon the sand, a little
farther onwards, people sitting near the empty
space.

Here the master said to me, "That you
may carry away full experience of this ring,
go and see their condition. Let your talk there
be brief. Till you return I will speak with
this beast, that he may lend us his strong
shoulders."

So I went by myself still farther along
the extreme margin of that seventh circle,
where the woeful people were seated. Their
grief was bursting forth through their eyes;
with their hands they defended themselves,
now here, now there, sometimes from the
flames, sometimes from the burning ground;

non altrimenti fan di state i cani
 or col ceffo or col piè, quando son morsi
 o da pulci o da mosche o da tafani.   *51*
Poi che nel viso a certi li occhi porsi,
 ne' quali 'l doloroso foco casca,
 non ne conobbi alcun; ma io m'accorsi *54*
che dal collo a ciascun pendea una tasca
 ch'avea certo colore e certo segno,
 e quindi par che 'l loro occhio si pasca. *57*
E com' io riguardando tra lor vegno,
 in una borsa gialla vidi azzurro
 che d'un leone avea faccia e contegno. *60*
Poi, procedendo di mio sguardo il curro,
 vidine un'altra come sangue rossa,
 mostrando un'oca bianca più che burro. *63*
E un che d'una scrofa azzurra e grossa
 segnato avea lo suo sacchetto bianco,
 mi disse: "Che fai tu in questa fossa? *66*
Or te ne va; e perché se' vivo anco,
 sappi che 'l mio vicin Vitalïano
 sederà qui dal mio sinistro fianco. *69*
Con questi Fiorentin son padoano:
 spesse fïate mi 'ntronan li orecchi
 gridando: 'Vegna 'l cavalier sovrano, *72*
che recherà la tasca con tre becchi!'"
 Qui distorse la bocca e di fuor trasse
 la lingua, come bue che 'l naso lecchi. *75*
E io, temendo no'l più star crucciasse
 lui che di poco star m'avea 'mmonito,
 torna'mi in dietro da l'anime lasse. *78*

not otherwise do the dogs in summer, now
with muzzle, now with paw, when they are
bitten by fleas, or flies, or gadflies. When I
set my eyes on the faces of some of these
on whom the grievous fire descends, I did not
recognize any of them, but I perceived that
from the neck of each hung a pouch, which
had a certain color and a certain device, and
thereon each seems to feast his eyes. And
when I came among them, looking about, I
saw, upon a yellow purse, azure that had the
form and bearing of a lion. Then, gazing
farther, I saw another, red as blood, display
a goose whiter than butter. And one, who
had his white wallet marked with an azure
and gravid sow, said to me, "What are you
doing in this ditch? Now get you gone! And
since you are still alive, know that my neigh-
bor Vitaliano shall sit here at my left side.
With these Florentines am I, a Paduan; often
they din my ears, shouting, 'Let the sovereign
knight come who will bring the pouch with
three goats!'" Then he twisted his mouth
and stuck out his tongue, like an ox that
licks its nose; and I, fearing lest a longer
stay should anger him who had admonished
me to stay but little, turned back from the
weary souls.

Trova' il duca mio ch'era salito
   già su la groppa del fiero animale,
   e disse a me: "Or sie forte e ardito.   *81*
Omai si scende per sì fatte scale;
   monta dinanzi, ch'i' voglio esser mezzo,
   sì che la coda non possa far male."   *84*
Qual è colui che sì presso ha 'l riprezzo
   de la quartana, c'ha già l'unghie smorte,
   e triema tutto pur guardando 'l rezzo,   *87*
tal divenn' io a le parole porte;
   ma vergogna mi fé le sue minacce,
   che innanzi a buon segnor fa servo forte.   *90*
I' m'assettai in su quelle spallacce;
   sì volli dir, ma la voce non venne
   com' io credetti: "Fa che tu m'abbracce."   *93*
Ma esso, ch'altra volta mi sovvenne
   ad altro forse, tosto ch'i' montai
   con le braccia m'avvinse e mi sostenne;   *96*
e disse: "Gerïon, moviti omai:
   le rote larghe, e lo scender sia poco;
   pensa la nova soma che tu hai."   *99*
Come la navicella esce di loco
   in dietro in dietro, sì quindi si tolse;
   e poi ch'al tutto si sentì a gioco,   *102*
là 'v' era 'l petto, la coda rivolse,
   e quella tesa, come anguilla, mosse,
   e con le branche l'aere a sé raccolse.   *105*
Maggior paura non credo che fosse
   quando Fetonte abbandonò li freni,
   per che 'l ciel, come pare ancor, si cosse;   *108*

I found my leader already mounted on the croup of the fierce beast, and he said to me, "Now be strong and bold: henceforward the descent is by such stairs as these. Mount in front, for I wish to be between, so that the tail may not harm you." As one who has the shivering-fit of the quartan so near that his nails are already pale, and he trembles all over at the mere sight of shade, such I became at these words of his; but shame rebuked me, which makes a servant brave in the presence of a good master. I seated myself on those ugly shoulders, and I wanted to say (but the voice did not come as I thought), "See that you embrace me!" But he who at other times had succored me in other peril clasped me in his arms and steadied me as soon as I was mounted up, then said, "Geryon, move on now; let your circles be wide, and your descending slow: remember the new burden that you have."

As the bark backs out little by little from its place, so Geryon withdrew thence; and when he felt himself quite free, he turned his tail to where his breast had been, and, stretching it out, moved it like an eel, and with his paws gathered the air to himself. I do not think that there was greater fear when Phaëthon let loose the reins, whereby the sky, as yet appears, was scorched,

né quando Icaro misero le reni
  sentì spennar per la scaldata cera,
    gridando il padre a lui "Mala via tieni!"   *111*
che fu la mia, quando vidi ch'i' era
  ne l'aere d'ogne parte, e vidi spenta
    ogne veduta fuor che de la fera.   *114*
Ella sen va notando lenta lenta;
  rota e discende, ma non me n'accorgo
    se non che al viso e di sotto mi venta.   *117*
Io sentia già da la man destra il gorgo
  far sotto noi un orribile scroscio,
    per che con li occhi 'n giù la testa sporgo.   *120*
Allor fu' io più timido a lo stoscio,
  però ch'i' vidi fuochi e senti' pianti;
    ond' io tremando tutto mi raccoscio.   *123*
E vidi poi, ché nol vedea davanti,
  lo scendere e 'l girar per li gran mali
    che s'appressavan da diversi canti.   *126*
Come 'l falcon ch'è stato assai su l'ali,
  che sanza veder logoro o uccello
    fa dire al falconiere "Omè, tu cali!"   *129*
discende lasso onde si move isnello,
  per cento rote, e da lunge si pone
    dal suo maestro, disdegnoso e fello;   *132*
così ne puose al fondo Gerïone
  al piè al piè de la stagliata rocca,
  e, discarcate le nostre persone,
si dileguò come da corda cocca.   *136*

nor when the wretched Icarus felt his loins
unfeathering by the melting wax, and his
father cried to him, "You go an ill way!"
than was mine when I saw that I was in the
air on every side, and saw extinguished every
sight, save of the beast. He goes swimming
slowly on, wheels and descends, but I per-
ceive it only by a wind upon my face and
from below. I heard now on our right the
whirlpool making a horrible roaring below
us, wherefore I stretch forth my head and
look down. Then I became more terrified at
the descent, for I saw fires and heard laments,
whereat, trembling, I cling the closer. And I
saw then—for I had not seen it before—the
descending and the circling, by the great evils
which were drawing near on every side.

As the falcon that has been long on the
wing—that, without seeing lure or bird, makes
the falconer cry, "Ah, ah, you're coming
down!"—descends weary, with many a wheel-
ing, to where it set out swiftly, and alights
disdainful and sullen, far from its master:
so, at the very foot of the jagged rock, did
Geryon set us down at the bottom, and, dis-
burdened of our persons, vanished like an
arrow from the string.

INFERNO

Luogo è in inferno detto Malebolge,
    tutto di pietra di color ferrigno,
    come la cerchia che dintorno il volge.   *3*
Nel dritto mezzo del campo maligno
    vaneggia un pozzo assai largo e profondo,
    di cui *suo loco* dicerò l'ordigno.   *6*
Quel cinghio che rimane adunque è tondo
    tra 'l pozzo e 'l piè de l'alta ripa dura,
    e ha distinto in dieci valli il fondo.   *9*
Quale, dove per guardia de le mura
    più e più fossi cingon li castelli,
    la parte dove son rende figura,   *12*
tale imagine quivi facean quelli;
    e come a tai fortezze da' lor sogli
    a la ripa di fuor son ponticelli,   *15*
così da imo de la roccia scogli
    movien che ricidien li argini e ' fossi
    infino al pozzo che i tronca e raccogli.   *18*

CANTO XVIII

THERE is a place in Hell called Malebolge, all of stone which is the color of iron, like the wall that goes round it. Right in the middle of this malign field yawns a pit very wide and deep, of whose structure I shall tell in its place. That belt, therefore, which remains between the pit and the foot of the high hard bank is circular, and it has its bottom divided into ten valleys. Such a figure as where, for guard of the walls, successive ditches encircle castles, the place where they are presents, such an image did these make here. And as in such strongholds from their thresholds to the outer bank are little bridges, so from the base of the cliff ran crags which traversed the embankments and the ditches as far as the pit, which cuts them off and collects them.

In questo luogo, de la schiena scossi
   di Gerïon, trovammoci; e 'l poeta
   tenne a sinistra, e io dietro mi mossi.   *21*
A la man destra vidi nova pieta,
   novo tormento e novi frustatori,
   di che la prima bolgia era repleta.   *24*
Nel fondo erano ignudi i peccatori;
   dal mezzo in qua ci venien verso 'l volto,
   di là con noi, ma con passi maggiori,   *27*
come i Roman per l'essercito molto,
   l'anno del giubileo, su per lo ponte
   hanno a passar la gente modo colto,   *30*
che da l'un lato tutti hanno la fronte
   verso 'l castello e vanno a Santo Pietro,
   da l'altra sponda vanno verso 'l monte.   *33*
Di qua, di là, su per lo sasso tetro
   vidi demon cornuti con gran ferze,
   che li battien crudelmente di retro.   *36*
Ahi come facean lor levar le berze
   a le prime percosse! già nessuno
   le seconde aspettava né le terze.   *39*
Mentr' io andava, li occhi miei in uno
   furo scontrati; e io sì tosto dissi:
   "Già di veder costui non son digiuno."   *42*
Per ch'ïo a figurarlo i piedi affissi;
   e 'l dolce duca meco si ristette,
   e assentio ch'alquanto in dietro gissi.   *45*
E quel frustato celar si credette
   bassando 'l viso; ma poco li valse,
   ch'io dissi: "O tu che l'occhio a terra gette,   *48*

In this place we found ourselves dropped
from the back of Geryon, and the poet held
to the left, and I came on behind. On the
right hand I saw new woe, new torments,
and new scourgers, with which the first ditch
was replete. At its bottom were the sinners,
naked; on our side of the middle they came
facing us, and, on the other side, along with
us, but with greater strides: thus the Romans,
because of the great throng, in the year of
the Jubilee, have taken measures for the peo-
ple to pass over the bridge, so that on one
side all face toward the Castle and go to St.
Peter's, and on the other they go toward the
Mount. Along the dark rock, on this side and
on that, I saw horned demons with large
scourges, who smote them fiercely from be-
hind. Ah, how they made them lift their
heels at the first blows! Truly none waited
for the second or the third!

While I was going on, my eyes were met
by one of them, and instantly I said, "This
fellow I've certainly seen before"; wherefore
I paused to make him out, and my gentle
leader stopped with me and gave me leave
to go back a little. And that scourged soul
thought to hide himself, lowering his face,
but it availed him little, for I said, "You
there, casting your eye on the ground,

se le fazion che porti non son false,
  Venedico se' tu Caccianemico.
  Ma che ti mena a sì pungenti salse?"   *51*
Ed elli a me: "Mal volontier lo dico;
  ma sforzami la tua chiara favella,
  che mi fa sovvenir del mondo antico.   *54*
I' fui colui che la Ghisolabella
  condussi a far la voglia del marchese,
  come che suoni la sconcia novella.   *57*
E non pur io qui piango bolognese;
  anzi n'è questo loco tanto pieno,
  che tante lingue non son ora apprese   *60*
a dicer 'sipa' tra Sàvena e Reno;
  e se di ciò vuoi fede o testimonio,
  rècati a mente il nostro avaro seno."   *63*
Così parlando il percosse un demonio
  de la sua scurïada, e disse: "Via,
  ruffian! qui non son femmine da conio."   *66*
I' mi raggiunsi con la scorta mia;
  poscia con pochi passi divenimmo
  là 'v' uno scoglio de la ripa uscia.   *69*
Assai leggeramente quel salimmo;
  e vòlti a destra su per la sua scheggia,
  da quelle cerchie etterne ci partimmo.   *72*
Quando noi fummo là dov' el vaneggia
  di sotto per dar passo a li sferzati,
  lo duca disse: "Attienti, e fa che feggia   *75*
lo viso in te di quest' altri mal nati,
  ai quali ancor non vedesti la faccia
  però che son con noi insieme andati."   *78*

if the features you wear are not false, are
Venedico Caccianemico. But what brings you
to such pungent sauces?"

And he to me, "Unwillingly I tell it, but
your plain speech, which makes me remem-
ber the former world, compels me. I was he
who brought Ghisolabella to do the will of
the Marquis, however the vile story may be
reported. And I am not the only Bolognese
who laments here; nay, this place is so full of
them, that so many tongues are not now
taught, between Savena and Reno, to say
sipa; and if of this you wish assurance or
testimony, recall to mind our avaricious na-
ture." As he spoke thus, a demon smote him
with his lash, and said, "Off, pander! There
are no women here to coin."

I rejoined my escort; then, with but a few
steps, we came to where a reef went out from
the bank. This we very easily ascended and,
turning to the right upon its jagged ridge,
we quitted those eternal circlings.

When we were at the place where it yawns
beneath to give passage to the scourged, my
leader said, "Stop, and let the sight of these
other ill-born souls strike on you, whose faces
you have not seen, for they have been going
along with us."

Del vecchio ponte guardavam la traccia
   che venìa verso noi da l'altra banda,
   e che la ferza similmente scaccia.   *81*
E 'l buon maestro, sanza mia dimanda,
   mi disse: "Guarda quel grande che vene,
   e per dolor non par lagrime spanda: *84*
quanto aspetto reale ancor ritene!
   Quelli è Iasón, che per cuore e per senno
   li Colchi del monton privati féne.   *87*
Ello passò per l'isola di Lenno
   poi che l'ardite femmine spietate
   tutti li maschi loro a morte dienno.   *90*
Ivi con segni e con parole ornate
   Isifile ingannò, la giovinetta
   che prima avea tutte l'altre ingannate.   *93*
Lasciolla quivi, gravida, soletta;
   tal colpa a tal martiro lui condanna;
   e anche di Medea si fa vendetta.   *96*
Con lui sen va chi da tal parte inganna;
   e questo basti de la prima valle
   sapere e di color che 'n sé assanna."   *99*
Già eravam là 've lo stretto calle
   con l'argine secondo s'incrocicchia,
   e fa di quello ad un altr' arco spalle.   *102*
Quindi sentimmo gente che si nicchia
   ne l'altra bolgia e che col muso scuffa,
   e sé medesma con le palme picchia.   *105*
Le ripe eran grommate d'una muffa,
   per l'alito di giù che vi s'appasta,
   che con li occhi e col naso facea zuffa.   *108*

From the old bridge we viewed the train
that was coming towards us on the other side,
likewise driven by the scourge. The good
master, without my asking, said to me, "Look
at that great one who comes, and seems to
shed no tear for pain. What a regal aspect he
yet retains! That is Jason, who by courage
and by craft despoiled the Colchians of the
ram. He passed by the isle of Lemnos when
the bold and pitiless women had given all
their males to death. There, with tokens and
with fair words, he deceived the young
Hypsipyle who first had deceived all the rest.
He left her there pregnant and forlorn: such
guilt condemns him to such torment; and
Medea too is avenged. With him go all who
practice such deceit; and let this suffice for
knowledge of the first valley and of those it
holds in its fangs."

We were now where the narrow path
intersects with the second embankment and
makes of that the abutment to another arch.
From there we heard people whining in the
next pouch, and puffing with their muzzles
and smiting themselves with their palms.
The banks were crusted over with a mold
from the vapor below that sticks on them
and that did battle with the eyes and with
the nose.

Lo fondo è cupo sì, che non ci basta
  loco a veder sanza montare al dosso
  de l'arco, ove lo scoglio più sovrasta.   *111*
Quivi venimmo; e quindi giù nel fosso
  vidi gente attuffata in uno sterco
  che da li uman privadi parea mosso.   *114*
E mentre ch'io là giù con l'occhio cerco,
  vidi un col capo sì di merda lordo,
  che non parëa s'era laico o cherco.   *117*
Quei mi sgridò: "Perché se' tu sì gordo
  di riguardar più me che li altri brutti?"
  E io a lui: "Perché, se ben ricordo,   *120*
già t'ho veduto coi capelli asciutti,
  e se' Alessio Interminei da Lucca:
  però t'adocchio più che li altri tutti."   *123*
Ed elli allor, battendosi la zucca:
  "Qua giù m'hanno sommerso le lusinghe
  ond' io non ebbi mai la lingua stucca."   *126*
Appresso ciò lo duca "Fa che pinghe,"
  mi disse, "il viso un poco più avante,
  sì che la faccia ben con l'occhio attinghe   *129*
di quella sozza e scapigliata fante
  che là si graffia con l'unghie merdose,
  e or s'accoscia e ora è in piedi stante.   *132*
Taïde è, la puttana che rispuose
  al drudo suo quando disse 'Ho io grazie
  grandi apo te?': 'Anzi maravigliose!'
  E quinci sian le nostre viste sazie."   *136*

The bottom is so deep that we could nowhere see it without mounting to the crown of the arch where the ridge rises highest. Hither we came, and thence I saw down in the ditch a people plunged in filth that seemed to have come from human privies.

And while I was searching down there with my eyes, I beheld one whose head was so befouled with ordure that it did not appear whether he was layman or cleric. He bawled to me, "Why are you so greedy to look more at me than at the other filthy ones?" And I to him, "Because, if I rightly recall, I have seen you before with your hair dry, and you are Alessio Interminei of Lucca; therefore do I eye you more than all the rest." And he, then, beating his pate, "Down to this the flatteries wherewith my tongue was never cloyed have sunk me."

Hereupon my leader said to me, "Now push your look a little further forwards, so that your eye may fully reach the face of that foul and disheveled wench who is scratching herself there with her filthy nails, now squatting, now standing. She is Thaïs the whore, who answered her paramour when he said, 'Have I great favor with you?'—'Nay, wondrous!' And therewith let our sight be satisfied."

INFERNO

O Simon mago, o miseri seguaci
   che le cose di Dio, che di bontate
   deon essere spose, e voi rapaci   *3*
per oro e per argento avolterate,
   or convien che per voi suoni la tromba,
   però che ne la terza bolgia state.   *6*
Già eravamo, a la seguente tomba,
   montati de lo scoglio in quella parte
   ch'a punto sovra mezzo 'l fosso piomba.   *9*
O somma sapïenza, quanta è l'arte
   che mostri in cielo, in terra e nel mal mondo,
   e quanto giusto tua virtù comparte!   *12*
Io vidi per le coste e per lo fondo
   piena la pietra livida di fóri,
   d'un largo tutti e ciascun era tondo.   *15*
Non mi parean men ampi né maggiori
   che que' che son nel mio bel San Giovanni,
   fatti per loco d'i battezzatori;   *18*

CANTO XIX

O Simon Magus! O you his wretched fol-
lowers that, rapacious, prostitute for gold and
silver the things of God which ought to be
the brides of rightcousness! now must the
trumpet sound for you, since you are in the
third pouch.

We were now at the next tomb, having
climbed to that part of the reef which hangs
directly over the middle of the ditch. O Su-
preme Wisdom, how great is the art which
Thou showest in heaven, on earth, and in the
evil world! and how justly does Thy Power
dispense!

Upon the sides and upon the bottom I saw
the livid stone full of holes, all of one size
and each was round. They seemed to me
not less wide or larger than those that are
made for the baptizings in my beautiful
San Giovanni;

l'un de li quali, ancor non è molt' anni,
   rupp' io per un che dentro v'annegava:
   e questo sia suggel ch'ogn' omo sganni.   *21*
Fuor de la bocca a ciascun soperchiava
   d'un peccator li piedi e de le gambe
   infino al grosso, e l'altro dentro stava.   *24*
Le piante erano a tutti accese intrambe;
   per che sì forte guizzavan le giunte,
   che spezzate averien ritorte e strambe.   *27*
Qual suole il fiammeggiar de le cose unte
   muoversi pur su per la strema buccia,
   tal era lì dai calcagni a le punte.   *30*
"Chi è colui, maestro, che si cruccia
   guizzando più che li altri suoi consorti,"
   diss' io, "e cui più roggia fiamma succia?"   *33*
Ed elli a me: "Se tu vuo' ch'i' ti porti
   là giù per quella ripa che più giace,
   da lui saprai di sé e de' suoi torti."   *36*
E io: "Tanto m'è bel, quanto a te piace:
   tu se' segnore, e sai ch'i' non mi parto
   dal tuo volere, e sai quel che si tace."   *39*
Allor venimmo in su l'argine quarto;
   volgemmo e discendemmo a mano stanca
   là giù nel fondo foracchiato e arto.   *42*
Lo buon maestro ancor de la sua anca
   non mi dipuose, sì mi giunse al rotto
   di quel che si piangeva con la zanca.   *45*
"O qual che se' che 'l di sù tien di sotto,
   anima trista come pal commessa,"
   comincia' io a dir, "se puoi, fa motto."   *48*

one of which, not many years ago, I broke to
save one who was drowning in it—and let
this be the seal to undeceive all men.

From the mouth of each projected the feet
of a sinner and his legs as far as the calf, and
the rest was within. They all had both their
soles on fire, because of which their joints
were twitching so hard that they would have
snapped ropes and withes. As flame on oily
things is wont to move only on their outer
surface, so it did there, from the heels to
the toes.

"Master, who is that who writhes himself,
twitching more than all his fellows," I said,
"and who is sucked by a ruddier flame?" And
he to me, "If you will have me carry you down
there by that more sloping bank, from him-
self you shall learn of him and of his wrongs."

And I, "Whatever pleases you is to my
liking: you are my lord and you know that
I depart not from your will; and you know
that which is left unsaid."

Then we came onto the fourth dike, turned
and descended on our left, down to the per-
forated and narrow bottom; and the good
master did not set me down from his side
till he had brought me to the hole of him who
was lamenting with his shanks.

"O wretched soul, whoever you are that,
planted like a stake, have your upper part
down under!" I began, "speak if you can."

Io stava come 'l frate che confessa
  lo perfido assessin, che, poi ch'è fitto,
  richiama lui per che la morte cessa.   *51*
Ed el gridò: "Se' tu già costì ritto,
  se' tu già costì ritto, Bonifazio?
  Di parecchi anni mi mentì lo scritto.   *54*
Se' tu sì tosto di quell' aver sazio
  per lo qual non temesti tòrre a 'nganno
  la bella donna, e poi di farne strazio?"   *57*
Tal mi fec' io, quai son color che stanno,
  per non intender ciò ch'è lor risposto,
  quasi scornati, e risponder non sanno.   *60*
Allor Virgilio disse: "Dilli tosto:
  'Non son colui, non son colui che credi' ";
  e io rispuosi come a me fu imposto.   *63*
Per che lo spirto tutti storse i piedi;
  poi, sospirando e con voce di pianto,
  mi disse: "Dunque che a me richiedi?   *66*
Se di saper ch'i' sia ti cal cotanto,
  che tu abbi però la ripa corsa,
  sappi ch'i' fui vestito del gran manto;   *69*
e veramente fui figliuol de l'orsa,
  cupido sì per avanzar li orsatti,
  che sù l'avere e qui me misi in borsa.   *72*
Di sotto al capo mio son li altri tratti
  che precedetter me simoneggiando,
  per le fessure de la pietra piatti.   *75*
Là giù cascherò io altresì quando
  verrà colui ch'i' credea che tu fossi,
  allor ch'i' feci 'l sùbito dimando.   *78*

I was standing there like the friar who con-
fesses the perfidious assassin who, after he is
fixed, recalls him in order to delay his death;
and he cried, "Are you already standing
there, are you already standing there, Boni-
fazio? By several years the writ has lied to
me. Are you so quickly sated with those gains
for which you did not fear to take by guile
the beautiful Lady, and then to do her out-
rage?"

I became like those who stand as if be-
mocked, not comprehending what is answered
them and unable to reply. Then Virgil said,
"Tell him quickly, 'I am not he, I am not he
whom you think!' and I answered as I was
bidden; whereat the spirit writhed hard both
his feet; then, sighing, and with tearful voice,
he said to me, "Then what is it you ask of
me? If to know who I am concerns you so
much that you have for that come down the
bank, know that I was vested with the great
mantle; and I was truly a son of the she-bear,
so eager to advance the cubs that up there I
pursed my gains, and here I purse myself.
Beneath my head are the others that preceded
me in simony, mashed down and flattened
through the fissures of the rock. I shall be
thrust down there in my turn when he comes
for whom I mistook you when I put my
sudden question.

Ma più è 'l tempo già che i piè mi cossi
e ch'i' son stato così sottosopra,
ch'el non starà piantato coi piè rossi: *81*
ché dopo lui verrà di più laida opra,
di ver' ponente, un pastor sanza legge,
tal che convien che lui e me ricuopra.   *84*
Nuovo Iasón sarà, di cui si legge
ne' Maccabei; e come a quel fu molle
suo re, così fia lui chi Francia regge."   *87*
Io non so s'i' mi fui qui troppo folle,
ch'i' pur rispuosi lui a questo metro:
"Deh, or mi dì: quanto tesoro volle   *90*
Nostro Segnore in prima da san Pietro
ch'ei ponesse le chiavi in sua balìa?
Certo non chiese se non 'Viemmi retro.'   *93*
Né Pier né li altri tolsero a Matia
oro od argento, quando fu sortito
al loco che perdé l'anima ria.   *96*
Però ti sta, ché tu se' ben punito;
e guarda ben la mal tolta moneta
ch'esser ti fece contra Carlo ardito.   *99*
E se non fosse ch'ancor lo mi vieta
la reverenza de le somme chiavi
che tu tenesti ne la vita lieta,   *102*
io userei parole ancor più gravi;
ché la vostra avarizia il mondo attrista,
calcando i buoni e sollevando i pravi.   *105*
Di voi pastor s'accorse il Vangelista,
quando colei che siede sopra l'acque
puttaneggiar coi regi a lui fu vista;   *108*

But longer already is the time that I have
cooked my feet and stood inverted thus than
he shall stay planted with glowing feet, for
after him shall come a lawless shepherd from
the west, of uglier deeds, one fit to cover both
him and me. A new Jason he will be, like
him we read of in Maccabees, but even as to
that one his king was pliant, so to this one
shall be he who governs France."

I do not know if here I was overbold, in
answering him in just this strain, "Pray now
tell me how much treasure did our Lord re-
quire of Saint Peter before he put the keys
into his keeping? Surely he asked nothing
save: 'Follow me.' Nor did Peter or the others
take gold or silver of Matthias when he was
chosen for the office which the guilty soul had
lost. Therefore stay right here, for you are
justly punished; and guard well the ill-got
gain that made you bold against Charles.
And were it not that reverence for the Great
Keys which you held in the glad life even
now forbids it to me, I would use yet harder
words, for your avarice afflicts the world,
trampling down the good and exalting the
bad. It was shepherds such as you that the
Evangelist had in mind when she that sitteth
upon the waters was seen by him committing
fornication with the kings:

quella che con le sette teste nacque,
   e da le diece corna ebbe argomento,
   fin che virtute al suo marito piacque.   *111*
Fatto v'avete dio d'oro e d'argento;
   e che altro è da voi a l'idolatre,
   se non ch'elli uno, e voi ne orate cento?   *114*
Ahi, Costantin, di quanto mal fu matre,
   non la tua conversion, ma quella dote
   che da te prese il primo ricco patre!"   *117*
E mentr' io li cantava cotai note,
   o ira o coscïenza che 'l mordesse,
   forte spingava con ambo le piote.   *120*
I' credo ben ch'al mio duca piacesse,
   con sì contenta labbia sempre attese
   lo suon de le parole vere espresse.   *123*
Però con ambo le braccia mi prese;
   e poi che tutto su mi s'ebbe al petto,
   rimontò per la via onde discese.   *126*
Né si stancò d'avermi a sé distretto,
   sì men portò sovra 'l colmo de l'arco
   che dal quarto al quinto argine è tragetto.   *129*
Quivi soavemente spuose il carco,
   soave per lo scoglio sconcio ed erto
   che sarebbe a le capre duro varco.
Indi un altro vallon mi fu scoperto.   *133*

she that was born with the seven heads, and
from the ten horns had her strength, so long
as virtue pleased her spouse. You have made
you a god of gold and silver; and wherein do
you differ from the idolators, save that they
worship one, and you a hundred? Ah, Con-
stantine, of how much ill was mother, not
your conversion, but that dowry which the
first rich Father took from you!" And while
I intoned these notes to him, whether anger
or conscience stung him, he kicked hard with
both his feet. And indeed I think it pleased
my guide, with so satisfied a look did he keep
listening to the sound of the true words
uttered. Thereupon he took me in his arms,
and when he had me quite on his breast, re-
mounted by the path where he had descended;
nor did he tire of holding me clasped to him-
self, but carried me up to the summit of the
arch which is the crossway from the fourth
to the fifth dike. Here he gently set down
his burden, gently because of the rugged and
steep crag, which would be a hard passage
for goats; and from there another valley was
disclosed to me.

INFERNO

Di nova pena mi conven far versi
e dar matera al ventesimo canto
de la prima canzon, ch'è d'i sommersi.   *3*
Io era già disposto tutto quanto
a riguardar ne lo scoperto fondo,
che si bagnava d'angoscioso pianto;   *6*
e vidi gente per lo vallon tondo
venir, tacendo e lagrimando, al passo
che fanno le letane in questo mondo.   *9*
Come 'l viso mi scese in lor più basso,
mirabilmente apparve esser travolto
ciascun tra 'l mento e 'l principio del casso,   *12*
ché da le reni era tornato 'l volto,
e in dietro venir li convenia,
perché 'l veder dinanzi era lor tolto.   *15*
Forse per forza già di parlasia
si travolse così alcun del tutto;
ma io nol vidi, né credo che sia.   *18*

CANTO XX

O<small>F NEW</small> punishment I must make verses, and give matter to the twentieth canto of the first canzone, which is of the submerged.

I was now all prepared to look into the depth disclosed to me, which was bathed with tears of anguish, and through the circular valley I saw a people coming, silent and weeping, at the pace made by litanies in this world. As my sight went lower on them, each seemed to be strangely distorted between the chin and the beginning of the chest, for the face was turned toward the loins, and they had to come backwards, since seeing forward was denied them. Perhaps some time by stroke of palsy a man has been thus twisted right around, but I have not seen it, nor do I believe it possible.

Se Dio ti lasci, lettor, prender frutto
   di tua lezïone, or pensa per te stesso
   com' io potea tener lo viso asciutto,   *21*
quando la nostra imagine di presso
   vidi sì torta, che 'l pianto de li occhi
   le natiche bagnava per lo fesso.   *24*
Certo io piangea, poggiato a un de' rocchi
   del duro scoglio, sì che la mia scorta
   mi disse: "Ancor se' tu de li altri sciocchi?   *27*
Qui vive la pietà quand' è ben morta;
   chi è più scellerato che colui
   che al giudicio divin passion comporta?   *30*
Drizza la testa, drizza, e vedi a cui
   s'aperse a li occhi d'i Teban la terra;
   per ch'ei gridavan tutti: 'Dove rui,   *33*
Anfïarao? perché lasci la guerra?'
   E non restò di ruinare a valle
   fino a Minòs che ciascheduno afferra.   *36*
Mira c'ha fatto petto de le spalle;
   perché volse veder troppo davante,
   di retro guarda e fa retroso calle.   *39*
Vedi Tiresia, che mutò sembiante
   quando di maschio femmina divenne,
   cangiandosi le membra tutte quante;   *42*
e prima, poi, ribatter li convenne
   li duo serpenti avvolti, con la verga,
   che rïavesse le maschili penne.   *45*
Aronta è quel ch'al ventre li s'atterga,
   che ne' monti di Luni, dove ronca
   lo Carrarese che di sotto alberga,   *48*

Reader, so God grant you to take profit of your reading, think now for yourself how I could keep my cheeks dry when near at hand I saw our image so contorted that the tears from the eyes bathed the buttocks at the cleft. Truly I wept, leaning on one of the rocks of the hard crag, so that my guide said to me, "Are you even yet among the other fools? Here pity lives when it is altogether dead. Who is more impious than he who sorrows at God's judgment?

"Raise, raise your head, and see him for whom the earth opened before the eyes of the Thebans, whereat they all cried, 'Whither are you rushing, Amphiaraus? Why are you leaving the war?' And he stopped not from falling headlong down to Minos, who seizes every one. See how he has made a breast of his shoulders: because he wished to see too far before him, he looks behind and makes his way backwards.

"See Tiresias, who changed semblance when from male he became female, transforming all his members; and afterwards he had to strike again the two entwined serpents with his rod before he could resume his manly plumes.

"He that backs up to the other's belly is Aruns who, in the hills of Luni where grubs the Carrarese who dwells beneath,

ebbe tra ' bianchi marmi la spelonca
　　per sua dimora; onde a guardar le stelle
　　e 'l mar non li era la veduta tronca.　　　　　*51*
E quella che ricuopre le mammelle,
　　che tu non vedi, con le trecce sciolte,
　　e ha di là ogne pilosa pelle,　　　　　*54*
Manto fu, che cercò per terre molte;
　　poscia si puose là dove nacqu' io;
　　onde un poco mi piace che m'ascolte.　　　　　*57*
Poscia che 'l padre suo di vita uscìo
　　e venne serva la città di Baco,
　　questa gran tempo per lo mondo gio.　　　　　*60*
Suso in Italia bella giace un laco,
　　a piè de l'Alpe che serra Lamagna
　　sovra Tiralli, c'ha nome Benaco.　　　　　*63*
Per mille fonti, credo, e più si bagna
　　tra Garda e Val Camonica e Pennino
　　de l'acqua che nel detto laco stagna.　　　　　*66*
Loco è nel mezzo là dove 'l trentino
　　pastore e quel di Brescia e 'l veronese
　　segnar poria, s'e' fesse quel cammino.　　　　　*69*
Siede Peschiera, bello e forte arnese
　　da fronteggiar Bresciani e Bergamaschi,
　　ove la riva 'ntorno più discese.　　　　　*72*
Ivi convien che tutto quanto caschi
　　ciò che 'n grembo a Benaco star non può,
　　e fassi fiume giù per verdi paschi.　　　　　*75*
Tosto che l'acqua a correr mette co,
　　non più Benaco, ma Mencio si chiama
　　fino a Govèrnol, dove cade in Po.　　　　　*78*

had a cave for his abode among the white
marbles, from which he could observe the
stars and the sea with unobstructed view.

"And she that covers her bosom, which you
cannot see, with her loose tresses, and has on
that side all her hairy parts was Manto, who
searched through many lands, then settled in
the place where I was born—and on this I
would have you hear me for a little. After her
father had departed from life and the city of
Bacchus had become enslaved, she wandered
for a long time about the world. Up in fair
Italy, at the foot of the mountains that bound
Germany above Tirol, lies a lake which is
called Benaco. By a thousand springs, I think,
and more, the region between Garda and
Val Camonica and Pennino is bathed by
the water which settles in that lake, and in
the middle of it is a spot where the pastors of
Trent and Brescia and Verona, if they went
that way, might give their blessing. Peschiera,
a beautiful and strong fortress to confront the
Brescians and the Bergamese, sits where the
shore around is lowest. There all the water
that in the bosom of Benaco cannot stay must
descend and make itself a river, down
through green pastures. Soon as the water
starts to run, it is no longer named Benaco,
but Mincio, as far as Govèrnolo, where it
falls into the Po;

Non molto ha corso, ch'el trova una lama,
　ne la qual si distende e la 'mpaluda;
　e suol di state talor esser grama.　　　　　　　　*81*
Quindi passando la vergine cruda
　vide terra, nel mezzo del pantano,
　sanza coltura e d'abitanti nuda.　　　　　　　　*84*
Lì, per fuggire ogne consorzio umano,
　ristette con suoi servi a far sue arti,
　e visse, e vi lasciò suo corpo vano.　　　　　　*87*
Li uomini poi che 'ntorno erano sparti
　s'accolsero a quel loco, ch'era forte
　per lo pantan ch'avea da tutte parti.　　　　　　*90*
Fer la città sovra quell' ossa morte;
　e per colei che 'l loco prima elesse,
　Mantüa l'appellar sanz' altra sorte.　　　　　　*93*
Già fuor le genti sue dentro più spesse,
　prima che la mattia da Casalodi
　da Pinamonte inganno ricevesse.　　　　　　　*96*
Però t'assenno che, se tu mai odi
　originar la mia terra altrimenti,
　la verità nulla menzogna frodi."　　　　　　　　*99*
E io: "Maestro, i tuoi ragionamenti
　mi son sì certi e prendon sì mia fede,
　che li altri mi sarien carboni spenti.　　　　　　*102*
Ma dimmi, de la gente che procede,
　se tu ne vedi alcun degno di nota;
　ché solo a ciò la mia mente rifiede."　　　　　　*105*
Allor mi disse: "Quel che da la gota
　porge la barba in su le spalle brune,
　fu – quando Grecia fu di maschi vòta,　　　　　*108*

and after a short course it comes to a level
where it spreads and makes a marsh that
sometimes in summer is unwholesome. The
cruel virgin, passing that way, saw land in
the middle of the fen, untilled and without
inhabitants. There, to shun all human fellow-
ship she stopped with her servants to practice
her arts, and lived, and left there her empty
body. Afterwards the people who were scat-
tered round about gathered to that place,
which was strong because of the marsh it
had on all sides. They built the city over
those dead bones, and for her who first chose
the place they called it Mantua, without other
augury. Once the people within it were more
numerous, before the folly of Casalodi was
tricked by Pinamonte. Therefore I charge
you, if you ever hear other origin given to
my city, let no falsehood defraud the truth."

And I, "Master, your words are to me so
certain and do so hold my confidence, that
all others would be to me as dead coals. But
tell me, of the people who are passing, if you
see any that are worthy of note, for to that
alone does my mind revert."

Then he to me, "That one, who from the
cheek spreads his beard over his swarthy
shoulders, was augur when Greece was left
so empty of males

sì ch'a pena rimaser per le cune –
   augure, e diede 'l punto con Calcanta
   in Aulide a tagliar la prima fune.   *111*
Euripilo ebbe nome, e così 'l canta
   l'alta mia tragedìa in alcun loco:
   ben lo sai tu che la sai tutta quanta.   *114*
Quell' altro che ne' fianchi è così poco,
   Michele Scotto fu, che veramente
   de le magiche frode seppe 'l gioco.   *117*
Vedi Guido Bonatti; vedi Asdente,
   ch'avere inteso al cuoio e a lo spago
   ora vorrebbe, ma tardi si pente.   *120*
Vedi le triste che lasciaron l'ago,
   la spuola e 'l fuso, e fecersi 'ndivine;
   fecer malie con erbe e con imago.   *123*
Ma vienne omai, ché già tiene 'l confine
   d'amendue li emisperi e tocca l'onda
   sotto Sobilia Caino e le spine;   *126*
e già iernotte fu la luna tonda:
   ben ten de' ricordar, ché non ti nocque
   alcuna volta per la selva fonda."
Sì mi parlava, e andavamo introcque.   *130*

that they scarcely remained for the cradles, and with Calchas he gave the moment for cutting the first cable at Aulis. Eurypylus was his name, and thus my high Tragedy sings of him in a certain passage—as you know well, who know the whole of it. That other who is so spare in the flanks was Michael Scot, who truly knew the game of magic frauds. See Guido Bonatti; see Asdente, who now would fain have attended to his leather and his thread, but too late repents. See the wretched women who left the needle, the spool, and the spindle, and became fortune-tellers; they wrought spells with herbs and with images.

"But now come, for already Cain with his thorns holds the confines of both the hemispheres, and touches the wave below Seville; and already last night the moon was round. You must remember it well, for it did you no harm sometimes in the deep wood."

Thus he spoke to me, and we went on the while.

Così di ponte in ponte, altro parlando
    che la mia comedìa cantar non cura,
    venimmo; e tenavamo 'l colmo, quando   *3*
restammo per veder l'altra fessura
    di Malebolge e li altri pianti vani;
    e vidila mirabilmente oscura.   *6*
Quale ne l'arzanà de' Viniziani
    bolle l'inverno la tenace pece
    a rimpalmare i legni lor non sani,   *9*
ché navicar non ponno – in quella vece
    chi fa suo legno novo e chi ristoppa
    le coste a quel che più vïaggi fece;   *12*
chi ribatte da proda e chi da poppa;
    altri fa remi e altri volge sarte;
    chi terzeruolo e artimon rintoppa – :   *15*
tal, non per foco ma per divin' arte,
    bollia là giuso una pegola spessa,
    che 'nviscava la ripa d'ogne parte.   *18*
I' vedea lei, ma non vedëa in essa
    mai che le bolle che 'l bollor levava,
    e gonfiar tutta, e riseder compressa.   *21*

CANTO XXI

T<small>HUS</small> from bridge to bridge we came along, talking of things of which my Comedy is not concerned to sing, and we had reached the summit, when we stopped to see the next cleft of Malebolge and the next vain lamentations: and I saw it strangely dark.

As in the Arsenal of the Venetians, in winter, the sticky pitch for caulking their unsound vessels is boiling, because they cannot sail then, and instead, one builds his ship anew and another plugs the ribs of his that has made many a voyage, one hammers at the prow and another at the stern, this one makes oars, that one twists ropes, another patches jib and mainsail; so, not by fire but by divine art, a thick pitch was boiling there below, which overglued the bank on every side. It I saw, but in it I saw nothing save the bubbles raised by the boiling, and all of it swelling up and settling down together.

Mentr' io là giù fisamente mirava,
   lo duca mio, dicendo "Guarda, guarda!"
   mi trasse a sé del loco dov' io stava.   *24*
Allor mi volsi come l'uom cui tarda
   di veder quel che li convien fuggire
   e cui paura sùbita sgagliarda,   *27*
che, per veder, non indugia 'l partire:
   e vidi dietro a noi un diavol nero
   correndo su per lo scoglio venire.   *30*
Ahi quant' elli era ne l'aspetto fero!
   e quanto mi parea ne l'atto acerbo,
   con l'ali aperte e sovra i piè leggero!   *33*
L'omero suo, ch'era aguto e superbo,
   carcava un peccator con ambo l'anche,
   e quei tenea de' piè ghermito 'l nerbo.   *36*
Del nostro ponte disse: "O Malebranche,
   ecco un de li anzïan di Santa Zita!
   Mettetel sotto, ch'i' torno per anche   *39*
a quella terra, che n'è ben fornita:
   ogn' uom v'è barattier, fuor che Bonturo;
   del no, per li denar, vi si fa *ita*."   *42*
Là giù 'l buttò, e per lo scoglio duro
   si volse; e mai non fu mastino sciolto
   con tanta fretta a seguitar lo furo.   *45*
Quel s'attuffò, e tornò sù convolto;
   ma i demon che del ponte avean coperchio,
   gridar: "Qui non ha loco il Santo Volto!   *48*
qui si nuota altrimenti che nel Serchio!
   Però, se tu non vuo' di nostri graffi,
   non far sopra la pegola soverchio."   *51*

While I was gazing fixedly down on it, my leader, saying, "Watch out, watch out!" drew me to himself from the place where I was standing. Then I turned round like one who is eager to see what he must shun, and who is dismayed by sudden fear, so that he looks back but does not delay his flight to look, and behind us I saw a black devil come running up along the crag. Ah, how savage he was in aspect and how fierce he seemed in act, with outspread wings and light on his feet. His shoulder, which was sharp and high, was laden by both haunches of a sinner, and he held him grasped by the tendons of the feet.

He spoke from our bridge, "O Malebranche, here's one of Saint Zita's Elders! Thrust him under, while I go back for more, to that city where there's a fine supply of them: every man there is a barrator, except Bonturo; there they make *Ay* of *No*, for cash."

Down he hurled him, and turned back on the hard crag, and never was an unleashed mastiff so swift in pursuit of a thief. The sinner sank under and rose again, rump up; but the devils, who were under cover of the bridge, cried, "Here's no place for the Holy Face! Here you'll swim otherwise than in the Serchio! And so, unless you want to feel our grapples, do not come out above the pitch."

Poi l'addentar con più di cento raffi,
   disser: "Coverto convien che qui balli,
   sì che, se puoi, nascosamente accaffi."   *54*
Non altrimenti i cuoci a' lor vassalli
   fanno attuffare in mezzo la caldaia
   la carne con li uncin, perché non galli.   *57*
Lo buon maestro "Acciò che non si paia
   che tu ci sia," mi disse, "giù t'acquatta
   dopo uno scheggio, ch'alcun schermo t'aia;   *60*
e per nulla offension che mi sia fatta,
   non temer tu, ch'i' ho le cose conte,
   per ch'altra volta fui a tal baratta."   *63*
Poscia passò di là dal co del ponte;
   e com' el giunse in su la ripa sesta,
   mestier li fu d'aver sicura fronte.   *66*
Con quel furore e con quella tempesta
   ch'escono i cani a dosso al poverello
   che di sùbito chiede ove s'arresta,   *69*
usciron quei di sotto al ponticello,
   e volser contra lui tutt' i runcigli;
   ma el gridò: "Nessun di voi sia fello!   *72*
Innanzi che l'uncin vostro mi pigli,
   traggasi avante l'un di voi che m'oda,
   e poi d'arrunciogliarmi si consigli."   *75*
Tutti gridaron: "Vada Malacoda!";
   per ch'un si mosse – e li altri stetter fermi –
   e venne a lui dicendo: "Che li approda?"   *78*
"Credi tu, Malacoda, qui vedermi
   esser venuto," disse 'l mio maestro,
   "sicuro già da tutti vostri schermi,   *81*

Then they struck him with more than a hundred prongs, and said, "Here you'll have to dance under cover, so grab on secretly, if you can." Just so cooks make their scullions plunge the meat down into the cauldron with their forks, that it may not float.

The good master said to me, "That it may not be seen that you are here, squat down behind a jag, so that you may have some screen for yourself; and whatever outrage be done to me, be not afraid, for I know about things here and was in a like fray once before."

Then he passed on beyond the head of the bridge, and when he arrived upon the sixth bank he had need to show a steadfast front. With the fury and uproar of dogs that rush out upon some poor beggar who straightway begs from where he stops, these rushed out from under the little bridge and turned all their hooks against him. But he cried, "Let none of you be savage! Before you touch me with your forks, let one of you come forward to hear me, and then decide about grappling me."

All cried, "Let Malacoda go"; whereon, while the rest stood still, one moved and came up to him, saying, "What will it avail him?"

"Do you think, Malacoda, to see me come here," said my master, "secure thus far against all your defenses,

sanza voler divino e fato destro?

　　Lascian' andar, ché nel cielo è voluto
　　ch'i' mostri altrui questo cammin silvestro." 　84
Allor li fu l'orgoglio sì caduto,
　　ch'e' si lasciò cascar l'uncino a' piedi,
　　e disse a li altri: "Omai non sia feruto." 　87
E 'l duca mio a me: "O tu che siedi
　　tra li scheggion del ponte quatto quatto,
　　sicuramente omai a me ti riedi." 　90
Per ch'io mi mossi e a lui venni ratto;
　　e i diavoli si fecer tutti avanti,
　　sì ch'io temetti ch'ei tenesser patto; 　93
così vid' ïo già temer li fanti
　　ch'uscivan patteggiati di Caprona,
　　veggendo sé tra nemici cotanti. 　96
I' m'accostai con tutta la persona
　　lungo 'l mio duca, e non torceva li occhi
　　da la sembianza lor ch'era non buona. 　99
Ei chinavan li raffi e "Vuo' che 'l tocchi,"
　　diceva l'un con l'altro, "in sul groppone?"
　　E rispondien: "Sì, fa che gliel' accocchi." 　102
Ma quel demonio che tenea sermone
　　col duca mio, si volse tutto presto
　　e disse: "Posa, posa, Scarmiglione!" 　105
Poi disse a noi: "Più oltre andar per questo
　　iscoglio non si può, però che giace
　　tutto spezzato al fondo l'arco sesto. 　108
E se l'andare avante pur vi piace,
　　andatevene su per questa grotta;
　　presso è un altro scoglio che via face. 　111

without divine will and propitious fate? Let us pass, for it is willed in Heaven that I show another this savage way." Then was his pride so fallen, that he let the hook drop at his feet, and said to the others, "Now let no one strike him."

And my leader to me, "Oh you that sit asquat among the splinters of the bridge, securely now return to me." Wherefore I moved and quickly came to him; and the devils all pressed forward, so that I feared they might not keep the pact. Thus I once saw the soldiers afraid who were coming out of Caprona under pledge, seeing themselves among so many enemies. I drew near to my leader, pressing in close to him, and did not turn my eyes from their looks, which were not good. And they lowered their forks, one of them saying, "Shall I touch him on the rump?" and another answering, "Yes, see that you nick it for him." But that demon who was speaking with my leader turned round instantly, saying, "Hold, hold, Scarmiglione!"

Then he said to us, "To go farther by this crag will not be possible, for the sixth arch lies all shattered at the bottom; but if it is still your pleasure to go forward, then proceed along this ridge: nearby is another crag that affords a way.

Ier, più oltre cinqu' ore che quest' otta,
   mille dugento con sessanta sei
   anni compié che qui la via fu rotta.   *114*
Io mando verso là di questi miei
   a riguardar s'alcun se ne sciorina;
   gite con lor, che non saranno rei."   *117*
"Tra'ti avante, Alichino, e Calcabrina,"
   cominciò elli a dire, "e tu, Cagnazzo;
   e Barbariccia guidi la decina.   *120*
Libicocco vegn' oltre e Draghignazzo,
   Cirïatto sannuto e Graffiacane
   e Farfarello e Rubicante pazzo.   *123*
Cercate 'ntorno le boglienti pane;
   costor sian salvi infino a l'altro scheggio
   che tutto intero va sovra le tane."   *126*
"Omè, maestro, che è quel ch'i' veggio?"
   diss' io, "deh, sanza scorta andianci soli,
   se tu sa' ir; ch'i' per me non la cheggio.   *129*
Se tu se' sì accorto come suoli,
   non vedi tu ch'e' digrignan li denti
   e con le ciglia ne minaccian duoli?"   *132*
Ed elli a me: "Non vo' che tu paventi;
   lasciali digrignar pur a lor senno,
   ch'e' fanno ciò per li lessi dolenti."   *135*
Per l'argine sinistro volta dienno;
   ma prima avea ciascun la lingua stretta
   coi denti, verso lor duca, per cenno;
ed elli avea del cul fatto trombetta.   *139*

Yesterday, five hours later than now, completed one thousand two hundred and sixty-six years since the road was broken here. I am sending some of my company that way, to see if any is out taking the air. Go with them, for they will not harm you."

"Come forward, Alichino and Calcabrina," he began to say, "and you, Cagnazzo; and let Barbariccia lead the ten. Let Libicocco come too, and Draghignazzo, and tusked Ciriatto and Graffiacane and Farfarello and crazy Rubicante. Search around the boiling glue. Let these two be safe as far as the next crag that all unbroken goes across the dens."

"O me! master, what is this I see?" I said. "Ah, let us go alone without escort, if you know the way, for, as for myself, I want none! If you are as wary as you are wont, do you not see how they grind their teeth and with their brows threaten harm to us?" And he to me, "I would not have you be afraid; let them grind on as they please, for they do it at the boiled wretches."

They wheeled round by the bank on the left, but first each pressed his tongue between his teeth at their leader for a signal, and he had made a trumpet of his arse.

INFERNO

Io vidi già cavalier muover campo,
   e cominciare stormo e far lor mostra,
   e talvolta partir per loro scampo;   *3*
corridor vidi per la terra vostra,
   o Aretini, e vidi gir gualdane,
   fedir torneamenti e correr giostra;   *6*
quando con trombe, e quando con campane,
   con tamburi e con cenni di castella,
   e con cose nostrali e con istrane;   *9*
né già con sì diversa cennamella
   cavalier vidi muover né pedoni,
   né nave a segno di terra o di stella.   *12*
Noi andavam con li diece demoni.
   Ahi fiera compagnia! ma ne la chiesa
   coi santi, e in taverna coi ghiottoni.   *15*
Pur a la pegola era la mia 'ntesa,
   per veder de la bolgia ogne contegno
   e de la gente ch'entro v'era incesa.   *18*

CANTO XXII

Ere now have I seen horsemen moving camp, and beginning an assault and making their muster, and sometimes retiring to escape; I have seen coursers over your land, O Aretines, and I have seen the starting of raids, the onset of tournaments, and the running of jousts, now with trumpets and now with bells, with drums and castle-signals, with native things and foreign—but never to so strange a pipe have I seen horsemen or footmen set forth, or ship by sign of land or star!

We were going along with the ten demons: ah, savage company! but "in church with saints and with guzzlers in the tavern!" My attention was all on the pitch, in order to see every condition of the pouch, and of the people who were burning in it.

Come i dalfini, quando fanno segno
  a' marinar con l'arco de la schiena
  che s'argomentin di campar lor legno,   *21*
talor così, ad alleggiar la pena,
  mostrav' alcun de' peccatori 'l dosso
  e nascondea in men che non balena.   *24*
E come a l'orlo de l'acqua d'un fosso
  stanno i ranocchi pur col muso fuori,
  sì che celano i piedi e l'altro grosso,   *27*
sì stavan d'ogne parte i peccatori;
  ma come s'appressava Barbariccia,
  così si ritraén sotto i bollori.   *30*
I' vidi, e anco il cor me n'accapriccia,
  uno aspettar così, com' elli 'ncontra
  ch'una rana rimane e l'altra spiccia;   *33*
e Graffiacan, che li era più di contra,
  li arrunciglió le 'mpegolate chiome
  e trassel sù, che mi parve una lontra.   *36*
I' sapea già di tutti quanti 'l nome,
  sì li notai quando fuorono eletti,
  e poi ch'e' si chiamaro, attesi come.   *39*
"O Rubicante, fa che tu li metti
  li unghioni a dosso, sì che tu lo scuoi!"
  gridavan tutti insieme i maladetti.   *42*
E io: "Maestro mio, fa, se tu puoi,
  che tu sappi chi è lo sciagurato
  venuto a man de li avversari suoi."   *45*
Lo duca mio li s'accostò allato;
  domandollo ond' ei fosse, e quei rispuose:
  "I' fui del regno di Navarra nato.   *48*

Like dolphins when with their arching backs
they give sign to mariners that they should
prepare to save their ship, so from time to
time one of the sinners would show his back
to alleviate his pain, and hide it again,
quicker than a lightning-flash. And as at the
edge of the water of a ditch the frogs lie with
only their muzzle out, so that they hide their
feet and the rest of their bulk, so were the
sinners on every side; but as Barbariccia ap-
proached, so would they draw back under
the boiling.

I saw—and my heart still shudders at it—
one waiting, just as it happens that one frog
stays and another jumps. And Graffiacane,
who was nearest to him, hooked him by his
pitchy locks, and haled him up so that to me
he seemed an otter. I already knew all their
names, having noted them well when they
were chosen, and then observed what they
called each other.

"O Rubicante, see that you set your claws
on him and flay him," shouted all the ac-
cursed crew together. And I, "Master, pray
learn, if you can, who is the hapless wretch
that has fallen into the hands of his enemies."

My leader drew up to his side, and asked
him whence he came; and he replied, "I was
born in the kingdom of Navarre.

Mia madre a servo d'un segnor mi puose,
 che m'avea generato d'un ribaldo,
 distruggitor di sé e di sue cose.   *51*
Poi fui famiglia del buon re Tebaldo;
 quivi mi misi a far baratteria,
 di ch'io rendo ragione in questo caldo."   *54*
E Cirïatto, a cui di bocca uscia
 d'ogne parte una sanna come a porco,
 li fé sentir come l'una sdruscia.   *57*
Tra male gatte era venuto 'l sorco;
 ma Barbariccia il chiuse con le braccia
 e disse: "State in là, mentr' io lo 'nforco."   *60*
E al maestro mio volse la faccia;
 "Domanda," disse, "ancor, se più disii
 saper da lui, prima ch'altri 'l disfaccia."   *63*
Lo duca dunque: "Or dì: de li altri rii
 conosci tu alcun che sia latino
 sotto la pece?" E quelli: "I' mi partii,   *66*
poco è, da un che fu di là vicino.
 Così foss' io ancor con lui coperto,
 ch'i' non temerei unghia né uncino!"   *69*
E Libicocco "Troppo avem sofferto,"
 disse; e preseli 'l braccio col runciglio,
 sì che, stracciando, ne portò un lacerto.   *72*
Draghignazzo anco i volle dar di piglio
 giuso a le gambe; onde 'l decurio loro
 si volse intorno intorno con mal piglio.   *75*
Quand' elli un poco rappaciati fuoro,
 a lui, ch'ancor mirava sua ferita,
 domandò 'l duca mio sanza dimoro: *78*

My mother placed me as servant of a lord, for she had borne me to a ribald destroyer of himself and of his substance. Then I was of the household of the good King Thibaut: there I set myself to practice barratry, for which I render reckoning in this heat."

Then Ciriatto, from whose mouth on either side protruded a tusk, as of a boar, made him feel how one of them could rip. The mouse had come among evil cats; but Barbariccia locked him in his arms and said, "Stand back while I enfork him," then turned to my master and said, "Ask on, if you would learn more from him before another mangles him."

My leader therefore, "Tell us, then: of the other sinners under the pitch, do you know any who are Italian?" And he, "I parted just now from one who was a neighbor of theirs. Would I were still under cover with him, for I should not fear claw or hook." And Libicocco cried, "We have endured too much!" and seized his arm with the grapple so that, tearing, he ripped out a muscle of it. Draghignazzo also made as if to hook him in the legs, at which their captain wheeled round on them all with an ugly look.

When they were a little quieted, my leader straightway asked him who was still gazing at his wound,

"Chi fu colui da cui mala partita
 di' che facesti per venire a proda?"
 Ed ei rispuose: "Fu frate Gomita,   *81*
quel di Gallura, vasel d'ogne froda,
 ch'ebbe i nemici di suo donno in mano,
 e fé sì lor, che ciascun se ne loda.   *84*
Danar si tolse e lasciolli di piano,
 sì com' e' dice; e ne li altri offici anche
 barattier fu non picciol, ma sovrano.   *87*
Usa con esso donno Michel Zanche
 di Logodoro; e a dir di Sardigna
 le lingue lor non si sentono stanche.   *90*
Omè, vedete l'altro che digrigna;
 i' direi anche, ma i' temo ch'ello
 non s'apparecchi a grattarmi la tigna."   *93*
E 'l gran proposto, vòlto a Farfarello
 che stralunava li occhi per fedire,
 disse: "Fatti 'n costà, malvagio uccello!"   *96*
"Se voi volete vedere o udire,"
 ricominciò lo spaürato appresso,
 "Toschi o Lombardi, io ne farò venire;   *99*
ma stieno i Malebranche un poco in cesso,
 sì ch'ei non teman de le lor vendette;
 e io, seggendo in questo loco stesso,   *102*
per un ch'io son, ne farò venir sette
 quand' io suffolerò, com' è nostro uso
 di fare allor che fori alcun si mette."   *105*
Cagnazzo a cotal motto levò 'l muso,
 crollando 'l capo, e disse: "Odi malizia
 ch'elli ha pensata per gittarsi giuso!"   *108*

"Who was that from whom you say you
made an ill departure to come ashore?"

And he answered, "That was Fra Gomita,
he of Gallura, vessel of every fraud, who had
his master's enemies in his hand, and did so
deal with them that they all praise him for
it. He took the cash and dismissed them
smoothly, as he says; and in his other affairs
too he was no petty barrator, but sovereign.
Don Michel Zanche of Logodoro keeps com-
pany with him, and in talking of Sardinia
their tongues are never weary. O me! see
that other one grinding his teeth! I would tell
more, but I fear he's preparing to scratch my
itch." And the great marshal, turning to
Farfarello, who was rolling his eyes to strike,
said, "Get back there, villainous bird!"

"If you would see or hear Tuscans or
Lombards," the frightened one then began
again, "I will make some of them come. But
let the Malebranche stand back a bit, so that
they may not fear their vengeance; and I,
sitting in this same place, for one that I am,
will make seven come when I whistle, as is
our custom when any of us gets out."

Cagnazzo at these words raised his muzzle
and said, shaking his head, "Hear the cun-
ning trick he has contrived to throw himself
down in."

Ond' ei, ch'avea lacciuoli a gran divizia,
    rispuose: "Malizioso son io troppo,
    quand' io procuro a' mia maggior trestizia."   *111*
Alichin non si tenne e, di rintoppo
    a li altri, disse a lui: "Se tu ti cali,
    io non ti verrò dietro di gualoppo,   *114*
ma batterò sovra la pece l'ali.
    Lascisi 'l collo, e sia la ripa scudo,
    a veder se tu sol più di noi vali."   *117*
O tu che leggi, udirai nuovo ludo:
    ciascun da l'altra costa li occhi volse,
    quel prima, ch'a ciò fare era più crudo.   *120*
Lo Navarrese ben suo tempo colse;
    fermò le piante a terra, e in un punto
    saltò e dal proposto lor si sciolse.   *123*
Di che ciascun di colpa fu compunto,
    ma quei più che cagion fu del difetto;
    però si mosse e gridò: "Tu se' giunto!"   *126*
Ma poco i valse: ché l'ali al sospetto
    non potero avanzar; quelli andò sotto,
    e quei drizzò volando suso il petto: *129*
non altrimenti l'anitra di botto,
    quando 'l falcon s'appressa, giù s'attuffa,
    ed ei ritorna sù crucciato e rotto.   *132*
Irato Calcabrina de la buffa,
    volando dietro li tenne, invaghito
    che quei campasse per aver la zuffa;   *135*

Whereon he, who had artifices in great store, replied, "I am indeed cunning when I contrive greater sorrow for my companions!" Alichino held in no longer and, in opposition to the others, said to him, "If you plunge, I won't follow you at a gallop, but I'll beat my wings above the pitch. Let the ridge be left, and let the bank be a screen, to see if you alone are more than a match for us."

Now, reader, you shall hear new sport. All turned their eyes toward the other side, he first who had most opposed it. The Navarrese chose well his time, planted his feet firmly on the ground, and in an instant leaped and broke away from their marshal. Thereat each was stung with his fault, but he most who was the cause of the blunder; wherefore he started and cried out, "You're caught!" But it availed him little, for wings could not outspeed the terror: the one went under, and the other, flying, turned his breast upward; not otherwise the wild duck that suddenly dives down, when the falcon approaches, and he returns upward, vexed and defeated. Calcabrina, furious at the trick, went flying after him, eager for the sinner to escape, so as to have a scuffle;

e come 'l barattier fu disparito,
   così volse li artigli al suo compagno,
   e fu con lui sopra 'l fosso ghermito.   *138*
Ma l'altro fu bene sparvier grifagno
   ad artigliar ben lui, e amendue
   cadder nel mezzo del bogliente stagno.   *141*
Lo caldo sghermitor sùbito fue;
   ma però di levarsi era neente,
   sì avieno inviscate l'ali sue.   *144*
Barbariccia, con li altri suoi dolente,
   quattro ne fé volar da l'altra costa
   con tutt' i raffi, e assai prestamente   *147*
di qua, di là discesero a la posta;
   porser li uncini verso li 'mpaniati,
   ch'eran già cotti dentro da la crosta.
E noi lasciammo lor così 'mpacciati.   *151*

and, when the barrator had disappeared, he turned his claws on his fellow and grappled with him above the ditch; but the other was indeed a full-grown hawk to claw him well, and both fell into the middle of the boiling pond. The heat at once unclutched them, but there was no getting out, they had so beglued their wings. Barbariccia, lamenting with the rest, made four of them fly to the other bank, each with his fork; and very quickly, on this side and on that, they descended to their posts and stretched their hooks toward the belimed ones, who were already cooked within their crust; and we left them thus embroiled.

Taciti, soli, sanza compagnia
  n'andavam l'un dinanzi e l'altro dopo,
  come frati minor vanno per via.   *3*
Vòlt' era in su la favola d'Isopo
  lo mio pensier per la presente rissa,
  dov' el parlò de la rana e del topo;   *6*
ché più non si pareggia "mo" e "issa"
  che l'un con l'altro fa, se ben s'accoppia
  principio e fine con la mente fissa.   *9*
E come l'un pensier de l'altro scoppia,
  così nacque di quello un altro poi,
  che la prima paura mi fé doppia.   *12*
Io pensava così: "Questi per noi
  sono scherniti con danno e con beffa
  sì fatta, ch' assai credo che lor nòi.   *15*
Se l'ira sovra 'l mal voler s'aggueffa,
  ei ne verranno dietro più crudeli
  che 'l cane a quella lievre ch'elli acceffa."   *18*

CANTO XXIII

Silent, alone, without escort, we went on, one before and the other behind, as Friars Minor go their way. My thought was turned by the present brawl on the fable of Aesop where he told of the frog and the mouse; for Ay and Yea are not more alike than the one case is to the other, if we compare the beginning and the end attentively. And just as one thought springs from another, so from that another was born which redoubled my first fear. I thought: they have been fooled because of us, and with such hurt and mockery as I believe must vex them greatly. If rage be added to their malice, they will come after us, fiercer than the dog to the leveret he snaps up.

Già mi sentia tutti arricciar li peli
   de la paura e stava in dietro intento,
   quand' io dissi: "Maestro, se non celi   *21*
te e me tostamente, i' ho pavento
   d'i Malebranche. Noi li avem già dietro;
   io li 'magino sì, che già li sento."   *24*
E quei: "S'i' fossi di piombato vetro,
   l'imagine di fuor tua non trarrei
   più tosto a me, che quella dentro 'mpetro.   *27*
Pur mo venieno i tuo' pensier tra ' miei,
   con simile atto e con simile faccia,
   sì che d'intrambi un sol consiglio fei.   *30*
S'elli è che sì la destra costa giaccia,
   che noi possiam ne l'altra bolgia scendere,
   noi fuggirem l'imaginata caccia."   *33*
Già non compié di tal consiglio rendere,
   ch'io li vidi venir con l'ali tese
   non molto lungi, per volerne prendere.   *36*
Lo duca mio di sùbito mi prese,
   come la madre ch'al romore è desta
   e vede presso a sé le fiamme accese,   *39*
che prende il figlio e fugge e non s'arresta,
   avendo più di lui che di sé cura,
   tanto che solo una camiscia vesta;   *42*
e giù dal collo de la ripa dura
   supin si diede a la pendente roccia,
   che l'un de' lati a l'altra bolgia tura.   *45*
Non corse mai sì tosto acqua per doccia
   a volger ruota di molin terragno,
   quand' ella più verso le pale approccia,   *48*

Already I felt my hair all bristling with fear
as I went along intent on what was behind
us, and I said, "Master, unless you quickly
hide yourself and me, I dread the Male-
branche. We have them after us already: I
so imagine them that I hear them now."

And he, "If I were of leaded glass, I should
not draw to me your outward semblance more
quickly than I receive your inward. Even
now came your thoughts among mine, with
like action and like look, so that of both I
have made one counsel. If it be that the slope
on the right lies so that we can descend into
the next ditch, we shall escape the imagined
chase."

He had not yet finished telling me his plan
when I saw them coming with outstretched
wings, not very far off, bent on taking us.
My leader instantly took me up, like a
mother who is awakened by the noise and
sees beside her the kindled flames, and
catches up her child and flies, and, more con-
cerned for him than for herself, does not stay
even to put on a shift; and, down from the
ridge of the hard bank he gave himself supine
to the sloping rock that closes one side of the
next pouch. Never did water run so fast
through a sluice to turn the wheel of a land-
mill when it approaches nearest to the paddles,

come 'l maestro mio per quel vivagno,
   portandosene me sovra 'l suo petto,
   come suo figlio, non come compagno.   *51*
A pena fuoro i piè suoi giunti al letto
   del fondo giù, ch'e' furon in sul colle
   sovresso noi; ma non lì era sospetto: *54*
ché l'alta provedenza che lor volle
   porre ministri de la fossa quinta,
   poder di partirs' indi a tutti tolle.   *57*
Là giù trovammo una gente dipinta
   che giva intorno assai con lenti passi,
   piangendo e nel sembiante stanca e vinta.   *60*
Elli avean cappe con cappucci bassi
   dinanzi a li occhi, fatte de la taglia
   che in Clugnì per li monaci fassi.   *63*
Di fuor dorate son, sì ch'elli abbaglia;
   ma dentro tutte piombo, e gravi tanto,
   che Federigo le mettea di paglia.   *66*
Oh in etterno faticoso manto!
   Noi ci volgemmo ancor pur a man manca
   con loro insieme, intenti al tristo pianto;   *69*
ma per lo peso quella gente stanca
   venìa sì pian, che noi eravam nuovi
   di compagnia ad ogne mover d'anca.   *72*
Per ch'io al duca mio: "Fa che tu trovi
   alcun ch'al fatto o al nome si conosca,
   e li occhi, sì andando, intorno movi."   *75*
E un che 'ntese la parola tosca,
   di retro a noi gridò: "Tenete i piedi,
   voi che correte sì per l'aura fosca!   *78*

as my master went down that bank, carrying
me along upon his breast, not as his com-
panion but as his child. Scarcely had his feet
reached the bed of the depth below when
they were on the height directly over us; but
there was nothing to fear, for the high Provi-
dence which willed to set them as ministers
of the fifth ditch deprives them all of power
to leave it.

There below we found a painted people
who were going round with very slow steps,
weeping and in their looks tired and over-
come. They wore cloaks with cowls down
over their eyes, of the cut that is made for
the monks of Cluny, so gilded outside that
they dazzle, but within, all of lead, and so
heavy that those Frederick imposed were of
straw. O toilsome mantle for eternity!

We turned, ever to the left, along with
them, intent on their dreary weeping. But,
because of the load, that tired folk came on
so slowly that our company was new at every
step we took; wherefore I said to my guide,
"Pray find someone who may be known by
deed or name, looking round as we go." And
one who caught the Tuscan speech cried after
us, "Stay your steps, you who run thus
through the dusky air!

Forse ch'avrai da me quel che tu chiedi."
　　Onde 'l duca si volse e disse: "Aspetta,
　　e poi secondo il suo passo procedi."　　　　　　*81*
Ristetti, e vidi due mostrar gran fretta
　　de l'animo, col viso, d'esser meco;
　　ma tardavali 'l carco e la via stretta.　　　　　*84*
Quando fuor giunti, assai con l'occhio bieco
　　mi rimiraron sanza far parola;
　　poi si volsero in sé, e dicean seco:　　　　　　*87*
"Costui par vivo a l'atto de la gola;
　　e s'e' son morti, per qual privilegio
　　vanno scoperti de la grave stola?"　　　　　　*90*
Poi disser me: "O Tosco, ch'al collegio
　　de l'ipocriti tristi se' venuto,
　　dir chi tu se' non avere in dispregio."　　　　*93*
E io a loro: "I' fui nato e cresciuto
　　sovra 'l bel fiume d'Arno a la gran villa,
　　e son col corpo ch'i' ho sempre avuto.　　　　*96*
Ma voi chi siete, a cui tanto distilla
　　quant' i' veggio dolor giù per le guance?
　　e che pena è in voi che sì sfavilla?"　　　　　*99*
E l'un rispuose a me: "Le cappe rance
　　son di piombo sì grosse, che li pesi
　　fan così cigolar le lor bilance.　　　　　　　*102*
Frati godenti fummo, e bolognesi;
　　io Catalano e questi Loderingo
　　nomati, e da tua terra insieme presi　　　　　*105*
come suole esser tolto un uom solingo,
　　per conservar sua pace; e fummo tali,
　　ch'ancor si pare intorno dal Gardingo."　　　　*108*

Perhaps you shall obtain from me what you
ask." At which my leader turned to me and
said, "Wait, and then proceed at his pace." I
stopped, and saw two show by their look
great haste of mind to be with me, but their
load and the narrow way retarded them.
When they came up, with eye askance they
gazed at me awhile without uttering a word;
then, turning to each other, they said, "This
man seems alive, by the action of his throat;
and if they are dead, by what privilege do
they go divested of the heavy stole?" Then
they said to me, "O Tuscan, who are come
to the assembly of the sad hypocrites, do not
disdain to tell us who you are."

And I to them, "I was born and grew up
on the fair stream of Arno, at the great town,
and I am in the body that I have always had;
but you, who are you, down whose cheeks
distils such woe as I see? And what penalty
is this upon you that glitters so?" And one
of them replied to me, "The orange cloaks
are of lead so thick that the weight thus
causes their scales to creak. We were Jovial
Friars, and Bolognese: I named Catalano,
and he Loderingo, and by your city chosen
together, as one man alone is usually chosen,
to maintain the peace; and we were such,
that it still appears around the Gardingo."

Io cominciai: "O frati, i vostri mali . . .";
   ma più non dissi, ch'a l'occhio mi corse
   un, crucifisso in terra con tre pali.   *111*
Quando mi vide, tutto si distorse,
   soffiando ne la barba con sospiri;
   e 'l frate Catalan, ch'a ciò s'accorse,   *114*
mi disse: "Quel confitto che tu miri,
   consigliò i Farisei che convenia
   porre un uom per lo popolo a' martìri.   *117*
Attraversato è, nudo, ne la via,
   come tu vedi, ed è mestier ch'el senta
   qualunque passa, come pesa, pria.   *120*
E a tal modo il socero si stenta
   in questa fossa, e li altri dal concilio
   che fu per li Giudei mala sementa."   *123*
Allor vid' io maravigliar Virgilio
   sovra colui ch'era disteso in croce
   tanto vilmente ne l'etterno essilio.   *126*
Poscia drizzò al frate cotal voce:
   "Non vi dispiaccia, se vi lece, dirci
   s'a la man destra giace alcuna foce   *129*
onde noi amendue possiamo uscirci,
   sanza costrigner de li angeli neri
   che vegnan d'esto fondo a dipartirci."   *132*
Rispuose adunque: "Più che tu non speri
   s'appressa un sasso che da la gran cerchia
   si move e varca tutt' i vallon feri,   *135*
salvo che 'n questo è rotto e nol coperchia;
   montar potrete su per la ruina,
   che giace in costa e nel fondo soperchia."   *138*

I began, "O Friars, your evil . . ."—but I said no more, for there caught my eye one crucified on the ground with three stakes. When he saw me he writhed all over, blowing in his beard with sighs; and Fra Catalano, observing this, said to me, "That transfixed one you are gazing at counseled the Pharisees that it was expedient to put one man to torture for the people. He is stretched out naked across the way, as you see, and needs must feel the weight of each that passes; and in like fashion is his father-in-law racked in this ditch, and the others of that council which was a seed of evil for the Jews." Then I saw Virgil wonder over him who was thus outstretched, as on a cross, so vilely in the eternal exile. Then he directed his words to the friar, "May it not displease you, if it be permitted, to tell us if there lies any passage on the right by which we two can get out of here, without requiring some of the black angels to come to deliver us from this bottom."

He then replied, "Nearer than you hope is a ridge of rock that starts from the great encircling wall and spans all the savage valleys, save that at this one it is broken down and does not cover it; you will be able to mount up by the ruin that lies against the side and piles up at the bottom."

Lo duca stette un poco a testa china;
   poi disse: "Mal contava la bisogna
   colui che i peccator di qua uncina."   *141*
E 'l frate: "Io udi' già dire a Bologna
   del diavol vizi assai, tra ' quali udi'
   ch'elli è bugiardo e padre di menzogna."   *144*
Appresso il duca a gran passi sen gì,
   turbato un poco d'ira nel sembiante;
   ond' io da li 'ncarcati mi parti'
dietro a le poste de le care piante.   *148*

My leader stood for a moment with bowed head, then said, "He that hooks the sinners back yonder gave a poor account of the matter." And the friar, "At Bologna once I heard it said that the devil has many vices, among which I heard that he is a liar and the father of lies."

Then my guide went on with great strides, somewhat disturbed with anger in his look; and I departed from those burdened souls, following the prints of the beloved feet.

INFERNO

In QUELLA parte del giovanetto anno
 che 'l sole i crin sotto l'Aquario tempra
  e già le notti al mezzo dì sen vanno,   *3*
quando la brina in su la terra assempra
 l'imagine di sua sorella bianca,
  ma poco dura a la sua penna tempra,   *6*
lo villanello a cui la roba manca,
 si leva, e guarda, e vede la campagna
  biancheggiar tutta; ond' ei si batte l'anca,   *9*
ritorna in casa, e qua e là si lagna,
 come 'l tapin che non sa che si faccia;
  poi riede, e la speranza ringavagna,   *12*
veggendo 'l mondo aver cangiata faccia
 in poco d'ora, e prende suo vincastro
  e fuor le pecorelle a pascer caccia.   *15*
Così mi fece sbigottir lo mastro
 quand' io li vidi sì turbar la fronte,
  e così tosto al mal giunse lo 'mpiastro;   *18*

CANTO XXIV

In that part of the youthful year when the sun tempers his locks beneath Aquarius, and the nights already wane towards half the day, when the hoarfrost copies on the ground the image of his white sister, but the temper of his pen lasts but short while—the peasant, whose fodder fails, rises and looks out and sees the fields all white; at which he smites his thigh, returns indoors and grumbles to and fro, like the poor wretch who knows not what to do; then comes out again and recovers hope when he sees how in but little time the world has changed its face, and taking his crook, drives forth his sheep to pasture. Thus my master caused me dismay when I saw his brow so troubled, and thus quickly came the plaster to the hurt.

ché, come noi venimmo al guasto ponte,
 lo duca a me si volse con quel piglio
 dolce ch'io vidi prima a piè del monte.   *21*
Le braccia aperse, dopo alcun consiglio
 eletto seco riguardando prima
 ben la ruina, e diedemi di piglio.   *24*
E come quei ch'adopera ed estima,
 che sempre par che 'nnanzi si proveggia,
 così, levando me sù ver' la cima   *27*
d'un ronchione, avvisava un'altra scheggia
 dicendo: "Sovra quella poi t'aggrappa;
 ma tenta pria s'è tal ch'ella ti reggia."   *30*
Non era via da vestito di cappa,
 ché noi a pena, ei lieve e io sospinto,
 potavam sù montar di chiappa in chiappa.   *33*
E se non fosse che da quel precinto
 più che da l'altro era la costa corta,
 non so di lui, ma io sarei ben vinto.   *36*
Ma perché Malebolge inver' la porta
 del bassissimo pozzo tutta pende,
 lo sito di ciascuna valle porta   *39*
che l'una costa surge e l'altra scende;
 noi pur venimmo al fine in su la punta
 onde l'ultima pietra si scoscende.   *42*
La lena m'era del polmon sì munta
 quand' io fui sù, ch'i' non potea più oltre,
 anzi m'assisi ne la prima giunta.   *45*
"Omai convien che tu così ti spoltre,"
 disse 'l maestro; "ché, seggendo in piuma,
 in fama non si vien, né sotto coltre;   *48*

For when we came to the ruined bridge my
leader turned to me with that sweet look
which I saw first at the foot of the mountain.
After taking some counsel with himself, look-
ing first well at the ruin, he opened his arms
and laid hold of me. And like one who works
and reckons, always seeming to provide be-
forehand, so, while lifting me up toward the
top of one great rock, he was looking out
another crag, saying, "Grapple next on that,
but try first if it will bear you." It was no
road for anyone wearing the mantle, for we—
he light and I pushed on—could scarcely
mount from jag to jag. And had it not been
that on that dike the slope was shorter than
on the other, I know not about him, but I
should have been quite vanquished. But be-
cause all Malebolge inclines toward the mouth
of the nethermost well, the site of each valley
is such that one side is higher and the other
lower. We, however, came at length to the
point where the last stone is broken off. The
breath was so spent from my lungs, when I
was up, that I could go no farther, but sat
down as soon as I got there.

"Now it behooves you thus to cast off
sloth," said my master, "for sitting on down
or under coverlet, no one comes to fame,

sanza la qual chi sua vita consuma,
  cotal vestigio in terra di sé lascia,
  qual fummo in aere e in acqua la schiuma.   51
E però leva sù; vinci l'ambascia
  con l'animo che vince ogne battaglia,
  se col suo grave corpo non s'accascia.   54
Più lunga scala convien che si saglia;
  non basta da costoro esser partito.
  Se tu mi 'ntendi, or fa sì che ti vaglia."   57
Leva'mi allor, mostrandomi fornito
  meglio di lena ch'i' non mi sentia,
  e dissi: "Va, ch'i' son forte e ardito."   60
Su per lo scoglio prendemmo la via,
  ch'era ronchioso, stretto e malagevole,
  ed erto più assai che quel di pria.   63
Parlando andava per non parer fievole;
  onde una voce uscì de l'altro fosso,
  a parole formar disconvenevole.   66
Non so che disse, ancor che sovra 'l dosso
  fossi de l'arco già che varca quivi;
  ma chi parlava ad ire parea mosso.   69
Io era vòlto in giù, ma li occhi vivi
  non poteano ire al fondo per lo scuro;
  per ch'io: "Maestro, fa che tu arrivi   72
da l'altro cinghio e dismontiam lo muro;
  ché, com' i' odo quinci e non intendo,
  così giù veggio e neente affiguro."   75
"Altra risposta," disse, "non ti rendo
  se non lo far; ché la dimanda onesta
  si de' seguir con l'opera tacendo."   78

without which whoso consumes his life leaves such vestige of himself on earth as smoke in air or foam on water. Rise, therefore; conquer your panting with the soul that wins every battle, if with its heavy body it sinks not down. A longer ladder must be climbed; it is not enough to have left these spirits. If you understand me, now act that it may profit you." I then rose, showing myself better furnished with breath than I felt, and said, "Go on, for I am strong and resolute."

We took the way up the ridge, which was rugged, narrow, and difficult, and far steeper than the last; and I talked as I went, so as not to seem exhausted, when a voice, ill-suited for forming words, came out from the next ditch. I do not know what it said, though I was already on the crown of the arch that crosses there, but he who was speaking seemed to be moving. I had turned my eyes downward, but because of the darkness my keen gaze could not reach the bottom; wherefore I said, "Master, pray go on to the next belt, and let us descend the wall, for from this point not only do I hear without understanding, but I look down and make out nothing."

"Other reply," he said, "I do not give you than the doing, for a fit request should be followed by the deed in silence."

Noi discendemmo il ponte da la testa
  dove s'aggiugne con l'ottava ripa,
  e poi mi fu la bolgia manifesta: *81*
e vidivi entro terribile stipa
  di serpenti, e di sì diversa mena
  che la memoria il sangue ancor mi scipa.   *84*
Più non si vanti Libia con sua rena;
  ché se chelidri, iaculi e faree
  produce, e cencri con anfisibena,   *87*
né tante pestilenzie né sì ree
  mostrò già mai con tutta l'Etïopia
  né con ciò che di sopra al Mar Rosso èe.   *90*
Tra questa cruda e tristissima copia
  corrëan genti nude e spaventate,
  sanza sperar pertugio o elitropia: *93*
con serpi le man dietro avean legate;
  quelle ficcavan per le ren la coda
  e 'l capo, ed eran dinanzi aggroppate.   *96*
Ed ecco a un ch'era da nostra proda,
  s'avventò un serpente che 'l trafisse
  là dove 'l collo a le spalle s'annoda.   *99*
Né o sì tosto mai né 1 si scrisse,
  com' el s'accese e arse, e cener tutto
  convenne che cascando divenisse;   *102*
e poi che fu a terra sì distrutto,
  la polver si raccolse per sé stessa
  e 'n quel medesmo ritornò di butto.   *105*
Così per li gran savi si confessa
  che la fenice more e poi rinasce,
  quando al cinquecentesimo anno appressa;   *108*

We descended at the end of the bridge where it joins the eighth bank, and then the ditch was manifest to me: I saw within it a fearful throng of serpents, of kinds so strange that the memory of it still chills my blood. Let Libya with her sands vaunt herself no more! for though she bring forth chelydri, jaculi, and phareae, and cenchres with amphisbaena, she never, with all Ethiopia, nor with the land that lies on the Red Sea, showed plagues so numerous or malignant. Amid this cruel and most dismal swarm were people running naked and terrified, without hope of hiding-place or heliotrope. They had their hands bound behind with serpents: these thrust through their loins the head and tail, which were knotted in front.

And lo! at one who was near our bank darted a serpent that transfixed him there where the neck is joined to the shoulders, and never was *o* or *i* written so fast as he took fire and burned, and must sink down all turned to ashes; and when he was thus destroyed on the ground, the dust drew together of itself and at once resumed the former shape; thus by great sages it is affirmed that the Phoenix dies and is born again when it approaches its five-hundredth year.

erba né biado in sua vita non pasce,
   ma sol d'incenso lagrime e d'amomo,
   e nardo e mirra son l'ultime fasce.   *111*

E qual è quel che cade, e non sa como,
   per forza di demon ch'a terra il tira,
   o d'altra oppilazion che lega l'omo,   *114*

quando si leva, che 'ntorno si mira
   tutto smarrito de la grande angoscia
   ch'elli ha sofferta, e guardando sospira: *117*

tal era 'l peccator levato poscia.
   Oh potenza di Dio, quant' è severa,
   che cotai colpi per vendetta croscia!   *120*

Lo duca il domandò poi chi ello era;
   per ch'ei rispuose: "Io piovvi di Toscana,
   poco tempo è, in questa gola fiera.   *123*

Vita bestial mi piacque e non umana,
   sì come a mul ch'i' fui; son Vanni Fucci
   bestia, e Pistoia mi fu degna tana."   *126*

E ïo al duca: "Dilli che non mucci,
   e domanda che colpa qua giù 'l pinse;
   ch'io 'l vidi omo di sangue e di crucci."   *129*

E 'l peccator, che 'ntese, non s'infinse,
   ma drizzò verso me l'animo e 'l volto,
   e di trista vergogna si dipinse;   *132*

poi disse: "Più mi duol che tu m'hai colto
   ne la miseria dove tu mi vedi,
   che quando fui de l'altra vita tolto.   *135*

Io non posso negar quel che tu chiedi;
   in giù son messo tanto perch' io fui
   ladro a la sagrestia d'i belli arredi,   *138*

In its life it feeds not on herb or grain, but only on tears of incense and amomum; and nard and myrrh are its last winding-sheet.

And as one who falls and knows not how, by force of some devil dragging him to the ground, or by some other obstruction that binds a man, who, when he rises, stares about him, all bewildered by the great anguish he has suffered and, looking, sighs: such was that sinner when he rose.

Oh power of God! how severe it is, that showers down such blows for vengeance!

My leader then asked him who he was; to which he answered, "Short while ago I rained down from Tuscany into this fierce gullet. A bestial life, not human, pleased me, mule that I was. I am Vanni Fucci, beast, and Pistoia was my fitting den." And I to my leader, "Tell him not to slip away, and ask what sin thrust him down here, for I have seen him a man of blood and rage." And the sinner, who heard, did not dissemble, but directed toward me his mind and look, and colored with dismal shame, then said, "It grieves me more that you have caught me in the misery where you see me than when I was taken from the other life. I cannot refuse you what you ask. I am put down so far because I was a thief in the sacristy of the fair adornments:

e falsamente già fu apposto altrui.
   Ma perché di tal vista tu non godi,
se mai sarai di fuor da' luoghi bui,   *141*
apri li orecchi al mio annunzio, e odi.
   Pistoia in pria d'i Neri si dimagra;
poi Fiorenza rinova gente e modi.   *144*
Tragge Marte vapor di Val di Magra
ch'è di torbidi nuvoli involuto;
e con tempesta impetüosa e agra   *147*
sovra Campo Picen fia combattuto;
   ond' ei repente spezzerà la nebbia,
sì ch'ogne Bianco ne sarà feruto.
E detto l'ho perché doler ti debbia!"   *151*

a deed that was once falsely put upon an-
other. But that you may not rejoice in this
sight, if ever you escape from these dark
regions, open your ears and hear what I an-
nounce: Pistoia first strips herself of Blacks;
then Florence renews her people and her
ways. Mars draws a vapor from Val di Magra
which is wrapt in turbid clouds, and with
impetuous and bitter storm there shall be
fighting on Campo Piceno, whence suddenly
it shall rend the mist, so that every White
shall be struck by it. And I have said this
that it may grieve you."

INFERNO

Aʟ ꜰɪɴᴇ de le sue parole il ladro
le mani alzò con amendue le fiche,
gridando: "Togli, Dio, ch'a te le squadro!"   *3*
Da indi in qua mi fuor le serpi amiche,
perch' una li s'avvolse allora al collo,
come dicesse "Non vo' che più diche";   *6*
e un'altra a le braccia, e rilegollo,
ribadendo sé stessa sì dinanzi,
che non potea con esse dare un crollo.   *9*
Ahi Pistoia, Pistoia, ché non stanzi
d'incenerarti sì che più non duri,
poi che 'n mal fare il seme tuo avanzi?   *12*
Per tutt' i cerchi de lo 'nferno scuri
non vidi spirto in Dio tanto superbo,
non quel che cadde a Tebe giù da' muri.   *15*
El si fuggì che non parlò più verbo;
e io vidi un centauro pien di rabbia
venir chiamando: "Ov' è, ov' è l'acerbo?"   *18*

CANTO XXV

At the end of his words the thief raised up his hands with both the figs, crying, "Take them, God, for I aim them at you!" From this time forth the serpents were my friends, for one then coiled itself about his neck, as if it said, "You shall say no more," and another about his arms and bound him again, so riveting itself in front that he could not give a jog with them.

Ah, Pistoia, Pistoia! why do you not decree to turn yourself to ashes and to last no longer, since you surpass your own seed in evil-doing? Through all the dark circles of Hell I saw no spirit so proud against God, not him who fell from the walls at Thebes.

He fled, speaking no more; and I saw a centaur full of rage come shouting, "Where is he, where is the unripe one?"

259

Maremma non cred' io che tante n'abbia,
   quante bisce elli avea su per la groppa
   infin ove comincia nostra labbia.   *21*
Sovra le spalle, dietro da la coppa,
   con l'ali aperte li giacea un draco;
   e quello affuoca qualunque s'intoppa.   *24*
Lo mio maestro disse: "Questi è Caco,
   che, sotto 'l sasso di monte Aventino,
   di sangue fece spesse volte laco.   *27*
Non va co' suoi fratei per un cammino,
   per lo furto che frodolente fece
   del grande armento ch'elli ebbe a vicino;   *30*
onde cessar le sue opere biece
   sotto la mazza d'Ercule, che forse
   gliene diè cento, e non sentì le diece."   *33*
Mentre che sì parlava, ed el trascorse,
   e tre spiriti venner sotto noi,
   de' quai né io né 'l duca mio s'accorse,   *36*
se non quando gridar: "Chi siete voi?"
   per che nostra novella si ristette,
   e intendemmo pur ad essi poi.   *39*
Io non li conoscea; ma ei seguette,
   come suol seguitar per alcun caso,
   che l'un nomar un altro convenette,   *42*
dicendo: "Cianfa dove fia rimaso?"
   per ch'io, acciò che 'l duca stesse attento,
   mi puosi 'l dito su dal mento al naso.   *45*
Se tu se' or, lettore, a creder lento
   ciò ch'io dirò, non sarà maraviglia,
   ché io che 'l vidi, a pena il mi consento.   *48*

Maremma, I do believe, has not so many
snakes as he upon his croup up to where our
form begins; and on his shoulders behind
the nape lay a dragon with outstretched wings
that sets on fire whomever it encounters. My
master said, "That is Cacus, who beneath the
rock of Mount Aventine full often made a
lake of blood. He goes not with his brothers
on one same road, because of the cunning
theft he made of the great herd that lay near
him; and for this his crooked ways were
ended under the club of Hercules, who
dealt him perhaps a hundred blows and he
felt not ten of them."

While he thus spoke, the centaur ran past,
and there came below us three spirits whom
neither I nor my guide perceived till they
cried out, "Who are you?" whereon we broke
off our talk and gave heed to them alone.
I did not know them; but it happened, as
often happens by some chance, that one had
occasion to name another, saying, "Where
can Cianfa be?" Wherefore, in order that my
leader might remain attentive, I placed my
finger upwards from my chin to my nose.

If, reader, you are now slow to credit that
which I shall tell, it will be no wonder, for I
who saw it do scarcely admit it to myself.

Com' io tenea levate in lor le ciglia,
  e un serpente con sei piè si lancia
    dinanzi a l'uno, e tutto a lui s'appiglia.   *51*
Co' piè di mezzo li avvinse la pancia
  e con li anterïor le braccia prese;
    poi li addentò e l'una e l'altra guancia;   *54*
li diretani a le cosce distese,
  e miseli la coda tra 'mbedue
    e dietro per le ren sù la ritese.   *57*
Ellera abbarbicata mai non fue
  ad alber sì, come l'orribil fiera
    per l'altrui membra avviticchiò le sue.   *60*
Poi s'appiccar, come di calda cera
  fossero stati, e mischiar lor colore,
    né l'un né l'altro già parea quel ch'era: *63*
come procede innanzi da l'ardore,
  per lo papiro suso, un color bruno
    che non è nero ancora e 'l bianco more.   *66*
Li altri due 'l riguardavano, e ciascuno
  gridava: "Omè, Agnel, come ti muti!
    Vedi che già non se' né due né uno."   *69*
Già eran li due capi un divenuti,
  quando n'apparver due figure miste
    in una faccia, ov' eran due perduti.   *72*
Fersi le braccia due di quattro liste;
  le cosce con le gambe e 'l ventre e 'l casso
    divenner membra che non fuor mai viste.   *75*
Ogne primaio aspetto ivi era casso:
  due e nessun l'imagine perversa
    parea; e tal sen gio con lento passo.   *78*

While I kept my eyes on them, lo! a serpent with six feet darts up in front of one
and fastens on him all over. With the middle
feet it clasped the belly, and with its fore
feet took his arms, then struck its teeth in
one and the other cheek; its hind feet it
spread upon his thighs, and put its tail between them, and bent it upwards on his
loins behind. Ivy was never so rooted to a
tree as the horrid beast entwined its own
limbs round the other's; then, as if they had
been of hot wax, they stuck together and
mixed their colors, and neither the one nor
the other now seemed what it was at first:
even as in advance of the flame a dark color
moves across the paper, which is not yet black
and the white dies away. The other two
were looking on, and each cried, "Oh me,
Agnello, how you change! Lo, you are already neither two nor one!"

Now the two heads had become one, when
we saw the two shapes mixed in one face,
where both were lost. Two arms were made
of the four lengths; the thighs with the
legs, the belly and the chest, became members
that were never seen before. Each former
feature was blotted out: the perverse image
seemed both and neither, and such, with
slow pace, it moved away.

Come 'l ramarro sotto la gran fersa
  dei dì canicular, cangiando sepe,
  folgore par se la via attraversa,   *81*
sì pareva, venendo verso l'epe
  de li altri due, un serpentello acceso,
  livido e nero come gran di pepe;   *84*
e quella parte onde prima è preso
  nostro alimento, a l'un di lor trafisse;
  poi cadde giuso innanzi lui disteso.   *87*
Lo trafitto 'l mirò, ma nulla disse;
  anzi, co' piè fermati, sbadigliava
  pur come sonno o febbre l'assalisse.   *90*
Elli 'l serpente e quei lui riguardava;
  l'un per la piaga e l'altro per la bocca
  fummavan forte, e 'l fummo si scontrava.   *93*
Taccia Lucano omai là dov' e' tocca
  del misero Sabello e di Nasidio,
  e attenda a udir quel ch'or si scocca.   *96*
Taccia di Cadmo e d'Aretusa Ovidio,
  ché se quello in serpente e quella in fonte
  converte poetando, io non lo 'nvidio;   *99*
ché due nature mai a fronte a fronte
  non trasmutò sì ch'amendue le forme
  a cambiar lor matera fosser pronte.   *102*
Insieme si rispuosero a tai norme,
  che 'l serpente la coda in forca fesse,
  e 'l feruto ristrinse insieme l'orme.   *105*
Le gambe con le cosce seco stesse
  s'appiccar sì, che 'n poco la giuntura
  non facea segno alcun che si paresse.   *108*

As the lizard under the great scourge of the dog days, darting from hedge to hedge, seems a lightning-flash, if it cross the way, so appeared, making for the bellies of the other two, a small fiery serpent, livid and black as a peppercorn; and it transfixed in one of them that part by which we first receive our nourishment, then fell down before him, stretched out. The transfixed one gazed at it, but said nothing, only standing there yawning as if sleep or fever had come upon him. He eyed the reptile, the reptile him; the one from his wound, the other from its mouth, smoked violently, and their smoke met.

Let Lucan now be silent, where he tells of the wretched Sabellus and of Nasidius, and let him wait to hear what now comes forth. Concerning Cadmus and Arethusa let Ovid be silent, for if he, poetizing, converts the one into a serpent and the other into a fountain, I envy him not; for two natures front to front he never so transmuted that both forms were prompt to exchange their substance. They mutually responded in such a way that the reptile cleft its tail into a fork, and the wounded one drew his feet together. The legs and thighs so stuck together that soon no mark of the juncture could be seen;

Togliea la coda fessa la figura
   che si perdeva là, e la sua pelle
   si facea molle, e quella di là dura.   *111*
Io vidi intrar le braccia per l'ascelle,
   e i due piè de la fiera, ch'eran corti,
   tanto allungar quanto accorciavan quelle.   *114*
Poscia li piè di rietro, insieme attorti,
   diventaron lo membro che l'uom cela,
   e 'l misero del suo n'avea due porti.   *117*
Mentre che 'l fummo l'uno e l'altro vela
   di color novo, e genera 'l pel suso
   per l'una parte e da l'altra il dipela,   *120*
l'un si levò e l'altro cadde giuso,
   non torcendo però le lucerne empie,
   sotto le quai ciascun cambiava muso.   *123*
Quel ch'era dritto, il trasse ver' le tempie,
   e di troppa matera ch'in là venne
   uscir li orecchi de le gote scempie;   *126*
ciò che non corse in dietro e si ritenne
   di quel soverchio, fé naso a la faccia
   e le labbra ingrossò quanto convenne.   *129*
Quel che giacëa, il muso innanzi caccia,
   e li orecchi ritira per la testa
   come face le corna la lumaccia;   *132*
e la lingua, ch'avëa unita e presta
   prima a parlar, si fende, e la forcuta
   ne l'altro si richiude; e 'l fummo resta.   *135*
L'anima ch'era fiera divenuta,
   suffolando si fugge per la valle,
   e l'altro dietro a lui parlando sputa.   *138*

the cloven tail took on the shape that was lost in the other; and its skin grew soft, the other's hard. I saw the arms drawing in at the armpits, and the brute's two feet, which were short, lengthening out in proportion as the other's arms were shortening. Then the hind paws, twisted together, became the member that man conceals, and from his the wretch had put forth two feet. While the smoke veils the one and the other with a new color, and generates hair on the one part and strips it from the other, the one rose upright and the other fell down, but neither turned aside the baleful lamps beneath which each was changing his muzzle. He that was erect drew his in toward the temples, and from the excess of matter that came in there the ears issued from the smooth cheeks; that which did not run back, but was retained, made of that excess a nose for the face and thickened the lips to due size. He that lay prone drives the snout forward and draws the ears back into the head as the snail does its horns; and the tongue, which before was whole and fit for speech, divides, and in the other the forked tongue joins up; and the smoke stops. The soul that was become a brute flees hissing along the valley; and the other, speaking, spits after it.

Poscia li volse le novelle spalle,
   e disse a l'altro: "I' vo' che Buoso corra,
   com' ho fatt' io, carpon per questo calle."   *141*
Così vid' io la settima zavorra
   mutare e trasmutare; e qui mi scusi
   la novità se fior la penna abborra.   *144*
E avvegna che li occhi miei confusi
   fossero alquanto e l'animo smagato,
   non poter quei fuggirsi tanto chiusi,   *147*
ch'i' non scorgessi ben Puccio Sciancato;
   ed era quel che sol, di tre compagni
   che venner prima, non era mutato;
l'altr' era quel che tu, Gaville, piagni.   *151*

Then he turned on it his new shoulders, and said to the third, "I'll have Buoso run on all fours along this road, as I have done!"

Thus I saw the seventh ballast change and transmute—and here let the novelty be my excuse, if my pen goes aught astray. And though my eyes were somewhat confused and my mind bewildered, these could not flee so covertly but that I clearly distinguished Puccio Sciancato, and it was he alone, of the three companions that came first, who was not changed; the other was he whom you, Gaville, lament.

INFERNO

Godi, Fiorenza, poi che se' sì grande
    che per mare e per terra batti l'ali,
    e per lo 'nferno tuo nome si spande!   *3*
Tra li ladron trovai cinque cotali
    tuoi cittadini onde mi ven vergogna,
    e tu in grande orranza non ne sali.   *6*
Ma se presso al mattin del ver si sogna,
    tu sentirai, di qua da picciol tempo,
    di quel che Prato, non ch'altri, t'agogna.   *9*
E se già fosse, non saria per tempo.
    Così foss' ei, da che pur esser dee!
    ché più mi graverà, com' più m'attempo.   *12*
Noi ci partimmo, e su per le scalee
    che n'avea fatto i borni a scender pria,
    rimontò 'l duca mio e trasse mee;   *15*
e proseguendo la solinga via,
    tra le schegge e tra ' rocchi de lo scoglio
    lo piè sanza la man non si spedia.   *18*

CANTO XXVI

Rejoice, O Florence, since you are so great that over sea and land you beat your wings, and your name is spread through Hell! Among the thieves I found five of your citizens, such that shame comes to me—and you rise thereby to no great honor. But if near morning our dreams are true, you shall feel ere long what Prato, as well as others, craves for you. And if it were already come, it would not be too soon. Would it were, since indeed it must, for it will weigh the more on me the more I age.

We departed thence, and by the stairs which the jutting rocks had made for our descent before, my leader remounted and drew me up; and pursuing the solitary way among the jags and rocks of the ridge, the foot could not advance without the hand.

Allor mi dolsi, e ora mi ridoglio
   quando drizzo la mente a ciò ch'io vidi,
   e più lo 'ngegno affreno ch'i' non soglio,   *21*
perché non corra che virtù nol guidi;
   sì che, se stella bona o miglior cosa
   m'ha dato 'l ben, ch'io stessi nol m'invidi.   *24*
Quante 'l villan ch'al poggio si riposa,
   nel tempo che colui che 'l mondo schiara
   la faccia sua a noi tien meno ascosa,   *27*
come la mosca cede a la zanzara,
   vede lucciole giù per la vallea,
   forse colà dov' e' vendemmia e ara: *30*
di tante fiamme tutta risplendea
   l'ottava bolgia, sì com' io m'accorsi
   tosto che fui là 've 'l fondo parea.   *33*
E qual colui che si vengiò con li orsi
   vide 'l carro d'Elia al dipartire,
   quando i cavalli al cielo erti levorsi,   *36*
che nol potea sì con li occhi seguire,
   ch'el vedesse altro che la fiamma sola,
   sì come nuvoletta, in sù salire: *39*
tal si move ciascuna per la gola
   del fosso, ché nessuna mostra 'l furto,
   e ogne fiamma un peccatore invola.   *42*
Io stava sovra 'l ponte a veder surto,
   sì che s'io non avessi un ronchion preso,
   caduto sarei giù sanz' esser urto.   *45*
E 'l duca, che mi vide tanto atteso,
   disse: "Dentro dai fuochi son li spirti;
   catun si fascia di quel ch'elli è inceso."   *48*

I sorrowed then, and sorrow now again, when I turn my mind to what I saw; and I curb my genius more than I am wont, lest it run where virtue does not guide it; so that, if a kindly star or something better has granted me the good, I may not grudge myself that gift.

As many as the fireflies which the peasant, resting on the hill—in the season when he that lights the world least hides his face from us, and at the hour when the fly yields to the mosquito—sees down along the valley, there perhaps where he gathers the grapes and tills: with so many flames the eighth ditch was all agleam, as I perceived as soon as I came where the bottom could be seen. And as he who was avenged by the bears saw Elijah's chariot at its departure, when the horses rose erect to heaven—for he could not so follow it with his eyes as to see aught save the flame alone, like a little cloud ascending: so each flame moves along the gullet of the ditch, for not one shows its theft, and each steals away a sinner.

I was standing on the bridge, having risen up to see, so that if I had not laid hold of a rock I should have fallen below without a push; and my leader, who saw me so intent, said, "Within the fires are the spirits: each swathes himself with that which burns him."

"Maestro mio," rispuos' io, "per udirti
    son io più certo; ma già m'era avviso
    che così fosse, e già voleva dirti: *51*
chi è 'n quel foco che vien sì diviso
    di sopra, che par surger de la pira
    dov' Eteòcle col fratel fu miso?"   *54*
Rispuose a me: "Là dentro si martira
    Ulisse e Dïomede, e così insieme
    a la vendetta vanno come a l'ira;   *57*
e dentro da la lor fiamma si geme
    l'agguato del caval che fé la porta
    onde uscì de' Romani il gentil seme.   *60*
Piangevisi entro l'arte per che, morta,
    Deïdamìa ancor si duol d'Achille,
    e del Palladio pena vi si porta."   *63*
"S'ei posson dentro da quelle faville
    parlar," diss' io, "maestro, assai ten priego
    e ripriego, che 'l priego vaglia mille,   *66*
che non mi facci de l'attender niego
    fin che la fiamma cornuta qua vegna;
    vedi che del disio ver' lei mi piego!"   *69*
Ed elli a me: "La tua preghiera è degna
    di molta loda, e io però l'accetto;
    ma fa che la tua lingua si sostegna.   *72*
Lascia parlare a me, ch'i' ho concetto
    ciò che tu vuoi; ch'ei sarebbero schivi,
    perch' e' fuor greci, forse del tuo detto."   *75*
Poi che la fiamma fu venuta quivi
    dove parve al mio duca tempo e loco,
    in questa forma lui parlare audivi: *78*

"Master," I replied, "I am the more certain for hearing you, but already I thought it was so, and already I wanted to ask: who is in that fire which comes so divided at its top that it seems to rise from the pyre where Eteocles was laid with his brother?"

He answered me, "Therewithin are tormented Ulysses and Diomedes, and they go together thus under the vengeance as once under the wrath; and in their flame they groan for the ambush of the horse which made the gate by which the noble seed of the Romans went forth; within it they lament the craft, because of which the dead Deidamia still mourns Achilles, and there for the Palladium they bear the penalty."

"If they can speak within those sparks," I said, "master, I earnestly pray you, and pray again, that my prayer avail a thousand, that you deny me not to wait until the horned flame comes hither: you see how with desire I bend towards it."

And he to me, "Your prayer deserves much praise and therefore I accept it; but do you restrain your tongue: leave speech to me, for I have understood what you wish—and perhaps, since they were Greeks, they would be disdainful of your words."

After the flame had come where it seemed to my leader the time and place, I heard him speak in this manner:

"O voi che siete due dentro ad un foco,
    s'io meritai di voi mentre ch'io vissi,
    s'io meritai di voi assai o poco   *81*
quando nel mondo li alti versi scrissi,
    non vi movete; ma l'un di voi dica
    dove, per lui, perduto a morir gissi."   *84*
Lo maggior corno de la fiamma antica
    cominciò a crollarsi mormorando,
    pur come quella cui vento affatica;   *87*
indi la cima qua e là menando,
    come fosse la lingua che parlasse,
    gittò voce di fuori e disse: "Quando   *90*
mi diparti' da Circe, che sottrasse
    me più d'un anno là presso a Gaeta,
    prima che sì Enëa la nomasse,   *93*
né dolcezza di figlio, né la pieta
    del vecchio padre, né 'l debito amore
    lo qual dovea Penelopè far lieta,   *96*
vincer potero dentro a me l'ardore
    ch'i' ebbi a divenir del mondo esperto
    e de li vizi umani e del valore;   *99*
ma misi me per l'alto mare aperto
    sol con un legno e con quella compagna
    picciola da la qual non fui diserto.   *102*
L'un lito e l'altro vidi infin la Spagna,
    fin nel Morrocco, e l'isola d'i Sardi,
    e l'altre che quel mare intorno bagna.   *105*
Io e' compagni eravam vecchi e tardi
    quando venimmo a quella foce stretta
    dov' Ercule segnò li suoi riguardi   *108*

"O you who are two within one fire, if I deserved of you while I lived, if I deserved of you much or little when in the world I wrote the lofty lines, move not; but let the one of you tell where he went, lost, to die."

The greater horn of the ancient flame began to wag, murmuring, like one that is beaten by a wind; then carrying to and fro its tip, as if it were a tongue that spoke, it flung forth a voice and said, "When I departed from Circe, who had detained me more than a year there near Gaeta, before Aeneas had so named it, neither fondness for my son, nor reverence for my aged father, nor the due love which would have made Penelope glad, could conquer in me the longing that I had to gain experience of the world, and of human vice and worth. But I put forth on the deep open sea with one vessel only, and with that small company which had not deserted me. The one shore and the other I saw as far as Spain, as far as Morocco, and Sardinia, and the other islands which that sea bathes round. I and my companions were old and slow when we came to that narrow outlet where Hercules set up his markers,

acció che l'uom più oltre non si metta;
   da la man destra mi lasciai Sibilia,
   da l'altra già m'avea lasciata Setta.   *111*
'O frati,' dissi, 'che per cento milia
   perigli siete giunti a l'occidente,
   a questa tanto picciola vigilia   *114*
d'i nostri sensi ch'è del rimanente
   non vogliate negar l'esperïenza,
   di retro al sol, del mondo sanza gente.   *117*
Considerate la vostra semenza:
   fatti non foste a viver come bruti,
   ma per seguir virtute e canoscenza.'   *120*
Li miei compagni fec' io sì aguti,
   con questa orazion picciola, al cammino,
   che a pena poscia li avrei ritenuti;   *123*
e volta nostra poppa nel mattino,
   de' remi facemmo ali al folle volo,
   sempre acquistando dal lato mancino.   *126*
Tutte le stelle già de l'altro polo
   vedea la notte, e 'l nostro tanto basso,
   che non surgëa fuor del marin suolo.   *129*
Cinque volte racceso e tante casso
   lo lume era di sotto da la luna,
   poi che 'ntrati eravam ne l'alto passo,   *132*
quando n'apparve una montagna, bruna
   per la distanza, e parvemi alta tanto
   quanto veduta non avëa alcuna.   *135*
Noi ci allegrammo, e tosto tornò in pianto;
   ché de la nova terra un turbo nacque
   e percosse del legno il primo canto.   *138*

that men should not pass beyond. On the right hand I left Seville, on the other I had already left Ceuta. 'O brothers,' I said, 'who through a hundred thousand dangers have reached the west, to this so brief vigil of our senses that remains to us, choose not to deny experience, following the sun, of the world that has no people. Consider your origin: you were not made to live as brutes, but to pursue virtue and knowledge.'

"With this little speech I made my companions so keen for the voyage that then I could hardly have held them back. And turning our stern to the morning, we made of our oars wings for the mad flight, always gaining on the left. The night now saw the other pole and all its stars, and ours so low that it did not rise from the ocean floor. Five times the light beneath the moon had been rekindled and as many quenched, since we had entered on the passage of the deep, when there appeared to us a mountain dark in the distance, and to me it seemed the highest I had ever seen. We rejoiced, but soon our joy was turned to grief, for from the new land a whirlwind rose and struck the forepart of the ship.

Tre volte il fé girar con tutte l'acque;
a la quarta levar la poppa in suso
e la prora ire in giù, com' altrui piacque,
infin che 'l mar fu sovra noi richiuso."   *142*

Three times it whirled her round with all the waters, and the fourth time it lifted the stern aloft and plunged the prow below, as pleased Another, till the sea closed over us."

INFERNO

Già era dritta in sù la fiamma e queta
   per non dir più, e già da noi sen gia
   con la licenza del dolce poeta,   *3*
quand' un'altra, che dietro a lei venìa,
   ne fece volger li occhi a la sua cima
   per un confuso suon che fuor n'uscia.   *6*
Come 'l bue cicilian che mugghiò prima
   col pianto di colui, e ciò fu dritto,
   che l'avea temperato con sua lima,   *9*
mugghiava con la voce de l'afflitto,
   sì che, con tutto che fosse di rame,
   pur el pareva dal dolor trafitto;   *12*
così, per non aver via né forame
   dal principio nel foco, in suo linguaggio
   si convertïan le parole grame.   *15*
Ma poscia ch'ebber colto lor vïaggio
   su per la punta, dandole quel guizzo
   che dato avea la lingua in lor passaggio,   *18*

CANTO XXVII

THE flame was already erect and quiet, having ceased to speak, and, with the consent of the gentle poet, now went away from us, when another that came on behind it made us turn our eyes to its tip for a confused sound that came from it. As the Sicilian bull (which bellowed first with the cry of him—and that was right—who had shaped it with his file) was wont to bellow with the voice of the victim, so that, though it was of brass, yet it seemed transfixed with pain: thus, having at first no course or outlet in the fire, the doleful words were changed into its language. But after they had found their way up through the tip, giving it the same vibration that the tongue had given in their passage,

udimmo dire: "O tu a cu' io drizzo
  la voce e che parlavi mo lombardo,
  dicendo 'Istra ten va, più non t'adizzo,' *21*
perch' io sia giunto forse alquanto tardo,
  non t'incresca restare a parlar meco;
  vedi che non incresce a me, e ardo! *24*
Se tu pur mo in questo mondo cieco
  caduto se' di quella dolce terra
  latina ond' io mia colpa tutta reco, *27*
dimmi se Romagnuoli han pace o guerra;
  ch'io fui d'i monti là intra Orbino
  e 'l giogo di che Tever si diserra." *30*
Io era in giuso ancora attento e chino,
  quando il mio duca mi tentò di costa,
  dicendo: "Parla tu; questi è latino." *33*
E io, ch'avea già pronta la risposta,
  sanza indugio a parlare incominciai:
  "O anima che se' là giù nascosta, *36*
Romagna tua non è, e non fu mai,
  sanza guerra ne' cuor de' suoi tiranni;
  ma 'n palese nessuna or vi lasciai. *39*
Ravenna sta come stata è molt' anni:
  l'aguglia da Polenta la si cova,
  sì che Cervia ricuopre co' suoi vanni. *42*
La terra che fé già la lunga prova
  e di Franceschi sanguinoso mucchio,
  sotto le branche verdi si ritrova. *45*
E 'l mastin vecchio e 'l nuovo da Verrucchio,
  che fecer di Montagna il mal governo,
  là dove soglion fan d'i denti succhio. *48*

we heard it say, "O you to whom I direct my voice and who just now spoke Lombard, saying, 'Now go your way, I do not urge you more,' although I have come perhaps some-what late, let it not irk you to stop and speak with me: you see it irks not me, and I am burning. If you are but now fallen into this blind world from that sweet land of Italy whence I bring all my guilt, tell me if the Romagnoles have peace or war; for I was of the mountains there between Urbino and the chain from which the Tiber springs."

I was still bent down and intent when my leader touched me on the side and said, "You speak: he is Italian." And I, who was already prepared to answer, began without delay, "O soul that are hidden down there, your Ro-magna is not, nor ever was, without war in the hearts of her tyrants; but no open war have I left there now. Ravenna is as it has been for many a year: the eagle of Polenta broods over it so that he covers Cervia with his wings. The city that once bore the long siege and made of the French a bloody heap, finds itself again under the green claws. And the old mastiff and the new of Verrucchio, who made the ill disposal of Montagna, ply their teeth where they are wont.

Le città di Lamone e di Santerno
   conduce il lïoncel dal nido bianco,
   che muta parte da la state al verno.   *51*
E quella cu' il Savio bagna il fianco,
   così com' ella sie' tra 'l piano e 'l monte,
   tra tirannia si vive e stato franco.   *54*
Ora chi se', ti priego che ne conte;
   non esser duro più ch'altri sia stato,
   se 'l nome tuo nel mondo tegna fronte."   *57*
Poscia che 'l foco alquanto ebbe rugghiato
   al modo suo, l'aguta punta mosse
   di qua, di là, e poi diè cotal fiato: *60*
"S'i' credesse che mia risposta fosse
   a persona che mai tornasse al mondo,
   questa fiamma staria sanza più scosse;   *63*
ma però che già mai di questo fondo
   non tornò vivo alcun, s'i' odo il vero,
   sanza tema d'infamia ti rispondo.   *66*
Io fui uom d'arme, e poi fui cordigliero,
   credendomi, sì cinto, fare ammenda;
   e certo il creder mio venìa intero,   *69*
se non fosse il gran prete, a cui mal prenda!,
   che mi rimise ne le prime colpe;
   e come e *quare*, voglio che m'intenda.   *72*
Mentre ch'io forma fui d'ossa e di polpe
   che la madre mi diè, l'opere mie
   non furon leonine, ma di volpe.   *75*
Li accorgimenti e le coperte vie
   io seppi tutte, e sì menai lor arte,
   ch'al fine de la terra il suono uscie.   *78*

The cities on Lamone and Santerno are
ruled by the young lion of the white lair, who
changes side from summer to winter. And
that city whose flank the Savio bathes, even
as it lies between the plain and the moun-
tain, so does it live between tyranny and
freedom. Now I pray you tell us who you
are; be not more grudging than another has
been to you, so may your name endure in the
world!"

After the flame had roared for a while in
its own fashion, the sharp point moved to
and fro, and then gave forth this breath, "If
I thought that my answer were to one who
might ever return to the world, this flame
would shake no more; but since from this
depth none ever returned alive, if what I
hear is true, I answer you without fear of
infamy.

"I was a man of arms, and then a corded
friar, trusting, so girt, to make amends; and
certainly my hope would have come full, but
for the High Priest—may ill befall him!—
who set me back in my first sins: and how
and wherefore I would have you hear from
me. While I was the form of the flesh and
bones my mother gave me, my deeds were
not those of the lion, but of the fox. I knew
all wiles and covert ways, and plied the art
of them so well that to the ends of the earth
their sound went forth.

Quando mi vidi giunto in quella parte
   di mia etade ove ciascun dovrebbe
   calar le vele e raccoglier le sarte,   *81*
ciò che pria mi piacëa, allor m'increbbe,
   e pentuto e confesso mi rendei;
   ahi miser lasso! e giovato sarebbe.   *84*
Lo principe d'i novi Farisei,
   avendo guerra presso a Laterano,
   e non con Saracin né con Giudei,   *87*
ché ciascun suo nimico era Cristiano,
   e nessun era stato a vincer Acri
   né mercatante in terra di Soldano,   *90*
né sommo officio né ordini sacri
   guardò in sé, né in me quel capestro
   che solea fare i suoi cinti più macri.   *93*
Ma come Costantin chiese Silvestro
   d'entro Siratti a guerir de la lebbre,
   così mi chiese questi per maestro   *96*
a guerir de la sua superba febbre;
   domandommi consiglio, e io tacetti
   perché le sue parole parver ebbre.   *99*
E' poi ridisse: 'Tuo cuor non sospetti;
   finor t'assolvo, e tu m'insegna fare
   sì come Penestrino in terra getti.   *102*
Lo ciel poss' io serrare e diserrare,
   come tu sai; però son due le chiavi
   che 'l mio antecessor non ebbe care.'   *105*
Allor mi pinser li argomenti gravi
   là 've 'l tacer mi fu avviso 'l peggio,
   e dissi: 'Padre, da che tu mi lavi   *108*

When I saw myself come to that part of my
life when every man should lower the sails
and coil up the ropes, that which before had
pleased me grieved me then, and with re-
pentance and confession I turned friar, and—
woe is me!—it would have availed.

"The Prince of the new Pharisees, having
war near the Lateran—and not with Saracens
or with Jews, for his every enemy was Chris-
tian, and none had been to conquer Acre, nor
been a merchant in the Soldan's land—re-
garded neither the supreme office and holy
orders in himself, nor, in me, that cord which
used to make its wearers leaner; but as Con-
stantine sought out Sylvester within Soracte
to cure his leprosy, so this one sought me out
as the doctor to cure the fever of his pride.
He asked counsel of me, and I kept silent, for
his words seemed drunken. Then he spoke
again, 'Let not your heart mistrust. I absolve
you here and now, and do you teach me how
I may cast Penestrino to the ground. I can
lock and unlock Heaven, as you know; for
the keys are two, which my predecessor did
not hold dear.' Thereon the weighty argu-
ments pushed me to where silence seemed to
me the worst, and I said, 'Father, since you
do wash me of that sin

di quel peccato ov' io mo cader deggio,
    lunga promessa con l'attender corto
    ti farà trïunfar ne l'alto seggio.'   *111*
Francesco venne poi, com' io fu' morto,
    per me; ma un d'i neri cherubini
    li disse: 'Non portar; non mi far torto.   *114*
Venir se ne dee giù tra ' miei meschini
    perché diede 'l consiglio frodolente,
    dal quale in qua stato li sono a' crini;   *117*
ch'assolver non si può chi non si pente,
    né pentere e volere insieme puossi
    per la contradizion che nol consente.'   *120*
Oh me dolente! come mi riscossi
    quando mi prese dicendomi: 'Forse
    tu non pensavi ch'io löico fossi!'   *123*
A Minòs mi portò; e quelli attorse
    otto volte la coda al dosso duro;
    e poi che per gran rabbia la si morse,   *126*
disse: 'Questi è d'i rei del foco furo';
    per ch'io là dove vedi son perduto,
    e sì vestito, andando, mi rancuro."   *129*
Quand' elli ebbe 'l suo dir così compiuto,
    la fiamma dolorando si partio,
    torcendo e dibattendo 'l corno aguto.   *132*
Noi passamm' oltre, e io e 'l duca mio,
    su per lo scoglio infino in su l'altr' arco
    che cuopre 'l fosso in che si paga il fio
a quei che scommettendo acquistan carco.   *136*

into which I now must fall, long promise
with short keeping will make you triumph
on the High Seat.'

"Then, when I died, Francis came for me;
but one of the black Cherubim said to him,
'Do not take him, wrong me not! He must
come down among my minions because he
gave the fraudulent counsel, since which till
now I have been at his hair; for he who re-
pents not cannot be absolved, nor is it pos-
sible to repent of a thing and to will it at the
same time, for the contradiction does not
allow it.'

"O wretched me! how I started when he
seized me, saying, 'Perhaps you did not think
that I was a logician!' He bore me to Minos,
who coiled his tail eight times round his
rough back, and then, biting it in great rage,
said, 'This is a sinner for the thievish fire';
wherefore here where you see me I am lost,
and go, thus robed, in bitterness."

When he had thus ended his words the
sorrowing flame departed, twisting and toss-
ing the pointed horn.

We passed onward, I and my guide, along
the reef as far as the next arch which spans
the ditch where they pay the fee who acquire
their load by sundering.

INFERNO

CHI PORIA mai pur con parole sciolte
dicer del sangue e de le piaghe a pieno
ch'i' ora vidi, per narrar più volte?   *3*
Ogne lingua per certo verria meno
per lo nostro sermone e per la mente
c'hanno a tanto comprender poco seno.   *6*
S'el s'aunasse ancor tutta la gente
che già, in su la fortunata terra
di Puglia, fu del suo sangue dolente   *9*
per li Troiani e per la lunga guerra
che de l'anella fé sì alte spoglie,
come Livïo scrive, che non erra,   *12*
con quella che sentio di colpi doglie
per contastare a Ruberto Guiscardo;
e l'altra il cui ossame ancor s'accoglie   *15*
a Ceperan, là dove fu bugiardo
ciascun Pugliese, e là da Tagliacozzo,
dove sanz' arme vinse il vecchio Alardo;   *18*

CANTO XXVIII

Wᴴᴼ could ever fully tell, even in un-
fettered words, though many times narrating,
the blood and the wounds that I now saw?
Surely every tongue would fail, because of
our speech and our memory which have little
capacity to comprehend so much.

Were all the people assembled again who
once in the fateful land of Apulia bewailed
their blood shed by the Trojans, and those
of the long war that made so vast a spoil of
rings—as Livy writes, who does not err—
together with those who felt the pain of
blows in the struggle with Robert Guiscard,
and those others whose bones are still heaped
up at Ceperano, where every Apulian was
false, and there by Tagliacozzo where old
Alardo conquered without arms;

e qual forato suo membro e qual mozzo
   mostrasse, d'aequar sarebbe nulla
   il modo de la nona bolgia sozzo.   *21*

Già veggia, per mezzul perdere o lulla,
   com' io vidi un, così non si pertugia,
   rotto dal mento infin dove si trulla.   *24*

Tra le gambe pendevan le minugia;
   la corata pareva e 'l tristo sacco
   che merda fa di quel che si trangugia.   *27*

Mentre che tutto in lui veder m'attacco,
   guardommi e con le man s'aperse il petto,
   dicendo: "Or vedi com' io mi dilacco!   *30*

vedi come storpiato è Mäometto!
   Dinanzi a me sen va piangendo Alì,
   fesso nel volto dal mento al ciuffetto.   *33*

E tutti li altri che tu vedi qui,
   seminator di scandalo e di scisma
   fuor vivi, e però son fessi così.   *36*

Un diavolo è qua dietro che n'accisma
   sì crudelmente, al taglio de la spada
   rimettendo ciascun di questa risma,   *39*

quand' avem volta la dolente strada;
   però che le ferite son richiuse
   prima ch'altri dinanzi li rivada.   *42*

Ma tu chi se' che 'n su lo scoglio muse,
   forse per indugiar d'ire a la pena
   ch'è giudicata in su le tue accuse?"   *45*

"Né morte 'l giunse ancor, né colpa 'l mena,"
   rispuose 'l mio maestro, "a tormentarlo;
   ma per dar lui esperïenza piena,   *48*

and one should show his limb pierced through, and another his cut off, it would be nothing to equal the foul fashion of the ninth pouch.

Truly a cask, through loss of mid-board or side-piece, gapes not so wide as one I saw, cleft from the chin to the part that breaks wind; his entrails were hanging between his legs, and the vitals could be seen and the foul sack that makes ordure of what is swallowed. While I was all absorbed in gazing on him, he looked at me and with his hands pulled open his breast, saying, "Now see how I rend myself, see how mangled is Mohammed! In front of me goes Ali weeping, cleft in the face from chin to forelock; and all the others whom you see here were in their lifetime sowers of scandal and of schism, and therefore are thus cleft. A devil is here behind that fashions us thus cruelly, putting again to the edge of the sword each of this throng when we have circled the doleful road; for the wounds are closed up before any of us pass again before him. But who are you that are musing on the ridge, perhaps to delay going to the punishment pronounced on your own accusations?"

"Neither has death yet reached him, nor does guilt bring him for torment," replied my master, "but in order to give him full experience,

a me, che morto son, convien menarlo
  per lo 'nferno qua giù di giro in giro;
  e quest' è ver così com' io ti parlo."   *51*
Più fuor di cento che, quando l'udiro,
  s'arrestaron nel fosso a riguardarmi
  per maraviglia, oblïando il martiro.   *54*
"Or dì a fra Dolcin dunque che s'armi,
  tu che forse vedra' il sole in breve,
  s'ello non vuol qui tosto seguitarmi,   *57*
sì di vivanda, che stretta di neve
  non rechi la vittoria al Noarese,
  ch'altrimenti acquistar non saria leve."   *60*
Poi che l'un piè per girsene sospese,
  Mäometto mi disse esta parola;
  indi a partirsi in terra lo distese.   *63*
Un altro, che forata avea la gola
  e tronco 'l naso infin sotto le ciglia,
  e non avea mai ch'una orecchia sola,   *66*
ristato a riguardar per maraviglia
  con li altri, innanzi a li altri aprì la canna,
  ch'era di fuor d'ogne parte vermiglia,   *69*
e disse: "O tu cui colpa non condanna
  e cu' io vidi in su terra latina,
  se troppa simiglianza non m'inganna,   *72*
rimembriti di Pier da Medicina,
  se mai torni a veder lo dolce piano
  che da Vercelli a Marcabò dichina.   *75*
E fa sapere a' due miglior da Fano,
  a messer Guido e anco ad Angiolello,
  che, se l'antiveder qui non è vano,   *78*

it behooves me, who am dead, to lead him
down here through Hell from circle to circle;
and this is as true as that I speak to you."

More than a hundred there were who,
when they heard him, stopped in the ditch
to look at me, forgetting their torment in
their wonder.

"Tell Fra Dolcino, then, you who perhaps
will see the sun before long, if he would not
soon follow me here, so to arm himself with
victuals that stress of snow may not bring
victory to the Novarese, which otherwise
would not be easy to attain."

After he had raised one foot to go on,
Mohammed said this to me, then set it on
the ground to depart.

Another who had his throat pierced through
and his nose cut off up to the eyebrows, and
only one ear left, stopped with the rest to
gaze in astonishment, and before the others
opened his gullet, which was all red outside,
and said, "O you whom guilt does not con-
demn and whom I saw above in the land of
Italy, if too great likeness does not deceive
me, if ever you return to see the sweet plain
that slopes from Vercelli to Marcabò, remem-
ber Pier da Medicina. And make it known to
the two best men of Fano, to messer Guido
and to Angiolello, that unless our foresight
here is vain,

gittati saran fuor di lor vasello
e mazzerati presso a la Cattolica
per tradimento d'un tiranno fello.   *81*
Tra l'isola di Cipri e di Maiolica
non vide mai sì gran fallo Nettuno,
non da pirate, non da gente argolica.   *84*
Quel traditor che vede pur con l'uno,
e tien la terra che tale qui meco
vorrebbe di vedere esser digiuno,   *87*
farà venirli a parlamento seco;
poi farà sì, ch'al vento di Focara
non sarà lor mestier voto né preco."   *90*
E io a lui: "Dimostrami e dichiara,
se vuo' ch'i' porti sù di te novella,
chi è colui da la veduta amara."   *93*
Allor puose la mano a la mascella
d'un suo compagno e la bocca li aperse,
gridando: "Questi è desso, e non favella.   *96*
Questi, scacciato, il dubitar sommerse
in Cesare, affermando che 'l fornito
sempre con danno l'attender sofferse."   *99*
Oh quanto mi pareva sbigottito
con la lingua tagliata ne la strozza
Curïo, ch'a dir fu così ardito!   *102*
E un ch'avea l'una e l'altra man mozza,
levando i moncherin per l'aura fosca,
sì che 'l sangue facea la faccia sozza,   *105*
gridò: "Ricordera'ti anche del Mosca,
che disse, lasso! 'Capo ha cosa fatta,'
che fu mal seme per la gente tosca."   *108*

they will be thrown out of their vessel and sunk near La Cattolica, through the treachery of a fell tyrant. Between the islands of Cyprus and Majorca Neptune never saw so great a crime, not of the pirates nor of the Argolic people. That traitor who sees with but one eye, and holds the city from sight of which one who is here with me would wish he had fasted, will make them come to parley with him, then will so deal with them that for the wind of Focara they will not need vow or prayer."

And I to him, "Show me and explain, if you would have me carry news of you above, who he is to whom that sight was bitter." Then he laid hold of the jaw of one of his companions and opened the mouth, saying, "This is he, and he does not speak: being banished, he quenched the doubt in Caesar, affirming that to a man prepared delay was always harmful." Ah, how aghast appeared to me, with tongue cut off in his throat, Curio who was so daring in his speech!

And one who had both hands lopped off, raising the stumps through the murky air so that the blood befouled his face, cried, "You will recall Mosca too who said, alas! 'A thing done has an end!' which was seed of ill to the Tuscan people"

E io li aggiunsi: "E morte di tua schiatta";
   per ch'elli, accumulando duol con duolo,
   sen gio come persona trista e matta.   *111*
Ma io rimasi a riguardar lo stuolo,
   e vidi cosa ch'io avrei paura,
   sanza più prova, di contarla solo;   *114*
se non che coscïenza m'assicura,
   la buona compagnia che l'uom francheggia
   sotto l'asbergo del sentirsi pura.   *117*
Io vidi certo, e ancor par ch'io 'l veggia,
   un busto sanza capo andar sì come
   andavan li altri de la trista greggia;   *120*
e 'l capo tronco tenea per le chiome,
   pesol con mano a guisa di lanterna:
   e quel mirava noi e dicea: "Oh me!"   *123*
Di sé facea a sé stesso lucerna,
   ed eran due in uno e uno in due;
   com' esser può, quei sa che sì governa.   *126*
Quando diritto al piè del ponte fue,
   levò 'l braccio alto con tutta la testa
   per appressarne le parole sue,   *129*
che fuoro: "Or vedi la pena molesta,
   tu che, spirando, vai veggendo i morti:
   vedi s'alcuna è grande come questa.   *132*
E perché tu di me novella porti,
   sappi ch'i' son Bertram dal Bornio, quelli
   che diedi al re giovane i ma' conforti.   *135*
Io feci il padre e 'l figlio in sé ribelli;
   Achitofèl non fé più d'Absalone
   e di Davìd coi malvagi punzelli.   *138*

—"and death to your own stock," I added then; whereat he, heaping sorrow on sorrow, went off as one crazed with grief.

But I stayed to view the troop, and saw a thing that I should be afraid even to relate without more proof, but that conscience, the good companion that emboldens a man under the hauberk of feeling itself pure, reassures me. Truly I saw, and seem to see it still, a trunk without the head going along as were the others of that dismal herd, and it was holding the severed head by the hair, swinging it in hand like a lantern, and it was gazing at us and saying: "O me!" Of itself it was making a lamp for itself, and they were two in one and one in two—how this can be, He knows who so ordains. When he was right at the foot of the bridge he raised high his arm with the head, in order to bring near to us his words, which were, "See now my grievous penalty, you who, breathing, go to view the dead: see if any other is so great as this! And that you may carry news of me, know that I am Bertran de Born, he who to the young king gave the evil counsels. I made the father and the son rebel against each other. Ahithophel did not more with Absalom and David by his wicked instigations.

Perch' io parti' così giunte persone,
  partito porto il mio cerebro, lasso!,
  dal suo principio ch'è in questo troncone.
Così s'osserva in me lo contrapasso." *142*

Because I parted persons thus united, I carry my brain parted from its source, alas! which is in this trunk. Thus is the retribution observed in me."

La molta gente e le diverse piaghe
  avean le luci mie sì inebrïate,
  che de lo stare a piangere eran vaghe.   *3*
Ma Virgilio mi disse: "Che pur guate?
  perché la vista tua pur si soffolge
  là giù tra l'ombre triste smozzicate?   *6*
Tu non hai fatto sì a l'altre bolge;
  pensa, se tu annoverar le credi,
  che miglia ventidue la valle volge.   *9*
E già la luna è sotto i nostri piedi;
  lo tempo è poco omai che n'è concesso,
  e altro è da veder che tu non vedi."   *12*
"Se tu avessi," rispuos' io appresso,
  "atteso a la cagion per ch'io guardava,
  forse m'avresti ancor lo star dimesso."   *15*
Parte sen giva, e io retro li andava,
  lo duca, già faccendo la risposta,
  e soggiugnendo: "Dentro a quella cava   *18*
dov' io tenea or li occhi sì a posta,
  credo ch'un spirto del mio sangue pianga
  la colpa che là giù cotanto costa."   *21*

CANTO XXIX

The many people and the strange wounds had made my eyes so drunken that they longed to stay and weep; but Virgil said to me, "What are you still gazing at? Why does your sight still rest down there among the dismal mutilated shades? You have not done so at the other pits. Consider, if you think to count them, that the valley circles two and twenty miles; and already the moon is beneath our feet. The time is now short that is allowed us, and there is more to see than you see here."

"If you had given heed to my reason for looking," I answered then, "perhaps you would have granted me a longer stay."

Meanwhile my leader was going on, and I was following after him, making my reply, and adding, "Within that hollow where I was but now holding my eyes so fixedly, I believe a spirit of my own blood laments the guilt that costs so dear down there."

Allor disse 'l maestro: "Non si franga
   lo tuo pensier da qui innanzi sovr' ello.
   Attendi ad altro, ed ei là si rimanga;   *24*
ch'io vidi lui a piè del ponticello
   mostrarti e minacciar forte col dito,
   e udi' 'l nominar Geri del Bello.   *27*
Tu eri allor sì del tutto impedito
   sovra colui che già tenne Altaforte,
   che non guardasti in là, sì fu partito."   *30*
"O duca mio, la vïolenta morte
   che non li è vendicata ancor," diss' io,
   "per alcun che de l'onta sia consorte,   *33*
fece lui disdegnoso; ond' el sen gio
   sanza parlarmi, sì com' ïo estimo:
   e in ciò m'ha el fatto a sé più pio."   *36*
Così parlammo infino al loco primo
   che de lo scoglio l'altra valle mostra,
   se più lume vi fosse, tutto ad imo.   *39*
Quando noi fummo sor l'ultima chiostra
   di Malebolge, sì che i suoi conversi
   potean parere a la veduta nostra,   *42*
lamenti saettaron me diversi,
   che di pietà ferrati avean li strali;
   ond' io li orecchi con le man copersi.   *45*
Qual dolor fora, se de li spedali
   di Valdichiana tra 'l luglio e 'l settembre
   e di Maremma e di Sardigna i mali   *48*
fossero in una fossa tutti 'nsembre,
   tal era quivi, e tal puzzo n'usciva
   qual suol venir de le marcite membre.   *51*

Then said the master, "Do not let your
thought distract itself on him henceforth;
attend to somewhat else, and let him stay
there; for I saw him there below the bridge
point at you and fiercely threaten with his
finger, and I heard them call him Geri del
Bello. You were then so wholly occupied with
him who once held Hautefort that you did
not look that way till he was gone."

"O my leader," I said, "the violent death
which is not yet avenged for him by any who
is partner in the shame made him indignant;
wherefore, as I judge, he went on without
speaking to me, and thereby has he made me
pity him the more."

Thus we spoke, up to the first place on
the crag which shows the next valley, had
there been more light, right to the bottom.
When we were above the last cloister of
Malebolge, so that its lay brothers could be
seen by us, strange lamentations assailed me
which had their shafts barbed with pity; at
which I covered my ears with my hands.
Such suffering as there would be if, between
July and September, the sick from the hos-
pitals of Valdichiana and of Maremma and
of Sardinia were all in one ditch together,
such was there here; and such a stench issued
thence as is wont to come from festered limbs.

Noi discendemmo in su l'ultima riva
  del lungo scoglio, pur da man sinistra;
  e allor fu la mia vista più viva   54
giù ver' lo fondo, là 've la ministra
  de l'alto Sire infallibil giustizia
  punisce i falsador che qui registra.   57
Non credo ch'a veder maggior tristizia
  fosse in Egina il popol tutto infermo,
  quando fu l'aere sì pien di malizia,   60
che li animali, infino al picciol vermo,
  cascaron tutti, e poi le genti antiche,
  secondo che i poeti hanno per fermo,   63
si ristorar di seme di formiche;
  ch'era a veder per quella oscura valle
  languir li spirti per diverse biche.   66
Qual sovra 'l ventre e qual sovra le spalle
  l'un de l'altro giacea, e qual carpone
  si trasmutava per lo tristo calle.   69
Passo passo andavam sanza sermone,
  guardando e ascoltando li ammalati,
  che non potean levar le lor persone.   72
Io vidi due sedere a sé poggiati,
  com' a scaldar si poggia tegghia a tegghia,
  dal capo al piè di schianze macolati;   75
e non vidi già mai menare stregghia
  a ragazzo aspettato dal segnorso,
  né a colui che mal volontier vegghia,   78
come ciascun menava spesso il morso
  de l'unghie sopra sé per la gran rabbia
  del pizzicor, che non ha più soccorso;   81

We descended onto the last bank of the long
crag, keeping ever to the left, and then my
sight was clearer down into the depth, where
the ministress of the High Lord, infallible
Justice, punishes the falsifiers whom she reg-
isters here.

I do not believe it was a greater sorrow to
see the whole people in Aegina sick, when the
air was so full of corruption that every ani-
mal, even to the little worm, fell dead, and
afterwards, as the poets hold for certain, the
ancient peoples were restored from seed of
ants, than it was to see, through that dark
valley, the spirits languishing in divers heaps.
One lay on his belly, one lay on the shoulders
of another, and one shifted on all fours along
the dismal way. Step by step we went in
silence, watching and listening to the sick,
who were unable to raise themselves.

I saw two sitting propped against each
other, as pan is leaned against pan to warm,
spotted from head to foot with scabs; and
never did I see currycomb plied by stable-
boy whose master waits for him, nor by one
who unwillingly stays awake, as each of these
plied thick the clawing of his nails upon
himself, for the great fury of the itch which
has no other succor;

e sì traevan giù l'unghie la scabbia,
  come coltel di scardova le scaglie
  o d'altro pesce che più larghe l'abbia.   *84*
"O tu che con le dita ti dismaglie,"
  cominciò 'l duca mio a l'un di loro,
  "e che fai d'esse tal volta tanaglie,   *87*
dinne s'alcun Latino è tra costoro
  che son quinc' entro, se l'unghia ti basti
  etternalmente a cotesto lavoro."   *90*
"Latin siam noi, che tu vedi sì guasti
  qui ambedue," rispuose l'un piangendo;
  "ma tu chi se' che di noi dimandasti?"   *93*
E 'l duca disse: "I' son un che discendo
  con questo vivo giù di balzo in balzo,
  e di mostrar lo 'nferno a lui intendo."   *96*
Allor si ruppe lo comun rincalzo;
  e tremando ciascuno a me si volse
  con altri che l'udiron di rimbalzo.   *99*
Lo buon maestro a me tutto s'accolse,
  dicendo: "Dì a lor ciò che tu vuoli";
  e io incominciai, poscia ch'ei volse: *102*
"Se la vostra memoria non s'imboli
  nel primo mondo da l'umane menti,
  ma s'ella viva sotto molti soli,   *105*
ditemi chi voi siete e di che genti;
  la vostra sconcia e fastidiosa pena
  di palesarvi a me non vi spaventi."   *108*
"Io fui d'Arezzo, e Albero da Siena,"
  rispuose l'un, "mi fé mettere al foco;
  ma quel per ch'io mori' qui non mi mena.   *111*

and the nails were dragging down the scab,
as a knife does the scales of bream or of
other fish that has them larger.

"O you who with your fingers dismail
yourself," my leader began to one of them,
"and who sometimes make pincers of them,
tell us if there is any Italian among these
who are here within, so may your nails suffice
you eternally in this work."

"We are Italians, both of us, whom you
see so disfigured here," replied the one, weep-
ing, "but who are you that inquire of us?"

And my leader said, "I am one who with
this living man descend from ledge to ledge,
and I mean to show him Hell."

Then their mutual support was broken,
and each turned toward me trembling, with
others who overheard him. The good master
drew quite close to me, saying, "Tell them
what you will." And I began, as he desired,
"So may memory of you in the first world
not fade away from the minds of men, but
may it live under many suns, tell me who
you are and of what people; let not your
ugly and disgusting punishment make you
fear to declare yourselves to me."

"I was of Arezzo," one of them replied,
"and Albero of Siena had me burned; but
what I died for does not bring me here.

Vero è ch'i' dissi lui, parlando a gioco:
  'I' mi saprei levar per l'aere a volo';
  e quei, ch'avea vaghezza e senno poco,   *114*
volle ch'i' li mostrassi l'arte; e solo
  perch' io nol feci Dedalo, mi fece
  ardere a tal che l'avea per figliuolo.   *117*
Ma ne l'ultima bolgia de le diece
  me per l'alchìmia che nel mondo usai
  dannò Minòs, a cui fallar non lece."   *120*
E io dissi al poeta: "Or fu già mai
  gente sì vana come la sanese?
  Certo non la francesca sì d'assai!"   *123*
Onde l'altro lebbroso, che m'intese,
  rispuose al detto mio: "Tra'mene Stricca
  che seppe far le temperate spese,   *126*
e Niccolò che la costuma ricca
  del garofano prima discoverse
  ne l'orto dove tal seme s'appicca;   *129*
e tra'ne la brigata in che disperse
  Caccia d'Ascian la vigna e la gran fonda,
  e l'Abbagliato suo senno proferse.   *132*
Ma perché sappi chi sì ti seconda
  contra i Sanesi, aguzza ver' me l'occhio,
  sì che la faccia mia ben ti risponda: *135*
sì vedrai ch'io son l'ombra di Capocchio,
  che falsai li metalli con l'alchìmia;
  e te dee ricordar, se ben t'adocchio,
com' io fui di natura buona scimia."   *139*

True it is, I said to him, speaking in jest,
'I would know how to raise myself through
the air in flight'; and he, who had a lively
desire and little wit, would have me show him
the art; and only because I did not make
him a Daedalus, he had me burned by one
who held him as a son. But, for the alchemy
I practiced in the world, Minos, to whom it
is not allowed to err, condemned me to this
last pouch of the ten."

And I said to the poet, "Now was ever a
people so vain as the Sienese? Surely not so
the French by far."

Whereat the other leper, who heard me,
responded to my words, "Except for Stricca,
who knew how to spend in moderation; and
except for Niccolò, who first devised the
costly use of the clove, in the garden where
such seed takes root; and except for the com-
pany in which Caccia d'Asciano squandered
the vineyard and the great purse, and Ab-
bagliato showed his wit. But, that you may
know who thus seconds you against the
Sienese, sharpen your eye toward me, that
my face may answer well to you, and you
will see that I am the shade of Capocchio,
who falsified the metals by alchemy; and you
must recall, if I rightly eye you, how good an
ape of nature I was."

INFERNO

Nᴇʟ ᴛᴇᴍᴘᴏ che Iunone era crucciata
   per Semelè contra 'l sangue tebano,
   come mostrò una e altra fïata,   *3*
Atamante divenne tanto insano,
   che veggendo la moglie con due figli
   andar carcata da ciascuna mano,   *6*
gridò: "Tendiam le reti, sì ch'io pigli
   la leonessa e ' leoncini al varco";
   e poi distese i dispietati artigli,   *9*
prendendo l'un ch'avea nome Learco,
   e rotollo e percosselo ad un sasso;
   e quella s'annegò con l'altro carco.   *12*
E quando la fortuna volse in basso
   l'altezza de' Troian che tutto ardiva,
   sì che 'nsieme col regno il re fu casso,   *15*
Ecuba trista, misera e cattiva,
   poscia che vide Polissena morta,
   e del suo Polidoro in su la riva   *18*

CANTO XXX

In the time when Juno was wroth for Semele against the Theban blood, as she showed more than once, Athamas became so insane that, seeing his wife go carrying their two children on either hand, he cried, "Let us spread the nets to take the lioness and the whelps at the pass!" and then stretched out his pitiless claws, grasping the one that was named Learchus, and whirled him round and dashed him on a rock; and she drowned herself with her other burden. And when Fortune brought low the all-daring pride of the Trojans, so that the king together with his kingdom was blotted out, Hecuba, sad, wretched and captive, after she had seen Polyxena slain and, forlorn, discerned her Polydorus on the sea-strand,

del mar si fu la dolorosa accorta,
 forsennata latrò sì come cane;
 tanto il dolor le fé la mente torta.   *21*
Ma né di Tebe furie né troiane
 si vider mäi in alcun tanto crude,
 non punger bestie, nonché membra umane, *24*
quant' io vidi in due ombre smorte e nude,
 che mordendo correvan di quel modo
 che 'l porco quando del porcil si schiude. *27*
L'una giunse a Capocchio, e in sul nodo
 del collo l'assannò, sì che, tirando,
 grattar li fece il ventre al fondo sodo. *30*
E l'Aretin che rimase, tremando
 mi disse: "Quel folletto è Gianni Schicchi,
 e va rabbioso altrui così conciando." *33*
"Oh," diss' io lui, "se l'altro non ti ficchi
 li denti a dosso, non ti sia fatica
 a dir chi è, pria che di qui si spicchi." *36*
Ed elli a me: "Quell' è l'anima antica
 di Mirra scellerata, che divenne
 al padre, fuor del dritto amore, amica. *39*
Questa a peccar con esso così venne,
 falsificando sé in altrui forma,
 come l'altro che là sen va, sostenne, *42*
per guadagnar la donna de la torma,
 falsificare in sé Buoso Donati,
 testando e dando al testamento norma." *45*
E poi che i due rabbiosi fuor passati
 sovra cu' io avea l'occhio tenuto,
 rivolsilo a guardar li altri mal nati. *48*

she, driven mad, barked like a dog, so had
the sorrow wrung her soul. But no fury of
Thebes or of Troy was ever seen so cruel
against any, in rending beasts, much less
human limbs, as were two pallid shades that
I saw biting and running like the pig when
it is let out of the sty. The one came at
Capocchio and fixed its tusks on his neck-
joint, so that, dragging him, it made his
belly scratch along the solid bottom. And the
Aretine, who was left, trembling said to me,
"That goblin is Gianni Schicchi, and he goes
rabid mangling others thus."

"Oh," said I to him, "so may the other not
fix its teeth on you, be pleased to tell who it
is, before it breaks away from here."

And he to me, "That is the ancient spirit
of infamous Myrrha, who became loving of
her father beyond rightful love. She came
to sin with him by falsifying herself in an-
other's form, even as the other, who goes off
there, ventured, that he might gain the lady
of the herd, to counterfeit in himself Buoso
Donati, making a will and giving it due
form."

And when the furious two on whom I had
kept my eyes had passed on, I turned to look
at the other ill-born shades, and

Io vidi un, fatto a guisa di lëuto,
   pur ch'elli avesse avuta l'anguinaia
   tronca da l'altro che l'uomo ha forcuto.   51
La grave idropesì, che sì dispaia
   le membra con l'omor che mal converte,
   che 'l viso non risponde a la ventraia,   54
faceva lui tener le labbra aperte
   come l'etico fa, che per la sete
   l'un verso 'l mento e l'altro in sù rinverte.   57
"O voi che sanz' alcuna pena siete,
   e non so io perché, nel mondo gramo,"
   diss' elli a noi, "guardate e attendete   60
a la miseria del maestro Adamo;
   io ebbi, vivo, assai di quel ch'i' volli,
   e ora, lasso!, un gocciol d'acqua bramo.   63
Li ruscelletti che d'i verdi colli
   del Casentin discendon giuso in Arno,
   faccendo i lor canali freddi e molli,   66
sempre mi stanno innanzi, e non indarno,
   ché l'imagine lor vie più m'asciuga
   che 'l male ond' io nel volto mi discarno.   69
La rigida giustizia che mi fruga
   tragge cagion del loco ov' io peccai
   a metter più li miei sospiri in fuga.   72
Ivi è Romena, là dov' io falsai
   la lega suggellata del Batista;
   per ch'io il corpo sù arso lasciai.   75
Ma s'io vedessi qui l'anima trista
   di Guido o d'Alessandro o di lor frate,
   per Fonte Branda non darei la vista.   78

I saw one shaped like a lute, if only he had
been cut short at the groin from the part
where a man is forked. The heavy dropsy
which, with its ill-digested humor, so un-
mates the members that the face does not
answer to the paunch, made him hold his
lips apart, like the hectic who, for thirst,
curls the one lip toward his chin and the
other upwards.

"Oh you who are without any punishment,
and I know not why, in this dismal world,"
he said to us, "behold and consider the misery
of Master Adam. Living, I had in plenty all
that I wished, and now, alas! I crave one drop
of water! The little brooks that from the
green hills of Casentino run down into the
Arno, making their channels cool and moist,
are always before me, and not in vain, for
the image of them parches me far more than
the malady that wastes my features. The rigid
justice that scourges me draws occasion from
the place where I sinned, to give my sighs a
quicker flight; there is Romena, where I
falsified the currency stamped with the Bap-
tist, for which on earth I left my body burnt.
But if I could see here the miserable soul of
Guido or of Alessandro or of their brother,
I would not give the sight for Fonte Branda.

Dentro c'è l'una già, se l'arrabbiate
   ombre che vanno intorno dicon vero;
   ma che mi val, c'ho le membra legate?   *81*
S'io fossi pur di tanto ancor leggero
   ch'i' potessi in cent' anni andare un'oncia,
   io sarei messo già per lo sentiero,   *84*
cercando lui tra questa gente sconcia,
   con tutto ch'ella volge undici miglia,
   e men d'un mezzo di traverso non ci ha.   *87*
Io son per lor tra sì fatta famiglia;
   e' m'indussero a batter li fiorini
   ch'avevan tre carati di mondiglia."   *90*
E io a lui: "Chi son li due tapini
   che fumman come man bagnate 'l verno,
   giacendo stretti a' tuoi destri confini?"   *93*
"Qui li trovai—e poi volta non dierno—,"
   rispuose, "quando piovvi in questo greppo,
   e non credo che dieno in sempiterno.   *96*
L'una è la falsa ch'accusò Gioseppo;
   l'altr' è 'l falso Sinon greco di Troia:
   per febbre aguta gittan tanto leppo."   *99*
E l'un di lor, che si recò a noia
   forse d'esser nomato sì oscuro,
   col pugno li percosse l'epa croia.   *102*
Quella sonò come fosse un tamburo;
   e mastro Adamo li percosse il volto
   col braccio suo, che non parve men duro,   *105*
dicendo a lui: "Ancor che mi sia tolto
   lo muover per le membra che son gravi,
   ho io il braccio a tal mestiere sciolto."   *108*

One of them is here within already, if the
raging shades who go around speak true; but
what does it avail me whose limbs are tied.
If I were only still so light that I could move
one inch in a hundred years, I would have set
out already on the road to seek him among
this disfigured people, for all it is eleven
miles around and not less than half a mile
across. Because of them am I in such a family:
they induced me to strike the florins that had
three carats of alloy."

And I to him, "Who are the two wretches
that are smoking like wet hands in winter,
lying close to your confines on the right?"

"Here I found them when I rained down
into this trough," he answered, "and since
then they have not given a turn, nor do I
think they will, to all eternity. The one is the
false woman who accused Joseph; the other
is the false Sinon, Greek from Troy. Burning
fever makes them reek so strongly."

And one of them, who took offense per-
haps at being named so darkly, with his
fist struck him on his stiff paunch; it sounded
like a drum; and Master Adam struck him
in the face with his arm, which seemed no
less hard, saying to him, "Though I am kept
from moving, by the weight of my limbs,
which are heavy, I have an arm free for such
a need."

Ond' ei rispuose: "Quando tu andavi
  al fuoco, non l'avei tu così presto;
  ma sì e più l'avei quando coniavi." *111*
E l'idropico: "Tu di' ver di questo:
  ma tu non fosti sì ver testimonio
  là 've del ver fosti a Troia richesto." *114*
"S'io dissi falso, e tu falsasti il conio,"
  disse Sinon; "e son qui per un fallo,
  e tu per più ch'alcun altro demonio!" *117*
"Ricorditi, spergiuro, del cavallo,"
  rispuose quel ch'avëa infiata l'epa;
  "e sieti reo che tutto il mondo sallo!" *120*
"E te sia rea la sete onde ti crepa,"
  disse 'l Greco, "la lingua, e l'acqua marcia
  che 'l ventre innanzi a li occhi sì t'assiepa!" *123*
Allora il monetier: "Così si squarcia
  la bocca tua per tuo mal come suole;
  ché, s'i' ho sete e omor mi rinfarcia, *126*
tu hai l'arsura e 'l capo che ti duole,
  e per leccar lo specchio di Narcisso,
  non vorresti a 'nvitar molte parole." *129*
Ad ascoltarli er' io del tutto fisso,
  quando 'l maestro mi disse: "Or pur mira,
  che per poco che teco non mi risso!" *132*
Quand' io 'l senti' a me parlar con ira,
  volsimi verso lui con tal vergogna,
  ch'ancor per la memoria mi si gira. *135*

To which he replied, "When you were
going to the fire you didn't have it thus ready;
but you did have it as ready, and more, when
you were coining."

And the dropsied one, "You speak the truth
in this; but you were not so true a witness
there at Troy where you were questioned
about the truth."

"If I spoke falsely, you falsified the coin,"
said Sinon, "and I am here for a single sin,
and you for more than any other demon."

"Remember, perjurer, the horse," he of the
swollen paunch replied, "and may it torture
you that all the world knows of it."

"And to you be torture the thirst that
cracks your tongue," said the Greek, "and
the foul water that makes your belly thus a
hedge before your eyes."

Then the coiner, "Thus for fever your jaws
gape wide, as usual; for if I have thirst and
if humor stuffs me, you have the burning and
an aching head, and to lick the mirror of
Narcissus you would not want many words of
invitation."

I was standing all intent to listen to them,
when the master said to me, "Now just you
keep on looking a little more and I will
quarrel with you!"

When I heard him speak to me in anger,
I turned to him with such shame that it
circles through my memory even yet.

Qual è colui che suo dannaggio sogna,
   che sognando desidera sognare,
   sì che quel ch'è, come non fosse, agogna,   *138*
tal mi fec' io, non possendo parlare,
   che disïava scusarmi, e scusava
   me tuttavia, e nol mi credea fare.   *141*
"Maggior difetto men vergogna lava,"
   disse 'l maestro, "che 'l tuo non è stato;
   però d'ogne trestizia ti disgrava.   *144*
E fa ragion ch'io ti sia sempre allato,
   se più avvien che fortuna t'accoglia
   dove sien genti in simigliante piato:
ché voler ciò udire è bassa voglia."   *148*

And as is he who dreams of something hurt-
ful to him and, dreaming, wishes that it were
a dream, so that he longs for that which is,
as if it were not, such I became that, unable
to speak, I wanted to excuse myself, and did
excuse myself all the while, not thinking I
was doing it.

"Less shame washes away a greater fault
than yours has been," said the master, "there-
fore disburden yourself of all sadness; and do
not forget that I am always at your side,
should it again fall out that fortune find you
where people are in a similar dispute, for the
wish to hear that is a base wish."

INFERNO

.

Una medesma lingua pria mi morse,
    sì che mi tinse l'una e l'altra guancia,
    e poi la medicina mi riporse;   *3*
così od' io che solea far la lancia
    d'Achille e del suo padre esser cagione
    prima di trista e poi di buona mancia.   *6*
Noi demmo il dosso al misero vallone
    su per la ripa che 'l cinge dintorno,
    attraversando sanza alcun sermone.   *9*
Quiv' era men che notte e men che giorno,
    sì che 'l viso m'andava innanzi poco;
    ma io senti' sonare un alto corno,   *12*
tanto ch'avrebbe ogne tuon fatto fioco,
    che, contra sé la sua via seguitando,
    dirizzò li occhi miei tutti ad un loco.   *15*
Dopo la dolorosa rotta, quando
    Carlo Magno perdé la santa gesta,
    non sonò sì terribilmente Orlando.   *18*

CANTO XXXI

ONE and the same tongue first stung me, so that it tinged both my cheeks, and then it supplied the medicine to me; thus I have heard that the lance of Achilles and of his father was wont to be the cause, first of a sad and then of a good gift.

We turned our backs to the wretched valley, going up by the bank that girds it round, crossing over it in silence. Here it was less than night and less than day, so that my sight went little ahead, but I heard a blast from a horn so loud that it would have made any thunderclap seem faint, and it directed my eyes, following back on its course, wholly to one place. After the dolorous rout when Charlemagne lost the holy gest, Roland did not sound a blast so terrible.

Poco portäi in là volta la testa,
 che me parve veder molte alte torri;
 ond' io: "Maestro, dì, che terra è questa?"   *21*
Ed elli a me: "Però che tu trascorri
 per le tenebre troppo da la lungi,
 avvien che poi nel maginare abborri.   *24*
Tu vedrai ben, se tu là ti congiungi,
 quanto 'l senso s'inganna di lontano;
 però alquanto più te stesso pungi."   *27*
Poi caramente mi prese per mano
 e disse: "Pria che noi siam più avanti,
 acciò che 'l fatto men ti paia strano,   *30*
sappi che non son torri, ma giganti,
 e son nel pozzo intorno da la ripa
 da l'umbilico in giuso tutti quanti."   *33*
Come quando la nebbia si dissipa,
 lo sguardo a poco a poco raffigura
 ciò che cela 'l vapor che l'aere stipa,   *36*
così forando l'aura grossa e scura,
 più e più appressando ver' la sponda,
 fuggiemi errore e crescémi paura;   *39*
però che, come su la cerchia tonda
 Montereggion di torri si corona,
 così la proda che 'l pozzo circonda   *42*
torreggiavan di mezza la persona
 li orribili giganti, cui minaccia
 Giove del cielo ancora quando tuona.   *45*
E io scorgeva già d'alcun la faccia,
 le spalle e 'l petto e del ventre gran parte,
 e per le coste giù ambo le braccia.   *48*

I had not long kept my head turned in that direction when I seemed to see many lofty towers; whereon I, "Master, say, what city is this?" And he to me, "It is because you pierce the darkness from too far off that you stray in your imagining; and when you reach the place you will see plainly how much the sense is deceived by distance; therefore, spur yourself on somewhat more." Then lovingly he took me by the hand and said, "Before we go further forward, in order that the fact may seem less strange to you, know that these are not towers, but giants, and every one of them is in the pit, round about the bank from the navel downward."

As when a mist is vanishing, the sight little by little shapes out that which the vapor hides that fills the air; so, as I pierced the thick and murky atmosphere and came on nearer and nearer to the brink, error fled from me and fear grew upon me; for, as on its round wall Montereggione crowns itself with towers, so here the horrible giants, whom Jove still threatens from heaven when he thunders, betowered with half their bodies the bank that encompasses the pit.

And already I discerned the face of one of them, his shoulders and his breast, and great part of his belly, and down along his sides both arms.

Natura certo, quando lasciò l'arte
  di sì fatti animali, assai fé bene
  per tòrre tali essecutori a Marte.   *51*
E s'ella d'elefanti e di balene
  non si pente, chi guarda sottilmente,
  più giusta e più discreta la ne tene;   *54*
ché dove l'argomento de la mente
  s'aggiugne al mal volere e a la possa,
  nessun riparo vi può far la gente.   *57*
La faccia sua mi parea lunga e grossa
  come la pina di San Pietro a Roma,
  e a sua proporzione eran l'altre ossa;   *60*
sì che la ripa, ch'era perizoma
  dal mezzo in giù, ne mostrava ben tanto
  di sovra, che di giugnere a la chioma   *63*
tre Frison s'averien dato mal vanto;
  però ch'i' ne vedea trenta gran palmi
  dal loco in giù dov' omo affibbia 'l manto.   *66*
"*Raphèl maì amècche zabì almi,*"
  cominciò a gridar la fiera bocca,
  cui non si convenia più dolci salmi.   *69*
E 'l duca mio ver' lui: "Anima sciocca,
  tienti col corno, e con quel ti disfoga
  quand' ira o altra passïon ti tocca!   *72*
Cércati al collo, e troverai la soga
  che 'l tien legato, o anima confusa,
  e vedi lui che 'l gran petto ti doga."   *75*
Poi disse a me: "Elli stessi s'accusa;
  questi è Nembrotto per lo cui mal coto
  pur un linguaggio nel mondo non s'usa.   *78*

Nature assuredly, when she gave up the art
of making creatures such as these, did right
well to deprive Mars of such executors; and
though she repents not of elephants and
whales, he who looks subtly holds her therein
more just and more discreet, for where the
instrument of the mind is added to an evil
will and to great power, men can make no
defense against it. His face seemed to me as
long and huge as the pine cone of St. Peter's
at Rome, and his other bones were in propor-
tion with it; so that the bank, which was an
apron to him from his middle downward
showed us fully so much of him above, that
three Frieslanders would have made ill
vaunt to have reached to his hair; for I saw
thirty great spans of him down from the
place where a man buckles his cloak.

"*Raphèl maỳ amecche zabì almi,*" the
fierce mouth, to which sweeter psalms were
not fitting, began to cry. And my leader
towards him, "Stupid soul, keep to your horn
and with that vent yourself when rage or
other passion takes you. Search at your neck
and you will find the belt that holds it tied,
O soul confused: see how it lies across your
great chest." Then he said to me, "He is his
own accuser: this is Nimrod, through whose
ill thought one language only is not used
in the world.

Lasciànlo stare e non parliamo a vòto;
   ché così è a lui ciascun linguaggio
   come 'l suo ad altrui, ch'a nullo è noto."   *81*
Facemmo adunque più lungo vïaggio,
   vòlti a sinistra; e al trar d'un balestro
   trovammo l'altro assai più fero e maggio.   *84*
A cigner lui qual che fosse 'l maestro,
   non so io dir, ma el tenea soccinto
   dinanzi l'altro e dietro il braccio destro   *87*
d'una catena che 'l tenea avvinto
   dal collo in giù, sì che 'n su lo scoperto
   si ravvolgëa infino al giro quinto.   *90*
"Questo superbo volle esser esperto
   di sua potenza contra 'l sommo Giove,"
   disse 'l mio duca, "ond' elli ha cotal merto.   *93*
Fïalte ha nome, e fece le gran prove
   quando i giganti fer paura a' dèi;
   le braccia ch'el menò, già mai non move."   *96*
E io a lui: "S'esser puote, io vorrei
   che de lo smisurato Brïareo
   esperïenza avesser li occhi mei."   *99*
Ond' ei rispuose: "Tu vedrai Anteo
   presso di qui che parla ed è disciolto,
   che ne porrà nel fondo d'ogne reo.   *102*
Quel che tu vuo' veder, più là è molto
   ed è legato e fatto come questo,
   salvo che più feroce par nel volto."   *105*
Non fu tremoto già tanto rubesto,
   che scotesse una torre così forte,
   come Fïalte a scuotersi fu presto.   *108*

Let us leave him alone and not speak in vain, for every language is to him as his is to others, which is known to none."

Then, turning to the left, we went farther on and, at the distance of a crossbow shot, we found the next, far more savage and bigger. Who had been the master to bind him I do not know, but he had his right arm shackled behind, and the other in front, by a chain which held him clasped from the neck downward, so that upon his uncovered part it was wound as far as the fifth coil.

"This proud one chose to try his strength against supreme Jove," said my guide, "wherefore he has such requital. Ephialtes he is called, and he made the great endeavors when the giants put the gods in fear. The arms he plied he moves no more."

And I to him, "If it were possible, I should wish my eyes might have experience of the immense Briareus." To which he replied, "Hard by here you shall see Antaeus, who speaks and is unfettered, and he will put us down into the bottom of all guilt. He whom you wish to see is much farther on, and he is bound and fashioned like this one, except that he seems more ferocious in his look."

Never did mighty earthquake shake a tower so violently as Ephialtes forthwith shook himself.

Allor temett' io più che mai la morte,
  e non v'era mestier più che la dotta,
  s'io non avessi viste le ritorte.   *111*
Noi procedemmo più avante allotta,
  e venimmo ad Anteo, che ben cinque alle,
  sanza la testa, uscia fuor de la grotta.   *114*
"O tu che ne la fortunata valle
  che fece Scipïon di gloria reda,
  quand' Anibàl co' suoi diede le spalle,   *117*
recasti già mille leon per preda,
  e che, se fossi stato a l'alta guerra
  de' tuoi fratelli, ancor par che si creda   *120*
ch'avrebber vinto i figli de la terra:
  mettine giù, e non ten vegna schifo,
  dove Cocito la freddura serra.   *123*
Non ci fare ire a Tizio né a Tifo:
  questi può dar di quel che qui si brama;
  però ti china e non torcer lo grifo.   *126*
Ancor ti può nel mondo render fama,
  ch'el vive, e lunga vita ancor aspetta
  se 'nnanzi tempo grazia a sé nol chiama."   *129*
Così disse 'l maestro; e quelli in fretta
  le man distese, e prese 'l duca mio,
  ond' Ercule sentì già grande stretta.   *132*
Virgilio, quando prender si sentio,
  disse a me: "Fatti qua, sì ch'io ti prenda";
  poi fece sì ch'un fascio era elli e io.   *135*
Qual pare a riguardar la Carisenda
  sotto 'l chinato, quando un nuvol vada
  sovr' essa sì, ched ella incontro penda: *138*

Then more than ever did I fear death, and nothing else was wanted for it but the fear, had I not seen his bonds. We then proceeded farther on and came to Antaeus, who stood full five ells, not reckoning his head, above the rock.

"O you that, in the fateful valley which made Scipio heir of glory, when Hannibal with his followers turned his back, did once take for prey a thousand lions, and through whom, had you been at the high war of your brothers, it seems that some still believe the sons of earth would have conquered, set us down below—and disdain not to do so— where the cold locks up Cocytus. Do not make us go to Tityus nor to Typhon: this man can give of that which is longed for here. Bend down, therefore, and do not curl your lip. He can yet restore your fame on earth, for he lives and expects long life yet, if grace does not untimely call him to itself."

Thus spoke my master; and the other in haste stretched out those hands of which Hercules once felt the mighty grip, and took my leader; and Virgil, when he felt their grasp, said to me, "Come here, that I may take you," and then of himself and me he made one bundle.

Such as the Garisenda seems to one's view, beneath the leaning side, when a cloud is passing over it against the direction in which it leans,

335

tal parve Antëo a me che stava a bada
di vederlo chinare, e fu tal ora
ch'i' avrei voluto ir per altra strada.   *141*
Ma lievemente al fondo che divora
Lucifero con Giuda, ci sposò;
né, sì chinato, lì fece dimora,
e come albero in nave si levò.   *145*

such did Antaeus seem to me as I watched
to see him stoop—and it was such a moment
that I should have wished to go by another
road! But he set us down gently on the bot-
tom that swallows Lucifer with Judas, nor did
he linger there thus bent, but raised himself
like the mast of a ship.

INFERNO

S'ïo AVESSI le rime aspre e chiocce,
   come si converrebbe al tristo buco
   sovra 'l qual pontan tutte l'altre rocce,   *3*
io premerei di mio concetto il suco
   più pienamente; ma perch' io non l'abbo,
   non sanza tema a dicer mi conduco;   *6*
ché non è impresa da pigliare a gabbo
   discriver fondo a tutto l'universo,
   né da lingua che chiami mamma o babbo.   *9*
Ma quelle donne aiutino il mio verso
   ch'aiutaro Anfïone a chiuder Tebe,
   sì che dal fatto il dir non sia diverso.   *12*
Oh sovra tutte mal creata plebe
   che stai nel loco onde parlare è duro,
   mei foste state qui pecore o zebe!   *15*
Come noi fummo giù nel pozzo scuro
   sotto i piè del gigante assai più bassi,
   e io mirava ancora a l'alto muro,   *18*
dicere udi'mi: "Guarda come passi:
   va sì, che tu non calchi con le piante
   le teste de' fratei miseri lassi."   *21*

CANTO XXXII

Iᴛ I had harsh and grating rhymes, as would befit the dismal hole on which all the other rocks converge and weigh, I would press out more fully the juice of my conception; but since I do not have them, it is not without fear that I bring myself to speak; for to describe the bottom of the whole universe is not an enterprise to be taken up in sport, nor for a tongue that cries mamma and daddy. But may those ladies aid my verse who aided Amphion to wall in Thebes, so that the telling may not be diverse from the fact. O you beyond all others misbegotten crowd who are in the place whereof it is hard to speak, better had you here been sheep or goats!

When we were down in the dark pit beneath the feet of the giant, far lower, and I was still gazing up at the high wall, I heard a voice say to me, "Look how you pass: take care not to tread on the heads of the wretched weary brothers."

Per ch'io mi volsi, e vidimi davante
  e sotto i piedi un lago che per gelo
  avea di vetro e non d'acqua sembiante.   *24*
Non fece al corso suo sì grosso velo
  di verno la Danoia in Osterlicchi,
  né Tanaï là sotto 'l freddo cielo,   *27*
com' era quivi; che se Tambernicchi
  vi fosse sù caduto, o Pietrapana,
  non avria pur da l'orlo fatto cricchi.   *30*
E come a gracidar si sta la rana
  col muso fuor de l'acqua, quando sogna
  di spigolar sovente la villana,   *33*
livide, insin là dove appar vergogna
  eran l'ombre dolenti ne la ghiaccia,
  mettendo i denti in nota di cicogna.   *36*
Ognuna in giù tenea volta la faccia;
  da bocca il freddo, e da li occhi il cor tristo
  tra lor testimonianza si procaccia.   *39*
Quand' io m'ebbi dintorno alquanto visto,
  volsimi a' piedi, e vidi due sì stretti,
  che 'l pel del capo avieno insieme misto.   *42*
"Ditemi, voi che sì strignete i petti,"
  diss' io, "chi siete?" E quei piegaro i colli;
  e poi ch'ebber li visi a me eretti,   *45*
li occhi lor, ch'eran pria pur dentro molli,
  gocciar su per le labbra, e 'l gelo strinse
  le lagrime tra essi e riserrolli.   *48*
Con legno legno spranga mai non cinse
  forte così; ond' ei come due becchi
  cozzaro insieme, tanta ira li vinse.   *51*

At this I turned and saw before me, and under my feet, a lake which through frost had the semblance of glass and not of water. Never did the Danube in Austria, nor the far-off Don under its cold sky, make in winter so thick a veil for their current as there was here: for had Tambernic fallen on it, or Pietrapana, it would not have given a creak, even at the edge. And as the frog lies to croak with muzzle out of the water, when the peasant girl dreams often of her gleaning, so, livid up to where the hue of shame appears, were the doleful shades within the ice, setting their teeth to the note of the stork. Each held his face turned downwards; by the mouth their cold, and by the eyes the misery of their hearts, is testified among them.

When I had looked round me awhile, I glanced down at my feet and saw two who were pressed so close together that they had the hair of their heads intermixed. "Tell me, you who thus press your breasts together," I said, "who are you?" And they bent back their necks, and when they had raised their faces towards me, their eyes, which before were moist only within, welled up with tears, which ran down over the lips, and the frost bound each to each and locked them even tighter; clamp never bound board on board so strongly; whereupon they butted together like two goats, such anger overcame them.

E un ch'avea perduti ambo li orecchi
    per la freddura, pur col viso in giùe,
    disse: "Perché cotanto in noi ti specchi?   *54*
Se vuoi saper chi son cotesti due,
    la valle onde Bisenzo si dichina
    del padre loro Alberto e di lor fue.   *57*
D'un corpo usciro; e tutta la Caina
    potrai cercare, e non troverai ombra
    degna più d'esser fitta in gelatina: *60*
non quelli a cui fu rotto il petto e l'ombra
    con esso un colpo per la man d'Artù;
    non Focaccia; non questi che m'ingombra   *63*
col capo sì, ch'i' non veggio oltre più,
    e fu nomato Sassol Mascheroni;
    se tosco se', ben sai omai chi fu.   *66*
E perché non mi metti in più sermoni,
    sappi ch'i' fu' il Camiscion de' Pazzi;
    e aspetto Carlin che mi scagioni."   *69*
Poscia vid' io mille visi cagnazzi
    fatti per freddo; onde mi vien riprezzo,
    e verrà sempre, de' gelati guazzi.   *72*
E mentre ch'andavamo inver' lo mezzo
    al quale ogne gravezza si rauna,
    e io tremava ne l'etterno rezzo;   *75*
se voler fu o destino o fortuna,
    non so; ma, passeggiando tra le teste,
    forte percossi 'l piè nel viso ad una.   *78*
Piangendo mi sgridò: "Perché mi peste?
    se tu non vieni a crescer la vendetta
    di Montaperti, perché mi moleste?"   *81*

And one who had lost both ears from the cold, with his face still downwards said, "Why do you gaze so much on us? If you would know who these two are, the valley whence the Bisenzio descends belonged to their father Albert and to them. They issued from one body; and all Caina you may search and not find a shade more fit to be fixed in ice; not him whose breast and shadow were pierced with a single blow from Arthur's hand; not Focaccia; not this one, who so obstructs me with his head that I see no farther, and who was named Sassol Mascheroni—if you are Tuscan you now know well who he was. And that you may not put me to further speech, know that I was Camiscion de' Pazzi, and I await Carlino to exculpate me."

After that I saw a thousand faces made purple by the cold, whence a shuddering comes over me, and always will, at frozen fords. And while we were going toward the center to which all gravity collects, and I was shivering in the eternal chill, whether it was will or fate or chance I do not know, but, walking among the heads, I struck my foot hard in the face of one.

Wailing he railed at me, "Why do you trample on me? If you do not come to increase the vengeance of Montaperti, why do you molest me?"

343

E io: "Maestro mio, or qui m'aspetta,
   sì ch'io esca d'un dubbio per costui;
   poi mi farai, quantunque vorrai, fretta."   *84*
Lo duca stette, e io dissi a colui
   che bestemmiava duramente ancora:
   "Qual se' tu che così rampogni altrui?"   *87*
"Or tu chi se' che vai per l'Antenora,
   percotendo," rispuose, "altrui le gote,
   sì che, se fossi vivo, troppo fora?"   *90*
"Vivo son io, e caro esser ti puote,"
   fu mia risposta, "se dimandi fama,
   ch'io metta il nome tuo tra l'altre note."   *93*
Ed elli a me: "Del contrario ho io brama.
   Lèvati quinci e non mi dar più lagna,
   ché mal sai lusingar per questa lama!"   *96*
Allor lo presi per la cuticagna
   e dissi: "El converrà che tu ti nomi,
   o che capel qui sù non ti rimagna."   *99*
Ond' elli a me: "Perché tu mi dischiomi,
   né ti dirò ch'io sia, né mosterrolti
   se mille fiate in sul capo mi tomi."   *102*
Io avea già i capelli in mano avvolti,
   e tratti glien' avea più d'una ciocca,
   latrando lui con li occhi in giù raccolti,   *105*
quando un altro gridò: "Che hai tu, Bocca?
   non ti basta sonar con le mascelle,
   se tu non latri? qual diavol ti tocca?"   *108*
"Omai," diss' io, "non vo' che più favelle,
   malvagio traditor; ch'a la tua onta
   io porterò di te vere novelle."   *111*

And I, "Master, now wait here for me, that I
may rid me of a doubt respecting this one,
then you shall make me hasten as much as
you wish." My leader stopped; and I said to
the shade who was still cursing bitterly, "Who
are you that thus reproach another?" "Nay,
who are you," he answered, "that go through
Antenora smiting the cheeks of others, so that,
were you alive, it would be too much."

"Alive I am," was my reply, "and if you
crave fame, it may be worth much to you that
I note your name among the rest." And he
to me, "The contrary is what I crave. Take
yourself hence and trouble me no more, for
ill do you know how to flatter in this depth."
Then I seized him by the hair of the nape
and said, "Either you'll name yourself, or not
a hair will be left on you here."

Whereon he to me, "Though you strip me
bald, I will not tell you or show you who I
am, though you should fall a thousand times
upon my head."

I had already twisted his hair in my hand
and had yanked out more than one tuft, he
barking and with his eyes kept close down,
when another cried, "What ails you, Bocca?
Is it not enough for you to make noise with
your jaws, but you must bark? What devil
is at you?"

"Now," said I, "I do not wish you to speak
more, accursed traitor, for to your shame will
I carry true news of you."

345

"Va via," rispuose, "e ciò che tu vuoi conta;
　　ma non tacer, se tu di qua entro eschi,
　　di quel ch'ebbe or così la lingua pronta.　　　*114*
El piange qui l'argento de' Franceschi:
　　'Io vidi,' potrai dir, 'quel da Duera
　　là dove i peccatori stanno freschi.'　　　*117*
Se fossi domandato 'Altri chi v'era?'
　　tu hai dallato quel di Beccheria
　　di cui segò Fiorenza la gorgiera.　　　*120*
Gianni de' Soldanier credo che sia
　　più là con Ganellone e Tebaldello,
　　ch'aprì Faenza quando si dormia."　　　*123*
Noi eravam partiti già da ello,
　　ch'io vidi due ghiacciati in una buca,
　　sì che l'un capo a l'altro era cappello;　　　*126*
e come 'l pan per fame si manduca,
　　così 'l sovran li denti a l'altro pose
　　là 've 'l cervel s'aggiugne con la nuca:　　　*129*
non altrimenti Tidëo si rose
　　le tempie a Menalippo per disdegno,
　　che quei faceva il teschio e l'altre cose.　　　*132*
"O tu che mostri per sì bestial segno
　　odio sovra colui che tu ti mangi,
　　dimmi 'l perché," diss' io, "per tal convegno,　　*135*
che se tu a ragion di lui ti piangi,
　　sappiendo chi voi siete e la sua pecca,
　　nel mondo suso ancora io te ne cangi,
se quella con ch'io parlo non si secca."　　　*139*

"Go away," he answered, "and tell what you will, but if you get out from here do not be silent about him that just now had his tongue so ready. He is lamenting here the silver of the French. 'I saw,' you can say, 'him of Duera, there where the sinners are put to cool.' Should you be asked who else was there, you have at your side him of the Beccheria whose gullet was slit by Florence. Gianni de' Soldanieri I think is farther on, with Ganelon, and with Tebaldello who opened Faenza while it slept."

We had already left him when I saw two frozen in one hole so close that the head of the one was a hood for the other; and as bread is devoured for hunger, so the upper one set his teeth upon the other where the brain joins with the nape. Not otherwise did Tydeus gnaw the temples of Menalippus for rage than this one was doing to the skull and the other parts.

"O you who by so bestial a sign show hatred against him whom you devour, tell me the wherefore," I said, "on this condition, that if you with reason complain of him, I, knowing who you are and his offense, may yet requite you in the world above, if that with which I speak does not dry up."

INFERNO

La bocca sollevò dal fiero pasto
quel peccator, forbendola a' capelli
del capo ch'elli avea di retro guasto.   3
Poi cominciò: "Tu vuo' ch'io rinovelli
disperato dolor che 'l cor mi preme
già pur pensando, pria ch'io ne favelli.   6
Ma se le mie parole esser dien seme
che frutti infamia al traditor ch'i' rodo,
parlare e lagrimar vedrai insieme.   9
Io non so chi tu se' né per che modo
venuto se' qua giù; ma fiorentino
mi sembri veramente quand' io t'odo.   12
Tu dei saper ch'i' fui conte Ugolino,
e questi è l'arcivescovo Ruggieri:
or ti dirò perché i son tal vicino.   15
Che per l'effetto de' suo' mai pensieri,
fidandomi di lui, io fossi preso
e poscia morto, dir non è mestieri;   18

CANTO XXXIII

Fʀᴏᴍ his savage repast the sinner raised his mouth, wiping it on the hair of the head he had spoiled behind, then began, "You will have me renew desperate grief, which even to think of wrings my heart before I speak of it. But if my words are to be seed that may bear fruit of infamy to the traitor whom I gnaw, you shall see me speak and weep together. I do not know who you are, nor by what means you have come down here; but truly you do seem to me Florentine when I hear you. You have to know that I was Count Ugolino, and this is the Archbishop Ruggieri. Now I will tell you why I am such a neighbor to him. How, by effect of his ill devising, I, trusting in him, was taken and thereafter put to death, there is no need to tell;

però quel che non puoi avere inteso,
   cioè come la morte mia fu cruda,
   udirai, e saprai s'e' m'ha offeso.   *21*
Breve pertugio dentro da la Muda,
   la qual per me ha 'l titol de la fame,
   e che conviene ancor ch'altrui si chiuda,   *24*
m'avea mostrato per lo suo forame
   più lune già, quand' io feci 'l mal sonno
   che del futuro mi squarciò 'l velame.   *27*
Questi pareva a me maestro e donno,
   cacciando il lupo e ' lupicini al monte
   per che i Pisan veder Lucca non ponno.   *30*
Con cagne magre, studïose e conte
   Gualandi con Sismondi e con Lanfranchi
   s'avea messi dinanzi da la fronte.   *33*
In picciol corso mi parieno stanchi
   lo padre e ' figli, e con l'agute scane
   mi parea lor veder fender li fianchi.   *36*
Quando fui desto innanzi la dimane,
   pianger senti' fra 'l sonno i miei figliuoli
   ch'eran con meco, e dimandar del pane.   *39*
Ben se' crudel, se tu già non ti duoli
   pensando ciò che 'l mio cor s'annunziava;
   e se non piangi, di che pianger suoli?   *42*
Già eran desti, e l'ora s'appressava
   che 'l cibo ne solëa essere addotto,
   e per suo sogno ciascun dubitava;   *45*
e io senti' chiavar l'uscio di sotto
   a l'orribile torre; ond' io guardai
   nel viso a' mie' figliuoi sanza far motto.   *48*

but what you cannot have heard, that is, how cruel my death was, you shall hear and you shall know if he has wronged me.

"A narrow hole in the Mew which because of me has the title of Hunger, and in which others are yet to be shut up, had, through its opening, already shown me several moons, when I had the bad dream that rent for me the veil of the future. This man appeared to me as master and lord, chasing the wolf and the whelps upon the mountain for which the Pisans cannot see Lucca. With trained hounds, lean and eager, he had put in front of him Gualandi with Sismondi and with Lanfranchi, and after a short run the father and the sons seemed to me weary, and it seemed to me I saw their flanks ripped by the sharp fangs.

"When I awoke before the dawn I heard my children, who were with me, crying in their sleep and asking for bread. You are cruel indeed if you do not grieve already, to think what my heart was foreboding; and if you weep not, at what do you ever weep?

"They were awake now, and the hour approached when our food was usually brought to us, and each was apprehensive because of his dream. And below I heard them nailing up the door of the horrible tower; whereat I looked in the faces of my children without a word.

351

Io non piangëa, sì dentro impetrai:
   piangevan elli; e Anselmuccio mio
   disse: 'Tu guardi sì, padre! che hai?'   *51*
Perciò non lagrimai né rispuos' io
   tutto quel giorno né la notte appresso,
   infin che l'altro sol nel mondo uscìo.   *54*
Come un poco di raggio si fu messo
   nel doloroso carcere, e io scorsi
   per quattro visi il mio aspetto stesso,   *57*
ambo le man per lo dolor mi morsi;
   ed ei, pensando ch'io 'l fessi per voglia
   di manicar, di sùbito levorsi   *60*
e disser: 'Padre, assai ci fia men doglia
   se tu mangi di noi: tu ne vestisti
   queste misere carni, e tu le spoglia.'   *63*
Queta'mi allor per non farli più tristi;
   lo dì e l'altro stemmo tutti muti;
   ahi dura terra, perché non t'apristi?   *66*
Poscia che fummo al quarto dì venuti,
   Gaddo mi si gittò disteso a' piedi,
   dicendo: 'Padre mio, ché non m'aiuti?'   *69*
Quivi morì; e come tu mi vedi,
   vid' io cascar li tre ad uno ad uno
   tra 'l quinto dì e 'l sesto; ond' io mi diedi, *72*
già cieco, a brancolar sovra ciascuno,
   e due dì li chiamai, poi che fur morti.
   Poscia, più che 'l dolor, poté 'l digiuno."   *75*
Quand' ebbe detto ciò, con li occhi torti
   riprese 'l teschio misero co' denti,
   che furo a l'osso, come d'un can, forti.   *78*

I did not weep, so was I turned to stone
within me. They wept, and my poor little
Anselm said, 'You look so, father, what ails
you?' I shed no tear for that, nor did I
answer all that day, nor the night after, until
the next sun came forth on the world. As soon
as a little ray made its way into the woeful
prison, and I discerned by their four faces
the aspect of my own, I bit both my hands
for grief. And they, thinking I did it for
hunger, suddenly rose up and said, 'Father,
it will be far less painful to us if you eat of
us; you did clothe us with this wretched
flesh, and do you strip us of it!'

"Then I calmed myself in order not to
make them sadder. That day and the next
we stayed all silent: Ah, hard earth! why did
you not open? When we had come to the
fourth day Gaddo threw himself outstretched
at my feet, saying, 'Father, why do you not
help me?' There he died; and even as you
see me, I saw the three fall, one by one, be-
tween the fifth day and the sixth; whence I
betook me, already blind, to groping over
each, and for two days I called them after
they were dead. Then fasting did more than
grief had done."

When he had said this, with eyes askance
he again took hold of the wretched skull with
his teeth, which were strong on the bone like
a dog's.

Ahi Pisa, vituperio de le genti
  del bel paese là dove 'l sì suona,
  poi che i vicini a te punir son lenti,   *81*
muovasi la Capraia e la Gorgona,
  e faccian siepe ad Arno in su la foce,
  sì ch'elli annieghi in te ogne persona!   *84*
Che se 'l conte Ugolino aveva voce
  d'aver tradita te de le castella,
  non dovei tu i figliuoi porre a tal croce.   *87*
Innocenti facea l'età novella,
  novella Tebe, Uguiccione e 'l Brigata
  e li altri due che 'l canto suso appella.   *90*
Noi passammo oltre, là 've la gelata
  ruvidamente un'altra gente fascia,
  non volta in giù, ma tutta riversata.   *93*
Lo pianto stesso lì pianger non lascia,
  e 'l duol che truova in su li occhi rintoppo,
  si volge in entro a far crescer l'ambascia;   *96*
ché le lagrime prime fanno groppo,
  e sì come visiere di cristallo,
  rïempion sotto 'l ciglio tutto il coppo.   *99*
E avvegna che, sì come d'un callo,
  per la freddura ciascun sentimento
  cessato avesse del mio viso stallo,   *102*
già mi parea sentire alquanto vento;
  per ch'io: "Maestro mio, questo chi move?
  non è qua giù ogne vapore spento?"   *105*
Ond' elli a me: "Avaccio sarai dove
  di ciò ti farà l'occhio la risposta,
  veggendo la cagion che 'l fiato piove."   *108*

Ah, Pisa! shame of the peoples of the fair land where the *sì* is heard, since your neighbors are slow to punish you, let Capraia and Gorgona shift, and make a hedge for Arno at its mouth, so that it drown every soul in you! For if Count Ugolino had the name of betraying you of your castles, you ought not to have put his children to such torture. Their youthful years, you modern Thebes, made Uguiccione and Brigata innocent, and the other two that my song names above.

We went farther on, where the frost roughly swathes another people, not bent downwards, but with faces all upturned. The very weeping there prevents their weeping, and the grief, which finds a barrier upon their eyes, turns inward to increase the agony, for the first tears form a knot and, like a crystal visor, fill all the cup beneath the eyebrow. And although, as in a callus, all feeling, because of the cold, had departed from my face, it now seemed to me as if I felt some wind, wherefore I, "Master, who moves this? Is not every vapor extinguished here below?

And he to me, "Soon shall you be where your eye itself, seeing the cause that rains down the blast, will make answer to you in this."

E un de' tristi de la fredda crosta
    gridò a noi: "O anime crudeli
    tanto che data v'è l'ultima posta, *111*
levatemi dal viso i duri veli,
    sì ch'io sfoghi 'l duol che 'l cor m'impregna,
    un poco, pria che 'l pianto si raggeli." *114*
Per ch'io a lui: "Se vuo' ch'i' ti sovvegna,
    dimmi chi se', e s'io non ti disbrigo,
    al fondo de la ghiaccia ir mi convegna." *117*
Rispuose adunque: "I' son frate Alberigo;
    i' son quel da le frutta del mal orto,
    che qui riprendo dattero per figo." *120*
"Oh," diss' io lui, "or se' tu ancor morto?"
    Ed elli a me: "Come 'l mio corpo stea
    nel mondo sù, nulla scïenza porto. *123*
Cotal vantaggio ha questa Tolomea,
    che spesse volte l'anima ci cade
    innanzi ch'Atropòs mossa le dea. *126*
E perché tu più volontier mi rade
    le 'nvetrïate lagrime dal volto,
    sappie che, tosto che l'anima trade *129*
come fec' ïo, il corpo suo l' è tolto
    da un demonio, che poscia il governa
    mentre che 'l tempo suo tutto sia vòlto. *132*
Ella ruina in sì fatta cisterna;
    e forse pare ancor lo corpo suso
    de l'ombra che di qua dietro mi verna. *135*
Tu 'l dei saper, se tu vien pur mo giuso:
    elli è ser Branca Doria, e son più anni
    poscia passati ch'el fu sì racchiuso." *138*

And one of the wretches of the cold crust cried out to us, "O souls so cruel that the last station is given to you, lift from my face the hard veils, so that, before the weeping freezes again, I may vent a little the misery that stuffs my heart." Wherefore I to him, "If you would have me help you, tell me who you are, and if I do not relieve you, may I have to go to the bottom of the ice."

He replied then, "I am Fra Alberigo; I am he of the fruits from the evil garden, and here I am paid date for fig."

"Oh," I said to him, "are you then dead already?"

And he to me, "How my body may fare in the world above I have no knowledge. Such vantage has this Ptolomea that often-times the soul falls down here before Atropos sends it forth; and that you may more will-ingly scrape the glazen tears from my face, know that as soon as the soul betrays as I did, its body is taken from it by a devil who thereafter rules it until its time has all re-volved. The soul falls headlong into this cistern, and perhaps the body of the shade that is wintering here behind me still appears above on earth: you must know if you are but now come down. He is ser Branca d'Oria, and many years have passed since he was shut up thus."

357

"Io credo," diss' io lui, "che tu m'inganni;
    ché Branca Doria non morì unquanche,
    e mangia e bee e dorme e veste panni."   *141*
"Nel fosso sù," diss' el, "de' Malebranche,
    là dove bolle la tenace pece,
    non era ancora giunto Michel Zanche,   *144*
che questi lasciò il diavolo in sua vece
    nel corpo suo, ed un suo prossimano
    che 'l tradimento insieme con lui fece.   *147*
Ma distendi oggimai in qua la mano;
    aprimi li occhi." E io non gliel' apersi;
    e cortesia fu lui esser villano.   *150*
Ahi Genovesi, uomini diversi
    d'ogne costume e pien d'ogne magagna,
    perché non siete voi del mondo spersi?   *153*
Ché col peggiore spirto di Romagna
    trovai di voi un tal, che per sua opra
    in anima in Cocito già si bagna,
e in corpo par vivo ancor di sopra.   *157*

"I believe you are deceiving me," I said to him, "for Branca d'Oria is not yet dead, and eats and drinks and sleeps and puts on clothes."

"In the ditch of the Malebranche above," he said, "where the sticky pitch is boiling, Michel Zanche had not yet arrived when this one left a devil in his stead in his own body, as did also a near kinsman of his who committed the treachery together with him. But now reach out your hand here: open my eyes"; and I opened them not for him—and to be rude to him was courtesy!

Ah Genoese! men strange to all good custom and full of all corruption, why are you not driven from the earth? For with the worst spirit of Romagna I found one of you who for his deeds even now is in soul bathed in Cocytus, and in body appears still alive on earth!

INFERNO

"*Vexilla regis prodeunt inferni*
   verso di noi; però dinanzi mira,"
   disse 'l maestro mio, "se tu 'l discerni."   *3*
Come quando una grossa nebbia spira,
   o quando l'emisperio nostro annotta,
   par di lungi un molin che 'l vento gira,   *6*
veder mi parve un tal dificio allotta;
   poi per lo vento mi ristrinsi retro
   al duca mio, ché non lì era altra grotta.   *9*
Già era, e con paura il metto in metro,
   là dove l'ombre tutte eran coperte,
   e trasparien come festuca in vetro.   *12*
Altre sono a giacere; altre stanno erte,
   quella col capo e quella con le piante;
   altra, com' arco, il volto a' piè rinverte.   *15*
Quando noi fummo fatti tanto avante,
   ch'al mio maestro piacque di mostrarmi
   la creatura ch'ebbe il bel sembiante,   *18*
d'innanzi mi si tolse e fé restarmi,
   "Ecco Dite," dicendo, "ed ecco il loco
   ove convien che di fortezza t'armi."   *21*

CANTO XXXIV

"*Vexilla regis prodeunt inferni* towards us;
look forward therefore," said my master, "see
if you discern him." As, when a thick fog
breathes, or when our hemisphere darkens to
night, a mill which the wind turns appears
from afar, such an edifice did I now seem to
see; then, because of the wind, I drew back
behind my leader, for there was no other
shelter there. I was now (and with fear I do
put in into verse!) where the shades were
wholly covered, showing through like straw
in glass. Some are lying, some are erect, this
with the head, that with the soles uppermost;
another, like a bow, bends his face to his feet.
When we had gone so far forward that it
pleased my master to show me the creature
who was once so fair, he took himself from
before me and made me stop, saying, "Lo
Dis!—and lo the place where you must arm
yourself with fortitude."

Com' io divenni allor gelato e fioco,
   nol dimandar, lettor, ch'i' non lo scrivo,
   però ch'ogne parlar sarebbe poco.   *24*
Io non mori' e non rimasi vivo;
   pensa oggimai per te, s'hai fior d'ingegno,
   qual io divenni, d'uno e d'altro privo.   *27*
Lo 'mperador del doloroso regno
   da mezzo 'l petto uscia fuor de la ghiaccia;
   e più con un gigante io mi convegno,   *30*
che i giganti non fan con le sue braccia:
   vedi oggimai quant' esser dee quel tutto
   ch'a così fatta parte si confaccia.   *33*
S'el fu sì bel com' elli è ora brutto,
   e contra 'l suo fattore alzò le ciglia,
   ben dee da lui procedere ogne lutto.   *36*
Oh quanto parve a me gran maraviglia
   quand' io vidi tre facce a la sua testa!
   L'una dinanzi, e quella era vermiglia;   *39*
l'altr' eran due, che s'aggiugnieno a questa
   sovresso 'l mezzo di ciascuna spalla,
   e sé giugnieno al loco de la cresta: *42*
e la destra parea tra bianca e gialla;
   la sinistra a vedere era tal, quali
   vegnon di là onde 'l Nilo s'avvalla.   *45*
Sotto ciascuna uscivan due grand' ali,
   quanto si convenia a tanto uccello:
   vele di mar non vid' io mai cotali.   *48*
Non avean penne, ma di vispistrello
   era lor modo; e quelle svolazzava,
   sì che tre venti si movean da ello: *51*

How frozen and faint I then became, ask
it not, reader, for I do not write it, because
all words would fail. I did not die and I did
not remain alive: now think for yourself, if
you have any wit, what I became, deprived
alike of death and life!

The emperor of the woeful realm stood
forth from mid-breast out of the ice; and I
in size compare better with a giant than
giants with his arms: see now how huge that
whole must be to correspond to such a part.
If he was once as beautiful as he is ugly
now, and lifted up his brows against his
Maker, well may all sorrow proceed from
him. Oh how great a marvel it was to me
when I saw three faces on his head: one in
front and it was red, and the other two joined
to this just over the middle of each shoulder,
and all were joined at the crown. The right
one seemed between white and yellow, and
the left one was such in appearance as are
those who come from whence the Nile
descends. From under each there came forth
two mighty wings, of size befitting such a
bird—sails at sea I never saw so broad. They
had no feathers, but were like a bat's. And
he was flapping them, so that three winds
went forth from him,

quindi Cocito tutto s'aggelava.
   Con sei occhi piangëa, e per tre menti
   gocciava 'l pianto e sanguinosa bava.   *54*
Da ogne bocca dirompea co' denti
   un peccatore, a guisa di maciulla,
   sì che tre ne facea così dolenti.   *57*
A quel dinanzi il mordere era nulla
   verso 'l graffiar, che tal volta la schiena
   rimanea de la pelle tutta brulla.   *60*
"Quell' anima là sù c'ha maggior pena,"
   disse 'l maestro, "è Giuda Scarïotto,
   che 'l capo ha dentro e fuor le gambe mena.   *63*
De li altri due c'hanno il capo di sotto,
   quel che pende dal nero ceffo è Bruto:
   vedi come si storce, e non fa motto!;   *66*
e l'altro è Cassio, che par sì membruto.
   Ma la notte risurge, e oramai
   è da partir, ché tutto avem veduto."   *69*
Com' a lui piacque, il collo li avvinghiai;
   ed el prese di tempo e loco poste,
   e quando l'ali fuoro aperte assai,   *72*
appigliò sé a le vellute coste;
   di vello in vello giù discese poscia
   tra 'l folto pelo e le gelate croste.   *75*
Quando noi fummo là dove la coscia
   si volge, a punto in sul grosso de l'anche,
   lo duca, con fatica e con angoscia,   *78*
volse la testa ov' elli avea le zanche,
   e aggrappossi al pel com' om che sale,
   sì che 'n inferno i' credea tornar anche.   *81*

whereby Cocytus was all congealed. With six eyes he was weeping, and down over three chins dripped tears and bloody foam. In each mouth he champed a sinner with his teeth, as with a heckle, and thus he kept three of them woeful. To the one in front the biting was nothing compared with the clawing, for sometimes his back remained all stripped of skin.

"The soul up there that has the greatest punishment," said the master, "is Judas Iscariot, who has his head within and plies his legs outside. Of the other two who have their heads below, the one that hangs from the black muzzle is Brutus: see how he writhes and utters not a word; the other is Cassius, who seems so stark of limb. But night is rising again, and now we must depart, for we have seen the whole."

As was his pleasure, I clasped him round the neck, and he took advantage of time and place, and when the wings were opened wide he caught hold on the shaggy flanks; down from shag to shag he descended between the matted hair and the frozen crusts. When we had come to where the thigh turns just on the thick of the haunch, my leader with labor and strain brought round his head to where his shanks had been and grappled on the hair like one who is climbing, so that I thought we were returning into Hell again.

"Attienti ben, ché per cotali scale,"
   disse 'l maestro, ansando com' uom lasso,
   "conviensi dipartir da tanto male."   *84*
Poi uscì fuor per lo fóro d'un sasso
   e puose me in su l'orlo a sedere;
   appresso porse a me l'accorto passo.   *87*
Io levai li occhi e credetti vedere
   Lucifero com' io l'avea lasciato,
   e vidili le gambe in sù tenere;   *90*
e s'io divenni allora travagliato,
   la gente grossa il pensi, che non vede
   qual è quel punto ch'io avea passato.   *93*
"Lèvati sù," disse 'l maestro, "in piede:
   la via è lunga e 'l cammino è malvagio,
   e già il sole a mezza terza riede."   *96*
Non era camminata di palagio
   là 'v' eravam, ma natural burella
   ch'avea mal suolo e di lume disagio.   *99*
"Prima ch'io de l'abisso mi divella,
   maestro mio," diss' io quando fui dritto,
   "a trarmi d'erro un poco mi favella: *102*
ov' è la ghiaccia? e questi com' è fitto
   sì sottosopra? e come, in sì poc' ora,
   da sera a mane ha fatto il sol tragitto?"   *105*
Ed elli a me: "Tu imagini ancora
   d'esser di là dal centro, ov' io mi presi
   al pel del vermo reo che 'l mondo fóra.   *108*
Di là fosti cotanto quant' io scesi;
   quand' io mi volsi, tu passasti 'l punto
   al qual si traggon d'ogne parte i pesi.   *111*

"Cling fast," said the master, panting like a man forspent, "for by such stairs as these we must depart from so much evil." Then he issued forth through the opening of a rock and placed me upon its edge to sit, then reached toward me his cautious step. I raised my eyes and thought to see Lucifer as I had left him, and saw him with his legs held upwards—and if I became perplexed then, let the dull crowd judge who do not see what is the point that I had passed.

"Rise to your feet," said the master. The way is long and the road is hard, and already the sun returns to mid-tierce."

It was no palace hall where we were, but a natural dungeon which had a bad floor and want of light. "Before I tear myself from the abyss, my master," I said, when I had risen, "speak to me a little, to draw me out of error. Where is the ice? And he there, how is it that he is fixed thus upside down? And how, in so brief a time, has the sun made transit from evening to morning?"

And he to me, "You imagine that you are still on the other side of the center, where I caught hold on the hair of the evil worm that pierces the world. As long as I descended you were on that side; when I turned myself you passed the point to which all weights are drawn from every part.

E se' or sotto l'emisperio giunto
   ch'è contraposto a quel che la gran secca
   coverchia, e sotto 'l cui colmo consunto   *114*
fu l'uom che nacque e visse sanza pecca;
   tu haï i piedi in su picciola spera
   che l'altra faccia fa de la Giudecca.   *117*
Qui è da man, quando di là è sera;
   e questi, che ne fé scala col pelo,
   fitto è ancora sì come prim' era.   *120*
Da questa parte cadde giù dal cielo;
   e la terra, che pria di qua si sporse,
   per paura di lui fé del mar velo,   *123*
e venne a l'emisperio nostro; e forse
   per fuggir lui lasciò qui loco vòto
   quella ch'appar di qua, e sù ricorse."   *126*
Luogo è là giù da Belzebù remoto
   tanto quanto la tomba si distende,
   che non per vista, ma per suono è noto   *129*
d'un ruscelletto che quivi discende
   per la buca d'un sasso, ch'elli ha roso,
   col corso ch'elli avvolge, e poco pende.   *132*
Lo duca e io per quel cammino ascoso
   intrammo a ritornar nel chiaro mondo;
   e sanza cura aver d'alcun riposo,   *135*
salimmo sù, el primo e io secondo,
   tanto ch'i' vidi de le cose belle
   che porta 'l ciel, per un pertugio tondo.
E quindi uscimmo a riveder le stelle.   *139*

And you are now come beneath the hem-
isphere opposite to that which canopies the
great dry land and underneath whose zenith
the Man was slain who was born and lived
without sin, and you have your feet upon a
little sphere which forms the other face of the
Judecca. Here it is morning when it is eve-
ning there, and this one who made a ladder
for us with his hair is still fixed as he was be-
fore. On this side he fell down from Heaven;
and the earth, which before stood out here,
for fear of him made a veil of the sea and
came to our hemisphere; and perhaps in order
to escape from him that which appears on
this side left here the empty space and rushed
upwards."

Down there, from Beelzebub as far re-
moved as his tomb extends, is a space not
known by sight, but by the sound of a rivulet
descending in it along the hollow of the rock
which it has eaten out in its winding and
gently sloping course. My leader and I en-
tered on that hidden road to return into the
bright world; and caring not for any rest,
we climbed up, he first and I second, so far
that through a round opening I saw some of
the beautiful things that Heaven bears; and
thence we issued forth to see again the stars.

NOTE

ON THE ITALIAN TEXT AND THE TRANSLATION

Dante's *Commedia*, like any poem, presents itself to us, there on the printed page, as a potential experience that can become actual only in the sustained act of a thoughtful reading.

"Homer is new this morning," wrote Charles Péguy, "and nothing is so old as yesterday's newspaper."

The best "introduction" to the *Divine Comedy*, it has long seemed to me, is no *Introduction* at all. Let the reader face the poem directly, begin his reading now, and see if Dante *can* be new again this morning—and *how* new.

The text of the poem given here is substantially that established by Giorgio Petrocchi in his authoritative critical edition of the work: Dante Alighieri, *La Commedia secondo l'antica vulgata*, a cura di Giorgio Petrocchi, Società Dantesca Italiana, Edizione Nazionale, Mondadori, 1966–68, in four volumes. I wish to express here my gratitude to the publisher of this notable edition for kind permission to present it here, as certainly the best text of the *Commedia* that we now have. I have ventured to depart from it at but a few points only, all of which are duly noted in my commentary at the appropriate place, together with my reasons for doing so.

Of English translations of the *Comedy* there is no end in sight; and one may well wonder why yet another should be added to that ceaseless flow. The answer must be that translation is interpretation, and that the version in prose here presented is but one more answer to the perennial question: How do we read this verse, this tercet, this canto? What do we conceive its essential meaning to be? Simple English prose (the ideal has been to make it as simple as Dante's own "humble" style—as he termed it, writing to Can Grande) can give but a partial answer, but it can and does give that.

Every "new" prose translation of the *Comedy* is doomed to display a coincidence of phraseology with other translations at every turn, and it would be a mistake to seek to avoid this and try to make one's effort strictly "original." Indeed it would be a mistake, I think, not to let the efforts of one's predecessors contribute to one's own. Let me clearly acknowledge, therefore, that I have constantly kept before me a considerable number of other English prose translations, and that I have let these efforts of others serve as my silent "readers," so to say, who constantly suggested to me ways of improving my own. Thus, with the many who before me have engaged in the rather desperate enterprise of attempting to translate Dante's verse into English prose I have incurred a great debt which, regretfully, cannot be acknowledged in any detail.

To Albert E. Trombly, David Paul, Francis Fergusson, Polly Hanford, as to readers of my efforts who were not so silent, but who generously made many suggestions for improvements in my poor phraseology, I remain deeply indebted and grateful.

Finally I may add that all the while I was enduring the

painful loss of the *poetry* of the *Comedy* that any prose translation inevitably brings about, I consoled myself with the thought that there are, after all, a great many readers who are able to make out the meaning, or some of the meaning at least, in the original Italian on the left-hand page. May this be the case with them ever more frequently, until they are able to "live along the lines" over there, on the left, in Dante's own words. The poem, the *poetry*, is there in its richness and true greatness—there, in the original, and almost nowhere else.

C. S. S.

INDEX

THIS LIST includes the names of persons and places mentioned in the *Inferno*. All names are given in their conventional English form where possible, according to the translation in this volume. Even though a name may occur more than once in a single passage or Canto, only its first occurrence there is listed. Italicized numbers of Cantos and verses indicate indirect reference to a person or place in the verse cited.